Humboldt Redwoods State Park
The Complete Guide

JERRY AND GISELA ROHDE

Illustrations by Larry Eifert

Miles & Miles
Eureka · 1992

Miles & Miles, Publishers
Post Office Box 6730
Eureka, California 95502

Dedicated to the place now called Humboldt Redwoods State Park, and to all that is, or once was, within it . . .

. . . to Kahs-cho, the coast redwood, and all the growing beings . . .

. . . to Sin-ke-kok, the South Fork Eel, and all the flowing beings . . .

. . . to Sa-bug-gah-nah, Eagle Point, and all the standing beings . . .

. . . to Nah-tos, the banana slug, and all the crawling beings . . .

. . . to Klo-kuk, the salmon, and all the swimming beings . . .

. . . to Chil-la-la, the kingfisher, and all the flying beings . . .

. . . to In-che, the black-tailed deer, and all the walking beings . . .

. . . to Ah-da-dil-law, and the other Lolangkoks, and all the vanished beings . . .

Table of Contents

FOREWORD

As tourism becomes more important to national and regional economies, guidebooks proliferate in the "Travel" sections of bookstores. On some shelves this compact guide may get lost among larger ones, but I hope its colorful cover will catch the eye of every browser interested in the redwoods of California's North Coast. Of the myriad books written about the redwood region, this one ranks among the very best. Before highlighting the qualities that make it special, let me introduce the talented team that has produced this, their first, book.

In the spring of 1990, as a Geography professor at Humboldt State University, I offered a new writing class called "American Places." Among the 20 topophiles (place lovers) who enrolled was a quiet 43-year-old named Jerry Rohde, who needed a few courses to renew his teaching credential. He soon confessed that his real interest lay less in teaching than in writing about places. The first night of class he expressed his desire in these words:

> I remember my mother telling me about places near where we lived, but which I had never visited. Places with magical names. . . that called forth images of steep mountain slopes and cascading water . . . . By now I've had the chance to match image with reality many times over, from the decaying meeting house of Parsonfield, Maine, to the sinkhole in Wyoming where the Little Popo Agie River drops below the ground. And each time I make another match . . . , my interest rises anew . . . . I want to go to these places . . . , [and] I want to share them, hoping that others will catch some of the magic I feel.

By the end of the semester Jerry had completed an impressive 60-page guide to what he called the "Hidden Side" of Humboldt Redwoods State Park. As I later learned, his wife Gisela, a library assistant at Humboldt State University, helped him with his field work. She has long shared Jerry's interest in places, particularly their flora and fauna. When German nurses first showed Gisela to her mother, she was holding an English daisy. She has clutched flowers ever since, while making a series of moves that eventually took her from southern Germany to southern California. She met and married Jerry while both studied in San Bernardino. Since their relocation to Humboldt County in 1979, they have made countless hikes together. As a self-taught naturalist, Gisela makes an ideal trail companion for Jerry, who would rather play with words than watch birds or identify plants.

The more I saw of Jerry's writing (and Gisela's editing), the more I encouraged him to expand his guide and make it more graphic. I thought it ought to include the better known "Avenue" side of the Park. And sensing the need for maps and illustrations to enhance the writing, Jerry and I approached Larry Eifert, one of the North Coast's finest landscape artists. Larry, as usual, had a dozen different projects in progress, including a mural commissioned by the same park about which Jerry was writing. But as a member of the board of the Humboldt Redwoods Interpretive Association, Larry could hardly decline an invitation to contribute a few drawings to a book focused on one of his favorite habitats. None of us, however, foresaw how many splendid graphics Eifert's zeal for the redwoods would add.

As a son of Illinois and two naturalists—one a writer, the other a museum curator—Larry started hiking at age five. Whether he was indoors or outdoors, his parents tried to contain his energies by keeping a pencil in his hand. Eventually they made an artist out of him. He moved to Ferndale in 1972 after reconnoitering much of North America's Pacific Coast for what he considered an ideal place to live and paint. Since then he has produced an incredible array of paintings, all designed to increase people's appreciation of places and concern for their environs.

After approaching several publishers, the Rohdes—through one of Gisela's friends—found a small company that recognized the potential of their manuscript. The owner has a son who, like the Rohdes, has lived in Humboldt County since 1979. For Matthew Miles, this Rohde-Eifert guide also marks a major milestone, since it is the first book he has taken to press by himself.

What Miles, Eifert, and the Rohdes have produced is an extraordinary guide to the complex place known as Humboldt Redwoods State Park. Besides providing, clearly and concisely, the essential information needed to explore the Park by foot, bike, or car, their book contains two elements that probe the habitats and history of the place. The first consists of plant profiles which combine Jerry's deft descriptions with Larry's precise line drawings. They will enable readers to identify many of the Park's common flora and fauna in their particular habitat. The second element features historical vignettes based on library research, interviews with old-timers, and hikes along every road and trail in the Park. Even local residents will learn much about the history of the region before it became a park. Jerry's almost poetic descriptions of cemeteries and his gripping descriptions of the 1955/1964 floods evoke both pathos and humor, as do Larry's sketches of abandoned barns and outhouses.

Whether visiting the Park for just a day on your way to somewhere else or savoring it for an extended period, you will find this guidebook invaluable. Passers-by should concentrate on the "Quick Guide to Enjoying the Park" and at least a sample of the Avenue section. Stayers should read about the areas of the Park they want to explore — either in advance or while there. Both groups of visitors will come away with a new appreciation of the Park and want to join me in asking the Rohde-Eifert-Miles team to produce a sequel for the redwood parks at the northern end of the North Coast. In the meantime I shall look for more students who can create similar guides to the many other fascinating towns and byroads that lie beyond the "Redwood Curtain."

Arcata, California   Lowell "Ben" Bennion
May, 1992

ACKNOWLEDGEMENTS

This book would not have been possible without the generous cooperation and assistance of many, many people. The authors would like to thank the following:

Lowell "Ben" Bennion, Professor of Geography, Humboldt State University, for his constant, enthusiastic support, which has ranged from inspiring the book to reviewing the manuscript to writing the foreward;

Larry Eifert, a consummate craftsman and the perfect artist for this book — his illustrations have brought to life the many places, plants, and people we've written about;

Matthew Miles, whose suggestions and encouragement as editor have made the book clearer, more relevant, and far more user-friendly;

John Rutherford, who created the cover graphics for the book;

Marilyn Corbeille, whose peerless proofreading caught the grammar glitches and spelling snafus we'd overlooked;

Karen Carlton, Associate Professor of English, Humboldt State University, who reviewed the manuscript and encouraged our work;

the dedicated Park Rangers who answered innumerable questions and offered their support: Chief District Ranger Joe Hardcastle, Supervising Ranger Tim Young, and State Park Unit rangers Jim Baird, Ron Jones, and Dan Ash;

the staff of the Park Visitors Center, especially manager Jack Rundell, former manager Bill Filsinger, and former assistant manager Fran Clever, for providing much helpful information and making available a variety of important documents;

Denise Philips and Dave Swisher of Beacon Printing, whose dedicated work assured quality reproductions of both the book's text and illustrations;

Darlene Magee, Librarian, Indian Action Council Library, Eureka, who reviewed sections of the manuscript pertaining to the Lolangkok Indians, and who often located obscure materials from her library's extensive collection;

Debbie Hill, Librarian, Humboldt County Library, who reviewed the book's index;

Erich Schimps, Special Collections Librarian, and Lincoln Kilian, Library Assistant, both of Humboldt State University, who helped locate documents within the library's Humboldt County Collection;

Susan O'Hara, Mike O'Hara, Margaret Pritchard, Jim Demulling, George Martin, and Christine Rising, who provided information about local history and geography;

Laura DeVere, Karen DeVere, Claude DeVere III, Tony Look, and Jan Perrott, who shared information about their families;

Carol Russell, Susan Smith Clark, and Dean Lewis, who arranged for interviews with "old-timer" relatives;

Tom Keeter, Archaeologist, U. S. Forest Service, Six Rivers National Forest, who shared his research on local Indian cultures and land use;

Dave Burnson, Engineering Geologist, California State Parks, for details about the geology of the Park region;

John Hewston, Emeritus Professor of Natural Resources, Humboldt State University, who answered questions about birds found in the Park;

Edie Butler, former Executive Director, Humboldt County Historical Society, and Claudia Israel, Director/Curator of the Clarke Museum, who provided photos and other historical information;

Susie Van Kirk, who helped locate historical records;

Gordon Leppig, Herbarium Botanist, Humboldt State University, and Carol Inyoue-Matthews, Steve Matthews, Norma Kirmsse, and Allan Borden, who helped us identify plants found in the Park;

Gisela and Herbert Haringer, who provided the equipment on which the book was word processed;

Jim Carley, Carolyn Mueller, William Mueller, Nancy Correll, Richard Dunning, and Nancy Austin, who biked and hiked the trails of Humboldt Redwoods with us;

the many current and former residents of the Park region who shared their accounts of local history — their names appear in the Sources section at the end of the book.

Humboldt Redwoods State Park:
The Complete Guide

A QUICK GUIDE
TO ENJOYING THE PARK

Tucked away in the narrow canyons of California's North Coast is a Fort Knox of the plant world — Humboldt Redwoods State Park. Within this botanical treasurehouse are some of the tallest and most magnificent trees to be found anywhere, colossal coast redwoods more than a thousand years old and over 300 feet high. And that is just the beginning; the Park is also home to congregations of calypso orchids, fleets of fetid adder's tongues, ranks of redwood sorrel — spectacular flowers that seldom grow so profusely elsewhere. Add in such striking upcountry inhabitants as canyon live oak, true baby stars, and two species of sweet-scented ceanothus, spread the lot of them over a series of steep ridges and deeply-shaded stream valleys, and the result is a setting that will both stimulate the senses and restore the spirit.

Humboldt Redwoods is by far the largest redwood park in the state system, but it offers more than mere size; a third of its 51,000-plus acres is covered by old-growth forest, while the remainder of its countryside contains dozens of creek canyons, prairies, and mixed woodlands that are intensely interesting in their own right. The Park's vast size and varied landscape offer a multitude of attractions for visitors — so many that it can be difficult knowing just where to start. The "Quick Guide" which follows will help orient the unknowing, free up time for the fast-paced, and brighten the way for the baffled; it's filled with references to more detailed descriptions found elsewhere in the book. If you're in a hurry to enjoy the Park, look here now, then read the rest of the book at your leisure.

*   *   *   *   *

For the most current information about Park regulations, river and trail conditions, and campground reservation procedures, check with the Humboldt Redwoods Visitor Center, located on the Avenue of the Giants between Myers Flat and Weott at Burlington; phone (707) 946-2263. Next door is the Park's headquarters; phone (707) 946-2311. (Contact the Park by mail at: P. O. Box 100, Weott, CA 95571.) At the Visitor Center, be sure to pick up a free copy of the *Eel River Current*, a fact-filled annual Park publication in newspaper format.

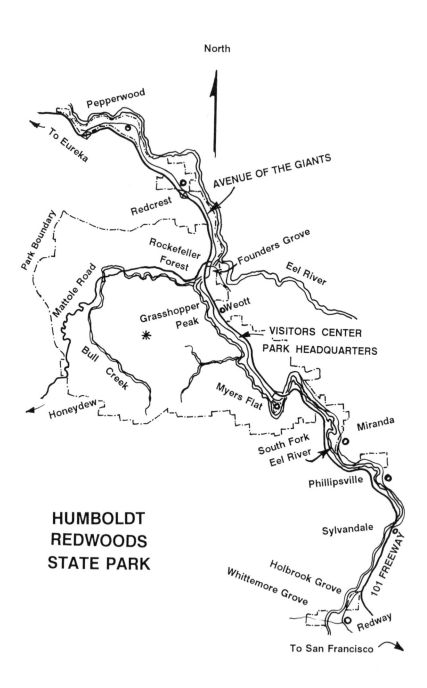

North

Pepperwood

To Eureka

AVENUE OF THE GIANTS

Redcrest

Park Boundary

Rockefeller
Forest

Founders Grove

Eel River

Mattole Road

Grasshopper
Peak

Weott

VISITORS CENTER
PARK HEADQUARTERS

Bull Creek

Myers Flat

Honeydew

Miranda

South Fork
Eel River

Phillipsville

**HUMBOLDT
REDWOODS
STATE PARK**

Sylvandale

101 FREEWAY

Holbrook Grove

Whittemore Grove

Redway

To San Francisco

Approaches by Auto:
The Avenue of the Giants and Mattole Road

The quickest way to see Humboldt Redwoods is to drive one or more sections of the Avenue of the Giants, a 31.5-mile Scenic Highway that runs through dozens of dazzling redwood groves. Both the sunny Southern Avenue [p. 93] and the wistful Northern Avenue [p. 164] have their share of charms, but for most travellers, it is the Central Avenue [p. 119] that forms the core of their Park experience. Located on this winding stretch of roadway are such attractions as the Visitor Center, a dozen delightful trails, five picnic areas, four swimming holes, and the stunning redwoods of the Dyerville Flats, including those in the world-famous Founders Grove. For the time-bound traveller, the Central Avenue can be "done" in an hour or less, although there is easily a week's worth of scenery watching and other activities along its eight-mile course.

Park Visitor Center, Burlington

Ranking with the Dyerville Flats as a redwood rendezvous is the magnificent Rockefeller Forest, reached via Mattole Road from the Freeway interchange at the mouth of the South Fork Eel [p. 198]. Again, an hour is all it takes to sample the area; this allows enough time for a stroll around the Rockefeller Loop Trail [p. 223] and also for a perusal of the Big Trees Area [p. 201]. If more time is available, the historic Bull Creek townsite lies just up the road.

Hiking Humboldt Redwoods:
Fifteen Favorite Routes

Over 50 trails and dirt roads run through the Park; they range in length from a few hundred yards to several miles and can often be combined to form longer routes. The following hikes are especially pleasant.

Note: 1) some trails, as indicated, are accessible only when temporary, "summer" bridges are in place across the South Fork Eel during the "low water" months of summer; 2) pets are allowed at Park beaches and campgrounds, but not on Park roads or trails.

Less than Two Miles (all distances are round trip)

1. *Percy's Path—French Grove Loop,* 0.7 mile [p. 192]. A delightful circuit, it cuts through a jungle of ferns and passes the bizarre, bark-shorn Girdled Tree.

2. *Hidden Springs Beach Loop,* 1.1 miles [p. 112]. Vanished Indian villages, a craggy point, many unusual plants, and a sunny swimming hole infuse this trail with interest.

3. *Hamilton Barn Road,* 1.4 miles [p. 216]. This rambling route crosses the Wheeler Mill site before ending at the old Hamilton Ranch, but the real highlight is Amos Cummings's beautiful apple orchard—a sight not to be missed in spring.

4. *Dyerville Flats Loop Trail Trio,* 1.4 miles. The Founders Tree, the fallen Dyerville Giant, a criterion goosepen tree, and the site of a historic confrontation—all this plus some of the loveliest ground cover to be found in the Park. Take the Founders Grove Nature Trail [p. 144] to the Dyerville Giant, and then turn left on a side trail, which curves around a large log and soon comes to a fork. Left leads to the Mahan Plaque Loop [p. 153], while right heads towards the Goosepen Loop [p. 145], which lies across the Avenue. Hike both of these magnificent short trails and then return to the Dyerville Giant and complete the Founder's loop.

5. *Canoe Creek Circuit,* 1.9 miles. A wistful byway, accessible only by summer bridge. Take the Garden Club-Burlington Trail [p. 159] north to the Canoe Creek Trail [p. 142]; follow this winding path up the lovely stream canyon, passing dogwood, Pacific yew, and a half dozen different kinds of ferns. The course fords the creek and returns to the Garden Club-Burlington Trail; turn right and go back to the route's start.

poison oak
(Toxicodendron diversilobum)

This is the first plant that Park visitors should learn to identify. Its leaves and stems both contain highly irritating oils that can cause welty, pustulant skin eruptions of several days' duration; many a pleasurable vacation has been transformed into a nightmare of itching due to inadvertent contact.

Poison oak provides certain clues as to its identity, but in other ways it disguises itself, so that close observation is often required to make a definite determination. The plant can grow as a small bush, as a ground cover, or as a large, almost tree-like shrub. In other situations, it produces long, thick vines, often encircling the bases of redwood trees and winding high up their trunks. Poison oak leaves form in clusters of three, with the leaf surfaces frequently covered with an oily sheen. The leaves are usually green in spring and summer, although they are sometimes tinged with red; the white springtime flowers turn into white berries during the summer. In fall, poison oak provides its best warning, its leaves first turning bright scarlet and then subsiding into a pale yellow. During winter, only the gray stems and dried berries remain, but even these still contain the volatile oils; at all other times of year, the admonition "leaves of three, let it be" provides a helpful warning. [blooms March-May]

Two to Four Miles

6. The Five Allens Ascent, 2.6 miles [p 188]. This steep, switch-backing climb offers three rewards: a dazzling waterfall, an assortment of flourishing ferns, and the haunting, hillside E. Achelis Grove.

7. High Rock Hike, 2.9 miles [p. 189]. Dark redwood groves, several deep creeks, and the promontory of High Rock highlight the only Park trail along the main Eel River.

8. To Look and Back, 3.1 miles [p. 238]. The lower part of Look Road takes you past Luke Prairie, then to the picturesque Look Prairie Barn, and on to the cascading upper Look Prairie. Turn left and climb onto the upper meadow, mile 1.5, and then either hike down the steep prairie slope to the barn or return by the road.

9. We Ought to Go to Weott, 3.2 miles [p. 140]. The Burlington-Weott Trail is a plant-filled hillside passage that connects campground with town. Some of Humboldt Redwoods' most stunning redwood lilies will be found midway along the route.

Five to Nine Miles

10. Indians and Poles, 5.2 miles. The Indian Orchard Trail [p. 234] climbs to a nearly-hidden homestead site that's dotted with old apple trees. Farther up the canyon, the route meets Pole Line Road [p. 245], which returns to the valley through a pair of sunny prairies. Near the bottom, turn right onto the Horse Trail [p. 219], ford Cuneo Creek, and complete the circuit back to the Cuneo Creek Horse Group Camp.

11. A Tramp to Tie Camp, 8.2 miles. The route leaves the Big Trees Area, crossing Bull Creek and proceeding east on the Bull Creek Flats Loop Trail [p. 212]. Turn right on the Johnson Camp Trail [p. 257] and follow it uphill through mixed forest to shaded, historic Johnson Tie Camp. Continue on the trail to its end at Grasshopper Road [p. 250]; bear right, returning by the road to the valley floor. There, at a small parking area, take the spur route, right, to the Big Trees-Albee Creek Loop [p. 208], and then follow the loop east past the Flatiron Tree and back to the Big Trees parking lot.

12. Rockefeller Reconnaissance, 8.8 miles. This double loop crosses most of the Bull Creek Flats, passing through the heart of the fabled Rockefeller Forest. Start on the Rockefeller Loop Trail [p. 223], which promptly connects you with the Bull Creek Flats Loop [p. 212]. Follow the creek upstream to the Big Trees Area and then return along the opposite side of Bull Creek. Complete the rest of the Rockefeller Loop and return to the parking area.

* * *

WATCH FOR DEER TICKS

Besides poison oak, the Park is home to only one other frequently found and dangerous inhabitant. The deer tick is only 1/4 inch long, but if it happens to be a carrier of Lyme disease, it can cause big trouble; fortunately, few of the ticks harbor the disease.

Deer ticks often perch on trailside foliage, where they wait to attach themselves to a passing host. The tick then engorges itself on its victim's blood, sometimes providing a dose of Lyme disease in exchange. Antibiotics will easily cure the ailment during its early stages, but if left untreated, it can cause a variety of symptoms that range from fever and headache to inflammation of the brain and heart.

To help avoid contact with deer ticks, take these precautions: 1) tuck pant legs into boots, 2) wear light-colored clothing, 3) wear a hat or other head covering, 4) make periodic body and scalp searches. Medical authorities advise that if bitten by a tick, use tweezers to gently pull it straight out; do not twist the tick, and do not touch it with your bare hands. Save the tick for identification and consult a physician.

Hillside hiking path —
Big Cut Trail above the Dyerville Flats

More than Ten Miles

13. Northside Loop, 10.4 miles. A rousing romp up, along, and down the hillside north of Bull Creek. Start on Look Prairie Road [p.238], take it to the ridgetop, and then turn left onto Peavine Road [p. 242]. Proceed west on Peavine to Thornton Road [p. 247]; turn left and descend to the Albee Creek Campground. Pick up the Horse Trail [p. 219] and follow it east to the parking area beside Look Prairie Road.

14. Bull Creek Ranch Ramble, 10.6 miles. Climb into the heart of the historic Bull Creek backcountry on this high-energy hike. Follow Bull

Creek Road [p. 266] south to Gould Road [p. 270]; turn left and climb to the site of the old Hazelton-Bull Creek Ranch. Continue on to the junction with South Prairie Road [p. 276]. Turn right and descend to Bull Creek Road; turn right again and return to the route's start.

15. *Grasshopper Trail,* 13.4 miles. From the riverside, through forests and prairies, to the highest point in the Park—a magnificent but demanding hike. Take the Garden Club-Burlington Trail [p. 159] to the southern spur of the Grasshopper Trail [p. 148]. Follow the Grasshopper Trail to the top of Grasshopper Peak; look around at the lookout—numerous mountain ranges rise in the distance—and then return by the same route, hopefully before it gets dark.

Biking Beyond the Big Trees:
Outrageous Roads Above Bull Creek

The word is out: the dozen-plus dirt roads in the Bull Creek section of Humboldt Redwoods provide some of the finest mountain bike routes in northwestern California. Most weekend mornings will find a contingent of cyclists chuffing up the gruesomely steep grades that rise to the rim of the Bull Creek drainage, while the afternoon air is rent by the whooshes of the bikers' wild and wheel-wrenching descents.

While no individual road is longer than seven-plus miles, there are numerous interconnections that allow for developing loop routes of many lengths. With a little planning, riders can make circuits of 20 miles or more, all with at least one major hill climb/descent. By using a car shuttle from paved Mattole Road, however, the downhill-racer types can eliminate the lung-lacerating ascents from the valley floor, some of which gain nearly a thousand feet in a mile.

Most of the roads offer well-graded dirt surfaces that are generally firm in dry weather but which turn into varying consistencies of mud when wet; a few are in poor condition throughout the year. Except as noted, locked metal gates block motor vehicle access; routes marked with an "AR" can be reached only via an approach road—see the Bull Creek area maps for connections. The routes are listed in approximate order of difficulty, based on steepness of grade and road condition, ranging from ultra-whimpy to totally post-awesome gnarly/gonzo.

1. *Hanson Ridge Road-AR:* Standard ridge running—up and down, shade and sun. Short, but a dead end means doubling back [p. 256] .

2. *Fox Camp Road:* Moderate excitement all the way along this high country course. The southern end runs through hilly prairies; it's an access road for local traffic, so you may have to dodge the odd pickup or logging truck. The northeastern section is often shaded, with switchbacks and gentle downgrades beyond Big Hill. A covering of leaves hides some nice, tire-trashing rocks along the way [p. 229].

Making the grade out of Bull Creek

3. Peavine Road-AR: A real ridgetop roller coaster — it dips and rises across several saddles; near each end of the road is a steep grade that drops from east to west. Partially shaded along most of the route, with some open stretches to the east [p. 242].

4. Squaw Creek Ridge Road-AR: The easiest way to get high in the Park. The first mile is steep but shaded, after which the route rises gradually through thick forest. You can wet your whiskers at Whiskey Flat Trail Camp along the way [p. 263].

5. Bull Creek Road: A horse highway, it provides the main access into the upper Bull Creek Canyon. The hoofprint-scarred northern section has been graveled because it turns to deep mud in wet weather; the southern third is steep and exposed [p. 266].

6. Grieg Road-AR: After a very steep start, Grieg calms down and follows a ridgeline to the southern shoulder of Grasshopper Peak; from there it serves as a backdoor approach to the mountaintop. Watch for washouts along the stretch southeast of the peak [p. 254].

7. Look Prairie Road: A generally steady climb with occasional tight turns. Its lower third often crosses prairie land and can be hot on summer days. Survivors of that stretch can chill out in the thick forest that then continues to the ridgetop [p. 238].

8. *Pole Line Road:* Steep and sunny, with a couple of semi-level prairie interludes to ease the way. Backcountry landowners travel on this road, so freewheeling around blind corners provides the chance to become a hood ornament on some rancher's pickup [p. 245].

Pole Line Road;
Grasshopper Peak in the distance

9. *Tanbark Road-AR:* Moderately steep grades and lots of curves along the bottom half make this an easygoing, fun descent; uphill is another story [p. 278].

10. *Kemp Road:* Sudden slopes and rough spots add interest to this medium-steep run. The water crossing at the bottom offers the obstacle of randomly placed rocks, some of which are visible [p. 273].

11. *Gould Road-AR:* The road surface is poor, the climb is abrupt, and there are boggy patches along the upper segment. In short, a perfect ride for your basic brute biker [p. 270].

12. *Preacher Gulch Road-AR:* Just when you thought you'd done all the difficult routes . . . . The initial climb from Bull Creek will crack most cyclists, and then, after a diabolically sharp drop to the headwaters of

Squaw Creek, there is another gruelling grind up the southwestern side of Grasshopper Peak [p. 260].

13. Grasshopper Road: This is the big boy: relatively long, lots of elevation gain, and an appallingly steep final section on the way to the top of Grasshopper Peak. How can anyone resist? Heavy shade makes it a good uphill route for hot days [p, 250].

14. South Prairie Road-AR: The lower half of this route is rumored to have once been a road, but it's lapsed into a rutted, barely discernable grass-covered track. And that's the good news. It also rises almost vertically, and it has a southern exposure with little shade. Survivors of this first stretch may want to jump in the watering trough beside the junction with Gould Road; from there on it's still a steep climb, but at least there's a real roadbed [p. 276].

15. Thornton Road: The graveyard of the gonzos. The route's moderately-sloped upper half will lull downhill cyclists into cheery complacency, but the litter of madrone leaves hides a rampage of rocks and ruts; then Thornton drops off the side of the earth, tumbling headlong towards Albee Creek through a ravine-ravaged remnant of a roadbed. Next of kin should be notified before attempting this one [p. 247].

Warning: Within Humboldt Redwoods, only roads are open to mountain bike use. All trails are off limits. Park rangers are willing to wait at parking areas until illegal bikers return to their vehicles in order to dispense tickets carrying a $100 fine.

All Kinds of Campgrounds

Reserving Campsites

Procedures for reserving Park campsites change periodically. For current information, contact the Visitor Center or Park headquarters.

Vehicle camping

The Park's three family campgrounds all have shaded sites, piped water, and wheelchair-accessible restrooms with showers and flush toilets; the Burlington and Hidden Springs campgrounds also have laundry tubs. Each campsite has a picnic table, food locker, and fire ring. The sites lack travel vehicle hookups, but the Williams Grove has a trailer sanitation station. All three campgrounds accommodate motorhomes up to 33 feet long; Hidden Springs and Burlington take trailers up to 24 feet in length and Albee takes those 21 feet long or less.

Hidden Springs Campground [p. 104] is located just east of Myers Flat on the Avenue of the Giants. Its 154 hillside sites offer twisting walkways, privacy, and a chance to safari through a jungle of second-growth tanoak. The campground is open only in summer. Nearby is Hidden Springs Beach, a scenery-packed swimming site.

Burlington Campground [p. 128] is next to the Visitor Center, midway between Myers Flat and Weott. Large stumps and young redwoods dot the 56 cozy sites—you'll find it easy to get to know your neighbors. Several trails are close by, as is a swimming area at the South Fork Eel. Burlington is the only family campground open all year.

Burlington Campground

Albee Creek Campground [p. 202] lies in the heart of the Bull Creek valley, five miles west of the Avenue on Mattole Road. Nestled next to a forested hillslope, it features a pair of creeks and a lovely old fruit orchard. Albee has 34 sites and is open only during summer. Biking, hiking, and horse routes all leave the campground.

Group Camping

Williams Grove Group Campground [p. 122], situated a short distance north of Myers Flat, has space for a single group of up to 125 people or for two smaller groups. There are large picnic tables, barbecues, and restrooms, but no showers; hiking trails and a swimming spot are nearby. The southern end of the Grove offers single-family picnic tables and a sanitary dump station.

Walk-In Camping

The Bull Creek canyon has two "environmental camps" that require a hike of about a hundred yards from the parking areas. They have untreated water and pit toilets, and each site has a fire ring, food locker, and picnic table. A gate key is available to provide vehicle access from Mattole Road to the parking sites.

Hamilton Barn Environmental Camp [p. 216] is situated above Bull Creek on what was once the Hamilton Ranch. There are five sites, four in the forest and one next to the old ranch orchard.

Baxter Environmental Camp [p. 208] lies across the creek from the Hamilton Barn site at the base of Squaw Creek Ridge. There are two campsites, one in a grove of redwoods and the other in mixed forest across a small bridge.

There are also specialized camps for backpackers, touring cyclists, and horseback riders; these are described in the following sections that cover each of those activities.

Backpacking:

The trails on and around Grasshopper Peak are dotted with five trail camps; each provides untreated water, a privy, and a primitive campsite. No open fires are allowed.

Johnson Trail Camp — perches upon the somber northern side of Grasshopper Peak along the Johnson Camp Trail [p. 257], 2.3 miles from the Big Trees Area. A camp for splitting railroad ties once stood here; four of the reconstructed shanties for the "tie hacks" now occupy the forest-enclosed spot. Be warned: one former resident noted the "sound of tiny saws buzzing," which came from "10 million mosquitoes."

Grasshopper Trail Camp — borders a beautiful sloping prairie at the junction of the Grasshopper Trail [p. 148] and Grieg Road [p. 254]. Nearby is the Grasshopper lookout with its panoramic, peaktop view. The main water source is at the lookout and is available only when the lookout is open. Check with Park headquarters for current information.

Whiskey Flat Trail Camp — situated on a shady, salal-surrounded benchland along Squaw Creek Ridge. Another springtime mosquito resort, it is reached by the Squaw Creek Ridge Road [p. 263].

Hanson Ridge Trail Camp/Hanson Ridge Group Trail Camp — both are found at the bottom of flower-filled Hanson Ridge Prairie. The lovely and remote setting is situated just off Hanson Ridge Road [p. 256]; parts of the upper Bull Creek watershed are visible from the prairie.

Bull Creek Trail Camp — lies 3.4 miles up Bull Creek Road [p. 266]; its pleasant streamside setting provides a starting point for excursions into the upper creek drainage.

Campers can watch for the nocturnal ringtail

Bicycle Touring:

Cyclists travelling along the Avenue of the Giants may stop over at the *Marin Garden Club Grove Hike and Bike Camp* [p. 134], located at the northern edge of Weott. The Bull Creek area's two environmental camps, Baxter [p. 208] and Hamilton Barn [p. 216], can be easily reached by cycling along short dirt routes from Mattole Road.

Warning: Beware of frequent narrow stretches and blind curves along both the Avenue of the Giants and Mattole Road. Cyclists using either route should realize that there are no bike lanes and that various vehicles, many of them quite large, often whiz by very close to the road shoulder.

Horseback Riding:

While horse use is not allowed on most of Humboldt Redwoods' hiking trails, the numerous dirt roads of the Bull Creek region provide ample routes for riding; in addition, the Horse Trail [p. 219] links several of the roads with the Cuneo Creek Horse Group Camp. There is a second horse trail, at Dry Creek on the Avenue of the Giants [p. 108], but it has a difficult stream crossing at its northern end and a poor

THE REDWOODS AND THE PARK

Morning fog covers the riverbottom; on a nearby flat, the first trilliums of spring brighten the forest floor. A varied thrush makes its hollow, haunting call, the sound soon swallowed by the shadows. Then, ever so gradually, the gigantic shapes are illuminated — they rise from the mist like ancient monuments, their trunks soaring into the dark foliage far above. Shafts of golden light angle through the heavy air; the great trees surround the space with a stillness that slows both time and thought. Within the grove, the silent redwoods grow in perfect peace, rooted by the riverside, poised at the edge of eternity.

Morning light in the grove

I. TREMENDOUS TREES

Redwoods — "the most perfect of vegetable growths."
                                        — Luther Burbank

Once there were a dozen species of redwoods, but now only three remain; California is home to the two largest, a pair of ruddy-barked giants that have long brought fame and fortune to the Golden State. The third, smaller type of redwood is found half a world away in China, but for many years, it wasn't believed to grow anywhere at all.

Coast redwood

Sometimes rising higher than 350 feet, *Sequoia sempervirens*, the coast redwood, is the world's tallest tree. Lumbermen have long lusted after its uniquely useful timber, while preservationists have fought for nearly a century to protect part of its old-growth habitat. Only scattered stands of the great trees now remain; most are located in either Redwood National Park or the 30-plus California state redwood parks.

Giant sequoia

Sequoiadendron giganteum, the giant sequoia, grows in the Sierra Nevada Mountains. While not as tall as the coast redwood, its enormous girth makes it the most massive of all trees. It is also one of the oldest living entities on Earth, with specimens reaching 3,200 years of age. Sometimes called "big tree," the giant sequoia inhabits several small sections of the Sierra, including groves in Yosemite, Kings Canyon, and Sequoia National parks.

The third species is the dawn redwood, *Metasequoia glyptostroboides;* experts considered it extinct until 1944, when it was discovered growing in a remote valley in China. After its identity was confirmed, this junior-size redwood created a furor among foresters and soon claimed a celebrity status similar to its larger

Dawn redwood

relatives. It grows to only a hundred feet or so in height but dazzles with a distinctive fall tinting of its needles.

At least nine additional redwood species existed during prehistoric times. Then, with the arrival of the Ice Age about one million years ago, cooler temperatures caused the forests to retreat southward. Previously both the dawn and coast redwoods had spread across Europe, Asia, and North America, while the giant sequoia blanketed much of Europe and the United States. The advancing ice pushed all three of these trees into drastically reduced ranges; the other varieties of redwood were even less fortunate — caught in the growing global deep freeze, they all eventually disappeared.

The coast redwood survived the Ice Age, but just barely. As the glaciers retreated, the tree found suitable habitat in only one location — a narrow strip of the North American continent near the Pacific Ocean. Seldom more than 20 miles wide, this band of forestland stretched from below present-day Big Sur, California northward to what is now the Chetco River, just across the Oregon border. In this small but hospitable region the coast redwood flourished for the next several hundred thousand years.

* * *

DID THE "CHINESE COLUMBUS" DISCOVER THE REDWOODS?

If an article that appeared in an 1890 New York newspaper had been taken seriously, we would no longer celebrate Columbus Day. Instead, the "discovery" of America would be commemorated on June 10th, and a Chinese mariner named Hee-li would be honored for the accomplishment. We would also credit him with being the first non-native to observe a redwood tree.

The century-old news story was written by a Dr. Shaw, who had recently returned from China after uncovering an interesting manuscript in the city archives at Si-Ngan-Foo. The report had been written by Hee-li, a local sea captain, more than 2,000 years earlier.

According to the account, Hee-li and his crew went sailing off the Chinese coast one day and became a little lost. A great storm blew up, sending their tiny junk far out to sea. There was no sight of land, so

Hee-li relied on his trusty compass to guide them towards the shores of home.

But strange things happened. After many days of sailing the men still hadn't found the coast, even though the storm couldn't have blown them that far off course. Then there was the problem with the sun. Each morning it now rose in the west, which wasn't right at all, and then in the evening it compounded the problem by setting in the east. When one of the crewmen pointed out this reversal of the heavens, Hee-li threw him overboard. No one else chose to continue the discussion, and so the ship sailed on.

Finally, four months after leaving port, the sailors again saw land. When they came ashore, however, they found themselves not back in China, but in some strange new place that had wonderful weather and grew gigantic trees with a thick, reddish bark.

Hee-li and his crew spent three months at the peaceful anchorage, which was probably located in what is now Monterey Bay. Early in their stay, a sailor who was polishing the captain's compass made an interesting discovery; a small cockroach had become wedged under the needle in such a way as to reverse the instrument's direction, thus explaining the captain's wrong-way trip. The problem solved, it was then an easy four-month voyage back to Si-Ngan-Foo. Hee-li wrote an account of his remarkable journey; the document was promptly filed away and forgotten. By the time Dr. Shaw uncovered it, Columbus had held sway for nearly 400 years as the supposed discoverer of America, and no one paid any heed to Hee-Li.

The misguided mariner deserved better, for besides recording the first sighting of a redwood tree, Hee-Li eventually proved himself a pretty good navigator—once he got the "bugs" out of his compass.

*   *   *

It wasn't easy for the *Sequoia sempervirens* to find a location that satisfied its unique and demanding lifestyle. To begin with, despite being called the coast redwood, it doesn't like to grow near the ocean. The tree needs lots of moisture, but coastal salt air has a harmful drying effect; moreover, redwoods have shallow roots, which render them vulnerable to the strong winds that often sweep onshore. So instead of perching beside the Pacific, the coast redwood prefers to grow near the frequently foggy streamcourses that twist through the inland canyons, such as the Eel and Klamath rivers and Redwood Creek; these areas provide the two elements essential to the tree's well-being: a massive supply of moisture and nutritious soil.

As with all trees, the coast redwood requires water, but it demands a much greater quantity than most other species. Because of its great size, a mature redwood can lose up to 500 gallons of moisture per day through its foliage—enough liquid to flush at least a hundred toilets. The cool fogs of river bottoms and creek canyons compensate for part of this loss, causing the water vapor emitted by the trees to condense into a rain-like drip. This recycled wetness is then returned to the redwoods' surroundings in amounts of up to 12 inches per year, a process that is especially important during the warm, dry months of summer. The coast redwood's enormous trunk also helps by storing a substantial reserve water supply, but some individual trees still become stressed from inadequate moisture. They then begin to die from their tops downward, creating withered, grey-brown "spiketops" that are devoid of foliage.

Osprey in spiketop redwood nest

River and creek canyons provide the redwoods not only with life-giving fogs, but also with a second essential—food. Over time, the alluvial silts and gravels that have washed down the streamcourses have been compacted into benches and flats; these low-lying landforms thereby become richer in nutrients than the soils on surrounding hill slopes. When supplemented by the fertility of fallen trees and other decaying plant life, the streamside collections of compressed sediment become banquet tables for a forest feast. The result is such well-fed redwoods as those of the Rockefeller Forest and the Founders Grove.

Periodic flooding of these canyon areas, if not too severe, will actually benefit the trees by creating new layers of nutritious alluvia; in some cases, coast redwoods will even grow an additional level of roots above their old ones to reach the fresh silt deposits. One tree was found to have survived four alluvium burials, each time sending up a new set of vertical roots from below. If the deposits become too compacted, however, as happened in the floods of 1955 and 1964, the affected trees receive too little air and may eventually die.

* * *

"WHITE" REDWOODS

Scattered mysteriously about the redwood forests are specimens of a strange, apparition-like plant. The ghostly objects are usually found clinging to the base of a healthy coast redwood; they appear to be sickly, miniature versions of their vigorous neighbors. These stunted treelets seldom grow more than 15 feet tall, and their foliage, while having some dead brown spots in it, is mostly pale white. Such wraiths of the woods are albino redwoods; they lack chlorophyll in their leaves and are thus compelled to derive their entire nourishment from the parent trees on which they've sprouted. The largest and oldest specimens grow in remote locations, but a few smaller ones struggle for survival near trails or roads. Avoiding direct contact with albino redwoods will help protect these rare and fragile foundlings of the forest.

* * *

While the coast redwood might expire from suffocation or thirst, it will seldom succumb to pests, for the tree protects itself with three separate lines of defense. First is its formidable bark, which can measure one to two feet thick on mature trees; it insures that many pestiferous critters will either give up their attempted entry or die of exhaustion before they succeed. Those attackers which survive this initial ordeal next meet a one-two chemical punch inside the tree: first come highly astringent tannins and then a pair of compounds called sequirins, one of which fights insects and the other fungi.

Redwood warriors with their gun sticks

that could weigh as much as a locomotive. Such a tree had bark thicker than the walls of a bank vault, and its trunk could be 15, or even 20, feet across. To combat such an adversary, the tree cutters equipped themselves with a formidable arsenal; it included two axes, two eight-foot saws, a 12-foot saw, two dozen plates, a dozen shims, 10 wedges, two sledge hammers, a pair of gun sticks for sighting the tree's fall, a plumb bob, and a set of 12 springboards and 6 pieces of staging used to stand upon when cutting high above the ground. Falling one of the giants took time, but the weapons did their work well; acre upon acre of weathering stumps came to mark the battlefields where the axes, shims, and saws had finally won their victories.

Several stands of northern redwoods gained special notice, including tracts along the Smith River and Mill Creek in Del Norte County and on Redwood Creek in northern Humboldt County. Magnificent as they were, it was generally agreed that the finest grove of all was located a considerable distance to the south, nestled in a shadowy stream canyon. According to one early admirer,

> . . . the world's greatest forest lies a mile or two from Dyerville near the South fork of the Eel river. This is known as the Bull creek forest. There are about 40 trees to the acre—more than 4,000,000 feet of timber. The trees are the largest in the redwood belt.

A few years later, another writer concurred, claiming that the "timber on the flat at the mouth of. . . Bull Creek is the finest and most valuable per acre of any in Humboldt County. . . . The timber is very dense, and little loss in logging will result."

And for a long time, logging was just about it; in the boom-days of the lumber industry, few people seemed to think that the giant trees deserved any fate but the mill saw or splitter's ax. Prompted by business-wise wood boosters, the public had come to embrace redwood as a construction material without equal, and the choppers and their cohorts strained to keep up with the demand.

*   *   *

THE "WONDER" WOOD

Stimulated by a strong advertising campaign, builders of all types, from creative craftsmen to city contractors, wanted redwood. One latter-day promoter dubbed it the "wonder wood," citing its capacity to hold paint and stain, its high insulation ability, its ease of working, and its resistance to both fire and weather. A list of testimonials to its utility stretches far into the past and across several continents:

. . . because so many redwood buildings emerged unscathed by the fire which followed San Francisco's 1906 earthquake, the mayor's emergency building committee dictated that all new structures had to be made of either galvanized iron or redwood . . .

. . . when asked to create the "most magnificently appointed train in the world," George Pullman selected redwood for the inside finish of the coaches . . .

. . . the King of Denmark was sent a folding bedstead of redwood by a San Francisco bank; it was placed in His Majesty's sleeping compartment for his "personal" use . . .

. . . redwood was shipped to both the Argentine Republic and the East Indian Islands, where it remained untouched by the voracious red ants that ate all other woods . . .

. . . *two Massachusetts piano makers required redwood for their piano cases, as it "made the most perfect sounding boards . . . [that] . . . would not warp, twist, or crack . . ."*

. . . *by the 1940s, sports fields across the continent contained seats made from redwood, including the football stadiums at Stanford, Pittsburgh, Michigan, Iowa, Virginia, Louisiana, and McGill universities, and also Fenway and Comiskey baseball parks . . .*

. . . *in 1874 the Santa Rosa Baptist Church was constructed from the timber of a single redwood tree, the congregation being apprised of this fact only after entering the building for the first service . . .*

. . . *the San Francisco-Oakland Bay Bridge used over seven million board feet of redwood lumber, including more than 105,000 ties selected especially for their durability and high insulating value . . .*

. . . *in addition, hundreds of smaller bridges were constructed out of rot-resistant redwood, along with countless pipelines, guard rails, posts, trestles, wharf piles, piers, grape stakes, silos, flood gates, feeders, water and septic tanks, irrigation flumes, wine vats, and cigar boxes.*

Garford truck with load of grapestakes

III. TOURISTS' TREASURE

While many early accounts of the redwoods focused on their worth as wood products, there was a growing awareness that the trees had value beyond merely being good sawtimber. One author who sang their praises as lumber also whistled this tune:

> Nature's masterpiece and unsurpassable! It took 1,500 years to produce them, and they are pillars in nature's grandest temples. Vacant must be the soul that can contemplate their stately grandeur without awe and reverence.

Other folk held similar sentiments, which soon spurred them to action. Early in the new century, a pair of redwood preserves were created, finally protecting a few of the magnificent but threatened trees. First came Big Basin State Park, created from the forests of northern Santa Cruz County in 1902 through the work of Phoebe A. Hearst and the earliest redwood preservationist organization, the Sempervirens Club. Next, in 1907, Congressman William Kent donated 510 acres of redwoods in Marin County for the establishment of Muir Woods National Monument. But the effort then slowed, and the mill saws whined unabated as grove after unprotected redwood grove was leveled to provide city homes, bleacher seats, railroad ties . . . and cigar boxes.

Much of Humboldt County's early redwood cutting had been in the coastal forests near Humboldt Bay. Only gradually had the skid trails and railroads snaked their way inland to the more remote stands of trees. In redwood-rich southern Humboldt, timber companies had long anticipated the arrival of the rail line, slowly buying up the early homesteads along the South Fork Eel. From 1902 to 1905, the Pacific Lumber Company pieced together an 8,000-acre tract of timberland on the flats of lower Bull Creek; as the early commentators had noted, it was the finest stand of redwoods to be seen anywhere, but the PL had purchased it to log, not to look at.

For a time, though, the company was busy elsewhere, logging the thick forests that lay to the north along the main branch of the Eel. The first cutters to descend on the canyon of the South Fork were instead the "split-stuff" and tanbark outfits; they purchased 40-acre parcels close to the county wagon road that, during the war years, was being converted into the "Redwood Highway."

tanoak, tanbark oak
(Lithocarpus densiflorus)

If the coast redwoods are the aristocrats of the Park's forestlands, then the tanoaks have become its derelicts — usually found huddled in unwanted spaces, dull and drab of appearance, easily overlooked. An uncaring world doesn't even spell the tree's name consistently, sometimes rendering it as tan oak, other times as tanoak, less frequently as tanbark oak. Worse yet, all three names are in a sense aliases, for the tree is neither a true oak nor tan in color.

Rather than being accepted into the staid and somewhat snobbish oak family, the tanoak is grouped with a collection of more than a hundred tree species found only in southeast Asia. This snub may be due in part to the tree's unusual acorns, which are much more bristly than those of true oaks. To muddy its pedigree still further, the tanoak produces flowers that are similar to those of chinkapins and chestnuts. As for its color, the leaves of the tanoak are actually an olive drab—about the shade of a war surplus jacket. The tree's name, as it turns out, was derived from one of its most useful features, the abundance of tannin that is found in its bark.

The tanoak's acorn, despite its bristles, was a primary food source for the Northern California Indians. Processing the acorns involved grinding, leaching, and drying; the resulting meal was used for soups and sometimes for bread. This now-neglected tree was thus close to being the Indians' "staff of life." The great tanoak grove along the Park's Peavine Ridge serves to commemorate the species' once high stature.

"SPLIT-STUFF" AND TANBARK

Although the logging of giant redwoods for lumber gained the most notoriety, the forests of southern Humboldt County were also depleted by the demand for two other types of wood products. At camps called "split-stuff layouts," redwoods were converted into specialized items like railroad ties, grapestakes, fence posts, and shingle bolts. Smaller trees were often used, since they usually split more easily. After a tree had been dropped, it was cut into short logs and then worked by hand; railroad ties, for instance, were "squared up" with an enormous, razor-sharp broadax that had a foot-long bit—the "tie hacks" who used this tool paid close attention to their work.

"Tanbarking" utilized the vast groves of tanoak trees that covered many of the hillslopes; as the name implies, the bark is high in tannin, and for many years it was used by tanneries in the Bay Area. Tanoak bark was best peeled between mid-May and mid-July of each year, when the sap level was at its highest. First the tree was girdled by a sharp ax cut near ground level, the incision going just through the bark; next came a similar scoring about four feet up the trunk. A vertical cut then opened the bark for peeling. After this first section of bark was removed, the tree was downed; the rest of the trunk and the larger limbs were then peeled. The cut bark was left to dry for a couple of months

before being bundled into packets and loaded onto mules for transport. The packets were usually sent to the tannery for processing, but some bark went to a plant in Briceland, which converted it into tannin extract. Not until the 1950s did the development of synthetic tannins render tanbark harvesting obsolete.

*   *   *

There were no new redwood parks for a decade after the establishment of Muir Woods, but then the flagging preservationist movement finally regained its vigor. The impetus for the revival came from the same Bull Creek forest that had charmed an earlier generation of observers; now the power of the great trees acted upon a group of prominent patricians who had been enjoying a fraternal retreat in the redwoods.

In the summer of 1917, three men left the Russian River's elite Bohemian Club and drove north, hoping to find "a forest wall reported to have mystery and charm unique among the living works of creation." Their interest was understandable, for they were among the country's most prestigious naturalists: Madison Grant, the wealthy founder of the New York Zoological Society; Henry Fairfield Osborn, President of the American Museum of Natural History; and John C. Merriam, a professor of paleontology and later President of the Carnegie Institution.

Upon reaching Bull Creek Flats they at last found their "wall," a stand of towering redwoods that surpassed all expectations. The men left the area awed by the magnificence of the great forest. For the next two years the three naturalists-turned-activists contacted a series of state officials, vainly attempting to gain government protection for the Bull Creek area. The men then shifted tactics, "enlisting the support of a group of patriotic Californians" to aid in their preservation efforts. In August of 1919, bolstered by the addition of other influential conservationists, the group organized itself into the "Save-the-Redwoods League." Franklin K. Lane, then Secretary of the Interior, was chosen as the League's first president.

After the meeting, Madison Grant again visited the South Fork Eel, accompanied this time by Stephen Tyng Mather, head of the recently formed National Park Service. Seeing the area after a two-year absence, Grant found that "the change was sickening." Forty-acre plots were being harvested right next to the roadside; 300-foot tall trees had been reduced to a mass of grapestakes that were then stacked in long, neat piles for shipment to the vineyards. Grant and Mather were stunned by the rapid destruction of the redwoods, made possible by the recent improvement of the roadway and by access to the railroad at the nearby town of South Fork.

Roadside along the South Fork Eel

They were not alone in their concern. Arriving at Bull Creek, the two men were met by a delegation from the Humboldt Chamber of Commerce, which then escorted them north to Eureka. There Mather gave a ringing speech at a large rally, urging the locals to join the effort to save the flats. The Chamber immediately launched a funding drive for the proposed redwood park, while a group of Humboldt women formed their own local Save-the-Redwoods League.

The fight to protect the forests on the Bull Creek and Dyerville flats now began in earnest. The participants at the fateful Eureka rally had managed to forge a powerful alliance of business and conservation interests, the like of which would never be seen again; it was well they did, for in the coming conflict every scrap of strength would be needed.

On his way south from Eureka, Grant stopped to see John Emert, President of the Pacific Lumber Company; Emert assured him that neither the Bull Creek nor the Dyerville flats would be cut for at least two years. Within a month, however, PL crews were logging part of the Dyerville area, and only after the combined protests of community leaders, the Eureka Chamber of Commerce, and Governor William D. Stephens did the company agree to reduce its harvest.

Meanwhile, the Save-the-Redwoods League moved quickly to gain control of land along the South Fork Eel. Once protected from cutting, such property could be held until a park was established; ownership would then be transferred to the State. The League began enrolling members and collecting donations, bolstered by a $55,000 contribution from Humboldt County and the approval of a state subsidy that would match private contributions on a 50-50 basis. Soon the League had acquired several groves of prime redwoods, all of them located along the new highway, and on June 16, 1922, the *Humboldt Beacon* was able to announce:

REDWOOD PARK

IS NOW OPEN

TO THE PUBLIC

Humboldt State Redwood Park, as it was then called, consisted of some 2,200 acres scattered along the highway from north of Miranda to Weott. More land was soon added as the League developed its highly successful "Memorial Grove" donation program, whereby groves were named in honor of persons selected by the donors. Yet despite the League's success, the forests of Bull Creek and Dyerville remained unprotected, and in the fall of 1924 there came reports that Pacific Lumber had recommenced logging the Dyerville Flats.

Camping in the redwoods

IV. TRAUMA AND TRIUMPH

Members of the Humboldt Women's Save-the-Redwoods League

LAURA AND JAMES MAHAN: PROTECTORS OF THE REDWOODS

As President of the Humboldt Women's Save-the-Redwoods League, Laura Mahan became a local leader in the drive to protect the great groves along the South Fork Eel. She was ably supported by her husband James, a prominent Eureka attorney.

Alarmed by rumors that the Pacific Lumber Company had begun to secretly log the Dyerville Flats, the Mahans drove down from Eureka to investigate. They found PL's choppers indeed busy at work, cutting a swath through the huge trees for a railroad right-of-way that would lead to the immense forest at Bull Creek. An outraged Laura Mahan alerted the Eureka newspapers by telephone. The reaction there was quick and decisive; within 48 hours the Board of Supervisors, with "virtually every town and organization in the County" urging protection, adopted a resolution binding the County to negotiate with the Pacific Lumber Company for the purchase of the Dyerville Flats. Newspaper editorials echoed the public's concern; one paper printed a letter from the *just-graduated Eureka High School Class of 1924 which offered a donation of $110 to help buy the threatened trees.*

The preservationists had won a round in the fight with PL, but there were more battles yet to come. In February of 1925, the Board of Supervisors met in special session to consider a proposal from the Save-the-Redwoods League to acquire both the Dyerville and the Bull Creek flats. Laura Mahan again rallied the tree savers, reading a telegram from the three million-member National Federation of Women's Clubs, which pledged its support to protect the threatened trees. Later in the meeting, tempers flared when James Mahan accused Donald McDonald, Treasurer of the Pacific Lumber Company, of having falsely claimed that PL was willing to sell the property. The two men then approached each other, McDonald "stiffening and straightening," and Mahan shaking his fist. Newton B. Drury, Secretary of the League, quickly intervened; a moment later, he was handed three telegrams in rapid succession, which he then read aloud:

"$700,000 in funds on hand to buy redwoods."

"$750,000 in funds on hand to buy redwoods."

"$750,000 in funds on hand to buy redwoods."

The telegrams were all signed, according to news reports, "by eminent San Francisco men, prominent bankers whose words carry national weight in financial matters." Bolstered by this showing of support, the County Supervisors voted unanimously to accept the League's proposal.

The fight to save the flats was still not finished, but thanks largely to the Mahans — and a trio of timely telegrams — victory was at last in sight.

*   *   *

Although the logging on the flats had been stopped, negotiations for the purchase of the area dragged on for six years; finally, Pacific Lumber and the League agreed to a compromise proposed by a Eureka bank president (and later League President), Arthur Connick. It had taken until 1931, but the unsurpassed redwoods of Dyerville and Bull Creek were finally protected. The Park, which until then had mainly been a scattering of relatively small groves, now had a heart.

It was a shining hour for the League, which had relied on some superlative fundraising to successfully complete the transaction. The flats could not have been purchased without a pair of million-dollar donations from John D. Rockefeller, Jr., who had been conducted through the redwoods by League officials and was suitably impressed. A state bond act, which the League strongly supported, had passed in 1928, and it now provided matching funds for the acquisition.

For a time the rapidly expanding Park had been supervised by the State Division of Forestry, but in 1929, the recently created Division of Beaches and Parks took over administration; two years later, Enoch "Percy" French became the first superintendent for the region's state parks. Part of Dyerville was purchased for a new headquarters, and the town's store was converted into Park offices and a museum.

Park headquarters, Dyerville, 1949

THE _TIMES_ REPORTS
THE PRESERVATION OF BULL CREEK

Although the Humboldt County "Save-the-Redwoods" movement lost its impetus in the late 1920s, the dedication of the long-sought Bull Creek grove was still treated as big news by the local papers. The story, entitled "Beautiful Bull Creek Redwoods Added to State Parks," was carried on page one of the September 15, 1931 edition of the Humboldt Times, right between "Slayer is Saved from Gallows" and "Radicals March on City Hall." The Times gave a lengthy account of the proceedings, including summaries of the numerous speeches that had been given from "a rustic platform, large enough for one person." The gathering, attended by 2,000 persons, concluded with a group of Eureka singers performing the "Hallelujah Chorus." It was a fitting end to what had been a big day for many people — be they slayers, radicals, or savers of the redwoods.

Other large tracts were added to the Park during the 1930s, as the League continued to find donors despite the effects of the Depression. When the Garden Club of America asked its members to fund the acquisition of a small grove on Kerr Creek, the response was so enthusiastic that the Club instead purchased a much larger stand downriver at Canoe Creek. By the end of the decade, Newton B. Drury, the League's affable and efficient secretary, was jokingly called the "biggest real estate man in California." There was actually much truth in the statement, for by then the League had purchased more than 30,000 acres of redwoods at a cost of six million dollars.

*   *   *

A TALE OF TWO TREES

The first of the two redwoods fell in Richardson Grove State Park, near the southern edge of Humboldt County. When it finally dropped in 1933, it had lived for 1,204 years, was 310 feet long, and was estimated to weigh an astonishing one million pounds. Professor Emmanual Fritz of the University of California examined the fallen giant and noted that a fire had damaged the tree extensively in 1820, killing 40 percent of its circumference and injuring its roots. The result was a tilting trunk that eventually caused the tree to topple, but only after a 113-year struggle. In all, the redoubtable redwood had been roasted in nine different fires, the earliest in 1147 — in that same year, half a world away, the ill-fated Second Crusade met disaster in Asia Minor. The tree, which was then already more than 400 years old, fared better than the crusaders, continuing to survive as other big fires burned it in 1595, 1789, and 1806. It was also assaulted by floods — seven major ones — but the tree compensated for these by sending up additional roots through the 11 feet of new soil that washed up around its base.

The second redwood may have faced less natural adversity, but it crashed to earth in 1943 the victim of forces that no tree could withstand. It was located on Big Creek, in Mendocino County, and stood 334 feet tall before expiring at age 1,728. This giant did not receive the exhaustive examination of the Humboldt County tree, for it had grown on the land of the Union Lumber Company, and its wood was used to provide fiber, not facts. The company was nonetheless able to offer some interesting information about this mill-filling mammoth — statistics to warm the cockles of a timber cruiser's heart: its stump diameter was 21 feet, 2 inches; the fallen log contained 140,800 board feet of lumber, enough to build more than eight houses; and it required 60 hours, or seven and a half working days, to be cut down.

Sixty hours versus 113 years: it was no contest. A power saw with a 22-foot blade easily outdid the combined forces of fire and flood.

Early "drag" saw bucking a redwood

In the late 1930s, the League began to promote the northward expansion of the Park along what it called the "Avenue of the Giants," a six-mile stretch of the Redwood Highway between Dyerville and Englewood. The League gradually purchased Pacific Lumber Company land which lay next to the road; in 1960, the initial "Avenue," now bordered by parkland, was superseded by the first segment of the new 101 Freeway, and the older route became a scenic and leisurely alternate. As more freeway was constructed during the following years, additional sections of the old highway were converted to Avenue. The Park meanwhile acquired groves in the Redcrest-Pepperwood area, which in 1969 formed the final section of the Avenue. In the middle of this project, the League learned of trouble back in Bull Creek.

PL truck crossing the Eel

Several years earlier, the December flood of 1955 had devastated the redwoods of the Rockefeller Forest, and a subsequent study of the incident determined that much of the damage resulted from intense logging in the upper Bull Creek watershed. The problem started in 1947; the post-World War II housing boom had created a demand for cheap lumber, and small logging operations began cutting the stands of Douglas fir that covered much of the higher canyon's steep and unstable terrain. Some redwood and tanoak were also taken out, and by 1954, a mass of skid trails and slash piles covered half of the upper drainage; a series of fires that burned 7,000 acres added to the devastation. When the torrential storms of 1955 hit, they unleashed a wall of water, mud, and debris that tore into the Rockefeller Forest, destroying scores of the sturdiest redwoods. Over the next few years, many trees that had survived the flood succumbed to the delayed effects of streambank undermining and silt burial, until over 500 giants had died.

Alarmed Park officials watched helplessly as huge mudflows choked Cuneo Creek and other side streams after every rain; it became clear that continued logging in the upper Bull Creek canyon would put the Rockefeller Forest at further risk. Accordingly, the Division of Beaches and Parks developed a plan to purchase the entire watershed and make it part of the Park. It was a massive undertaking, for thousands of acres needed to be protected as quickly as possible; funding pleas, featuring photos of the flood-wracked canyon, quickly appeared in the League's bulletin. Contributions poured in, and between 1963 and 1984, almost every privately-owned acre in Bull Creek became state property. Residents were forced to relocate, often over their protests, and all but a few of the buildings were demolished. The Park initiated projects for tree planting and stream rehabilitation that are still in progress; today, much of the damaged countryside is covered with young forest, although the scars on some eroded hillslopes yet remain.

By the mid-1980s, Humboldt Redwoods seemed almost complete; a nearly continuous string of protected redwood groves lined the Avenue, while the massive Bull Creek-Grasshopper Peak backcountry

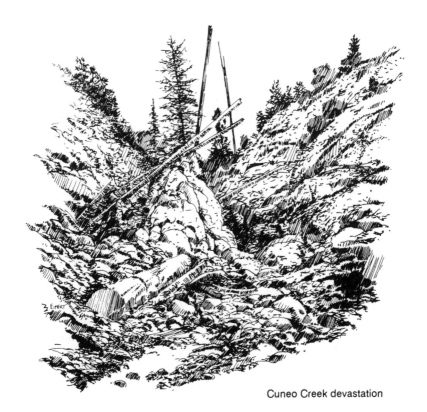

Cuneo Creek devastation

gave the Park a diverse second section of equal size and interest. Then, in 1986, a flood undercut more than a hundred redwoods along the Avenue, recalling the problems that had earlier plagued Bull Creek. The solution was the same — acquire the land upslope of the endangered trees. The League's current program targets four such areas for inclusion within the Park: 1) a long stretch of hillside above Redcrest and Pepperwood; 2) the Elk Creek drainage, north of Miranda; 3) areas southeast of the Founders Grove, including Camp Grant and part of Mail Ridge; and 4) land across the main Eel River from old Dyerville.

Since its early years, the Save-the-Redwoods League and its allies have helped protect many other redwood groves besides those in Humboldt Redwoods; in 1923 the League had already targeted forestlands on the San Francisco Peninsula and in northern Humboldt County for acquisition. Although over 30 state redwood parks were eventually established, it was not until 1968 that Congress finally acted to create Redwood National Park, preserving several sites in Humboldt and Del Norte counties where patches of magnificent old-growth forest still existed. A decade later, a major addition was tacked on to the federal park, partly to help protect creekside stands of trees that were threatened by erosion from heavy upstream logging. Some officials wondered if the action was necessary; they had only to look southward — to Bull Creek — to find out.

*   *   *

STILL SAVING THE REDWOODS

When Grant, Merriam, and Osborn made their 1917 trip in search of the fabled "wall" of trees, they likely had little inkling of what would ensue from their dusty drive down the valley of the South Fork. Were they to set out from San Francisco again today, there are few sights along the route they would recognize — until they reached the protected confines of Humboldt Redwoods State Park. There, centuries-old giants still shade the fern-covered flats where the men had once walked, the then-threatened trees now safe from the splitter's ax. In other places, the stumps of stands once laid low are now sprouting a new generation of redwoods, infant groves that will grow in peaceful perpetuity. The forest wall has flourished.

The sights the men saw in 1917 gave birth to a vision, out of which came a movement, and from that, a park. As Humboldt Redwoods now nears completion, the vision and the movement remain alive and active, inspiring the protection of other forests and the growth of other parks. Like the resilient redwoods themselves, the effort has been infused with a powerful, life-giving force. Today, more than 70 years after it originated, the drive to "Save-the-Redwoods" still continues.

Over 250,000 acres of coast redwood habitat, some of it virgin forest and some of it previously logged, is now preserved in state and national parks, but the vast majority of redwood acreage, including a few still-uncut stands of old-growth, belongs to large timber companies. On these private lands, the chainsaws roar, the skidders creak, and the logging trucks rumble as each tall tree begins its transformation from living legend into lucrative lumber. The technology has changed, but much else has remained the same since Walt Whitman wrote, more than a century ago, of redwood timber being cut . . .

With crackling blows of axes sounding musically driven by strong arms,

Riven deep by the sharp tongues of the axes, there in the redwood forest dense,

I heard the mighty tree its death-chant chanting.

The choppers heard not, the camp shanties echoed not,

The quick-ear'd teamsters and chain and jack-screw men heard not,

As the wood-spirits came from their haunts of a thousand years to join the refrain,

But in my soul I plainly heard.

—Song of the Redwood Tree

Listening to a redwood

RIDGES, ROCKS, RAINS, AND RIVERS

Humboldt Redwoods State Park nestles in shadowy seclusion among the mountains and valleys of southern Humboldt County, far from the winter roar of the rumbling Pacific, farther still from the bright lights that surround San Francisco Bay. It is a place of startling contrasts: of low mountains and tall trees, of hot noonday sun and cool morning mist, of flat river bottoms and 70-degree mountain slopes. Yet there is a sense of harmony here, too, where great groves of redwoods stand in a silence that seems to have endured for centuries, and where the surrounding hillsides that were once ravaged by chainsaw, ax, and flood have slowly begun to heal themselves.

Like many parks, Humboldt Redwoods encloses an area where nature seems to have worked overtime, creating features that are grander and more awe inspiring than those which adorn other, less-favored landscapes. Yellowstone has its geysers, Yosemite its granite; here, the "Big R" predominates — the coast REDWOOD. But while the huge trees are the stars of the Park's production, they are also supported by a cast of hundreds: flowers, ferns, bushes, other trees, and many species of wildlife. Worth noting, too, is the stage on which the performance is played; it is composed of the four "little r's" — ridges, rocks, rains, and rivers.

ridges

The mountains that surround the Park were once mere masses of sediment, lying on the bottom of the ocean. Then, about 200 million years ago, huge pieces of the earth's crust, called plates, began to move around a bit, and the plate which was the floor of the Pacific Ocean started sliding under the North American continental plate. When the two plates rubbed together, sediment was scraped off the ocean floor, lodging against the edge of the continent; the accumulated material was later crushed and compressed into many folded layers. Eventually these compacted sediments emerged from the ocean as a group of infant ridges, still wet behind the peaks, so to speak, but ready to rise to mountain-size maturity. The first to form were the Sierra Nevada and Klamath ranges; some 40 million years ago the Coast Range then began to surface. At the start it was just a series of hilly islands, but it gradually rose higher to become a continuous string of mountains. This growing ridgeline eventually isolated the ocean waters to the east, turning them into an inland sea. In time the water dried up and the empty basin collected a layer of sediment, becoming what is now the Central Valley.

The earth-moving forces which formed the Coast Range have continued operating into the present, adding to the crumpled and convoluted contours that characterize these low-elevation but highly unstable mountains. Earthquakes regularly rattle the area, littering the ground with redwood limbs and covering trails with madrone bark. Historically, the region has seen a major quake about once every 300 years; the last was in 1720, and the clock is ticking. The cause of this long-standing instability is a group of tectonic troublemakers situated near Humboldt Redwoods: the San Andreas Fault runs near the coast southwest of the Park, while a few miles offshore lies the Mendocino triple junction, a site of submerged seismic activity where three plates — the North American, Pacific, and Gorda — converge. Several small inland faults also add their landscape-altering effects, resulting in a knot of geologic chaos that some experts have called "a nightmare of rocks."

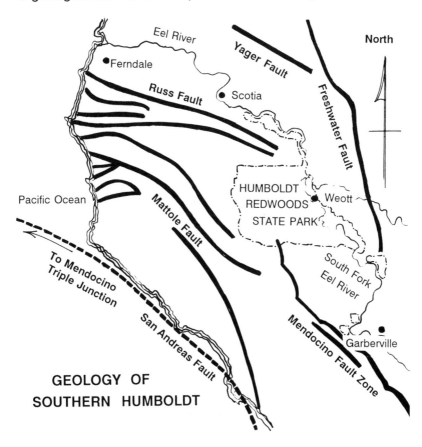

GEOLOGY OF SOUTHERN HUMBOLDT

rocks

The rocks which comprise this "nightmare" are actually a rather sedate collection of marine sediments called siltstones or mudstones. The sediments have been compressed into numerous, very thin layers that were severely twisted and folded during the formation of the Coast Range, creating a fine-grained strata that is often visible at roadcuts.

Siltstones from three distinct time periods run through the Park. Oldest are the Franciscan sediments; they curve in an arc around the western and northern sides of the Bull Creek canyon, continuing eastward from Peavine Ridge to the Eel River at High Rock. Next oldest is the Yager Formation, which underlies most of the land within Humboldt Redwoods; a thick section of Yager sandstone is exposed at the Narrows, an impressive gorge located in upper Bull Creek. Rock from the Wildcat Group, the youngest formation in the Park, is found at the northern end of the Avenue of the Giants and is visible in just one location — the high roadbank between Chadd and Bear creeks, south of Pepperwood. Canyon bottoms often contain a mix of alluvial rock that has been washed down from the higher reaches of the drainage.

The Park's siltstones are composed of particles that gradate through a wide range of sizes; the individual sediments thus absorb and evaporate moisture at different rates, which makes the rock friable — easily crumbled. The result is a mass of weakly bound material that is susceptible to severe erosion. Frequent fracturing by earthquake activity tends to loosen and further disrupt the rock, which is often precariously positioned on steep ridgesides. By the mid-1950s, logging and fires had exposed large areas of the upper Bull Creek watershed to the region's heavy rainfall, and many of the already unstable hillslopes broke loose, creating massive mud slides of catastrophic proportions.

rains

The precipitation that has helped form the Park's topography falls mostly as rain, with only Grasshopper Peak and the ridges above Bull Creek receiving regular coverings of snow. Normally there is little rainfall in summer, when the redwoods must slake their immense thirst with moisture from the canyon fogs, but between October and May frequent storms pound the countryside. The downpours are especially intense during the winter months, and a pair of Christmas-time deluges attained legendary proportions — the 1955 and 1964 floods. Even in "average" years the rainfall totals are substantial: some 55 to 60 inches fall on the towns along the main Eel and South Fork Eel rivers, while the totals increase up the Bull Creek drainage to an ark-activating high of 115 inches at Panther Gap.

The Narrows,
from Bull Creek Road

THE 1955 FLOOD:
BEDLAM IN BULL CREEK

Since 1931 the heart of Humboldt Redwoods State Park has been the Rockefeller Forest, an 8,000-acre tract of majestic trees on the flats of lower Bull Creek. By the mid-fifties, however, much of the creek's upper watershed was a wasteland, its hillsides laid bare by a decade of intensive logging and a series of severe wildfires.

In December of 1955 a terrific storm hit. During the first day it dumped an incredible 21.2-inch-rainfall on the hamlet of Honeydew, over the ridge west of the Park. By the time the soaking ended, Bull Creek itself had received over three feet of rain.

Above the Bull Creek village, water poured off the denuded slopes. Piles of logging debris lodged in the ravines, forming small dams that temporarily caught and held the muddy runoff. When the blockages broke away, the clots of water, wood, and mud plunged downward with ever-increasing force. A major disaster was in the making.

Residents began to evacuate; high up in the drainage, Don Gould left his ranch and headed for Weott, some 15 miles away. Behind him came the flood.

As Gould made his way down onto the flats, he found the creekbed in chaos. At the lower end of town, the surging water had torn into the log deck of the Bee River Mill, jumbling two million board feet of timber into a huge dam. The blocked runoff then began backing into the town of Bull Creek. Soon the jam broke loose, but immediately another tangle of timber formed opposite Albee Creek, just above the first Bull Creek bridge. The rapidly rising water began to use Mattole Road, along which Gould was now driving, as an outlet. In moments the escape route was awash.

His car splashing along the flooded roadway, Gould passed the mill and gingerly made his way across the bridge. Moments later the Albee Creek jam burst, crashing into the wooden span like a runaway locomotive and smashing it to smithereens.

Gould's luck continued after his close call at the bridge. He navigated the sodden depths of the Rockefeller Forest, safely crossed the raging South Fork Eel, and at last reached his home in Weott. His house there was on high ground, far above the wave of water that washed over the highway and rearranged the lower part of town.

After the flooding subsided, Bull Creek found itself isolated from the rest of the region. Emergency food supplies were airlifted into the canyon by plane and dropped by parachute; later, teams of volunteers packed in goods by hiking over the mountains from Rio Dell. When Lloyce Chadbourne fell into a side creek while carrying in 15 dozen eggs, her hungry companions first pulled the precious cargo from the water before they rescued the struggling woman. Lloyce was soaked but unharmed, and the eggs — all 180 of them — survived intact.

Teenager Bill Beat devised an ingeneous, if somewhat risky, way of reaching Bull Creek from his home in Weott; he simply shimmied across the South Fork Eel on the town's waterline, which hung above the raging river, and then traversed the soggy side of Grasshopper Peak via an old trail. It was a route no one else chose to follow.

When the residents of Bull Creek tallied up the damage, the results were staggering: the store and about 35 houses were gone, and many of the surviving buildings were filled with mud. Even the Bull Creek cemetery was swept away; some of its coffins were found caught in the trees of the Rockefeller Forest. No one could argue — it had truly been a flood to raise the dead.

*   *   *

The 1955 storm was of such magnitude that it was called a "hundred-year flood." When a greater washout came within a decade, the new one was dubbed the "thousand-year" flood. Despite the damage wrought by the waters of 1955, there had been few improvements in flood preparedness by the time the storms of 1964 hit. Perhaps little could have been done to anticipate or deal with a flood of such magnitude — water stood 35 feet deep along the Avenue of the Giants — but in its aftermath, an improved "early warning" system took shape.

A multi-agency "river watch" center was soon established — it combined the expertise of the National Weather Service, the U. S. Geological Survey, the California Department of Water Resources, and the Office of Emergency Services. Today, the center conducts a high-tech monitoring program that includes hourly, computerized measurement of rainfall and river heights, round-the-clock staffing of the Weather Service office, and a crew of computer-carrying meteorologists, who can use their portable terminals to track river conditions whether at home, work, or play. It's good to know that the watch center is now so well prepared; after all, it's been more than 25 years since the last "thousand-year" flood.

rivers

Most of the rain which falls so abundantly within the Park enters the drainage of the South Fork Eel, a major tributary of the Eel River. In all, the Eel has four large branches, spread over a system that covers more than 3,000 square miles — an area about the size of Delaware and Rhode Island combined. The South Fork is the most accessible branch; one of the country's few north-flowing rivers, it originates in Mendocino County near Laytonville, encounters the 101 Freeway below Leggett, later runs past Garberville and Redway, and then accompanies the Avenue of the Giants to a point just north of the Founders Grove, where it flows under the roadway and meets the main Eel.

The Middle Fork Eel starts the highest of any branch of the river, at more than 7,000 feet, but drops quickly in its early stages. The rest of the river system generally runs on a gentle gradient, flowing through nearly flat valleys on its 160-mile run to the sea. When the South Fork

Eel passes by Phillipsville, it is still some 40 miles from the ocean, yet during that distance its elevation will drop scarcely more than 200 feet.

Although relatively short in length, the Eel ranks as the country's most erosive river; a study done in the 1970s found that it was moving some 31 million tons of rock and soil each year—the equivalent of a dump truck load every 12 seconds. The Mississippi River, by comparison, transports only about two million tons of earth annually, despite being called "the Big Muddy." Government researchers attribute the Eel's washy wastefulness to steep slopes, heavy rains, and unstable soils— they neglect to mention the effects of massive clearcutting in many parts of the drainage. During the rainy season, the river will often run brown for days at a time as it carries off layers of the exposed upstream mountainsides.

Enough of the Eel's soil-rich runoff is deposited before reaching the ocean to maintain some of the most fertile bottomlands in northern California. Early homesteaders were quick to discover this, converting the river benches next to Phillipsville, Myers Flat, Pepperwood, and Shively into prime garden spots. If the settlers proved too zealous in their efforts and overworked the land, there was usually a good flood every decade or so that replenished the riverside topsoil. Sometimes, however, the washouts did more than that, as was the case with the tragic 1964 flood.

* * *

THE 1964 FLOOD:
TOO MUCH FOR PEPPERWOOD

Nine years to the day after the start of the 1955 flood, another terrific storm swept into Humboldt County. According to official reports, a warm mass of tropical air brought "torrential rain approaching cloud-burst proportions." In the higher elevations, the downpour began melting a snowpack that was more than two feet deep.

On December 21, the Eel was five feet above flood stage; by the next day it had risen another five feet, and most of the low-lying areas along the river were being evacuated.

Rancher Henry Millsap, 82, had lived in Pepperwood for most of his life. The family house had survived the 1955 flood, suffering only mud damage; now, with another washout in the offing, Millsap was reluctant to leave, but he finally departed at about 2:30 a.m. on the 23rd. Before going, he moved many of the family's possessions into the attic.

At daylight, Millsap and his grandson, John Hower, rowed their boat back to the house to check on it. As they watched, the floodwater lifted the structure from its foundation and began moving it downriver.

"There are things in there I don't want to lose," Millsap yelled to his grandson, and the pair began rowing after the runaway house. In a few moments they had pulled alongside, and as Millsap steadied the boat, Hower scrambled through a window into the attic. Inside, he grabbed Millsap's guns, riding boots, spurs, and a few other items, pitching them through the window and into the boat. Once back with his grandfather, Hower looked on as the current swept the house away.

Although the Millsaps had lost their home, others fared even worse. Longtime Pepperwood rancher Albert Porter, 78, rowed to the Tower Auto Court and picked up two men, but the swirling water became too much for his wife, Florence, who was also in the boat. According to Porter ". . . my wife was just horror stricken. I told her to stay with me in the boat but she wouldn't do it." The 70-year-old woman climbed into the top floor of the motel building, joining four other refugees there; her husband reluctantly departed, taking the two men to safety.

Tower Auto Court

Porter tried to return to the auto court, but he could now make no headway against the increasing current; Millsap and Hower set out in their boat, but they, too, were stymied by the force of the flood. Porter surveyed the rising deluge and estimated that the people trapped at the Tower had only a couple of hours before the water would reach them. He contacted the sheriff's office to ask for help, but the area's lone rescue helicopter was busy elsewhere—there was nothing to be done.

The water continued rising, rushing though what was once Pepperwood, pushing buildings into trees or smashing them against one another. Newspaper photographer Neil Hulbert flew over the shattered community later on the 23rd and reported that "Pepperwood is completely gone. It's just a huge pile of debris. Houses are stacked on top of houses. The entire area is floating. Nothing is standing . . . nothing but debris."

Pepperwood after the flood

By the next day the floodwaters had begun to recede, and Albert Porter returned to the ruins of Pepperwood, riding in on a road grader with two other men; when they reached the remains of the auto court, he let the others enter without him. Inside were the bodies of Florence Porter and her four companions.

A disconsolate Porter decided to leave the farm he'd worked for 35 years. "This flood was worse than the one in '55 and for me, I'm through," Porter said. "First a flood in '37, then one in '55 and now this. That's enough."

PLENTY OF OTHER PLANTS

From windy ridgetop to fertile riverbottom, from shadowed canyon to sunny hillslope, the landscapes of Humboldt Redwoods State Park are covered with a blanket of plant life. Within this vast and varied area, differences in such influences as rainfall, elevation, and temperature have created several distinct environments that each support a specific association, or community, of plants. Although botanists would offer additional sub-categories, here are five basic plant communities that the layperson can easily identify and enjoy when exploring the Park:

Redwood Forest:

The largest and most magnificent stands of redwood are found on canyon bottomlands. It is here that silts, rocks, and gravels – alluvia – have washed down from the surrounding mountainsides and formed compact, nutrient-rich masses of soil that rise in terraces above the creeks and rivers. Atop the packed sediment, great galleries of redwoods stand in shadowy silence, the air barely penetrated by sound or light. Other trees are scarce, although a few tanoaks and California laurels occasionally grow as an understory. A sprinkling of delicate California hazels often dots the lower forest, their spreading limbs contrasting with the redwoods' massive, vertical trunks. Sword fern is a common inhabitant, and bracken fern grows in sunny openings; lady fern, giant chain fern, and five-fingered fern are sometimes found in moister locations. Near ground level is a wealth of flowers: redwood and smooth yellow violets, Smith's and Hooker's fairybells, Siberian candy-flower, milkmaids, Pacific windflower, thin false Solomon's seal, sugar scoop, vanilla leaf, calypso orchid, trillium, trail plant, and, most common of all, redwood sorrel.

Old-growth redwood resident –
spotted owl

55

Bottomland groves of redwood grow in the Rockefeller Forest on the flats of lower Bull Creek, at the Founders Grove and nearby areas of the Dyerville Flats, on the west bank of the South Fork Eel beneath Grasshopper Peak, and in various groves along the Avenue of the Giants. Occasionally redwoods also form nearly pure stands at higher elevations, such as in the E. Achelis Grove at the end of the Five Allens Trail.

Mixed Forest:

On less-fertile canyon bottoms and lower hillsides, the coast redwood is joined by another large, thick-trunked tree, Douglas fir; the consorting conifers are often supported by a lower level of tanoak. Upslope, madrone begins to replace the redwoods, while the tanoaks increase in height. Black huckleberry usually forms the main ground cover, although salal sometimes occupies wetter areas. There are fewer flowering plants than on the flats, but fetid adder's tongue, redwood lily, fat false Solomon's seal, Pacific starflower, redwood inside-out flower, and clintonia surface sporadically. Three members of the heath family grow here: pipsissewa and both bog and white-veined wintergreen; also present are rattlesnake, calypso, and phantom orchids, and the related spotted coral root. Some orchid and heath species may exist in a non-green form, deriving their nutrients parasitically from other plants.

Many of the Park's trails and roads pass through mixed forest settings on their way from valley bottom to ridgetop; some impressive routes include the lower portion of the Grasshopper Trail, the Johnson Camp Trail, Squaw Creek Ridge Road, and Grasshopper Road. Almost the entire Hidden Springs-Williams Grove Trail crosses through lower-elevation mixed forest, and a stunning stand of large redwoods, Douglas firs, and tanoaks enhances Peavine Road a short distance east of its junction with Thornton Road.

Prairies and Wooded Uplands:

The sunny grasslands and smaller openings found on upcountry hillsides are usually covered with bracken fern and grasses, along with a variety of wildflowers that may include California poppy, miniature lupine, winecup clarkia, true baby stars, and western blue flax. Many of the grass species are non-natives that were introduced by the early homesteaders, but upper Look Prairie still contains a good sampling of the original grass cover. Trees and brush spread thickly over most of the hillslopes, often forming borders of lush foliage at prairie perimeters; Oregon white oak, California black oak, canyon live oak, madrone, and Douglas fir are common constituents, along with such shrubs as blueblossom, snowbrush, and occasionally hairy manzanita. Small open areas, like roadbanks, may have coverings of yerba de selva, Pacific starflower, or intermittent clumps of Bolander's phacelia.

Douglas fir
(Pseudotsuga menziesii)

Despite its name, this frequently seen tree is not truly part of the fir family, although it has fir-like foliage. Some scientists categorize it as a type of spruce, but others include it in the pine family. Its Latin name means "false hemlock," which helps not a bit. Worse yet, early lumbermen called it "Oregon pine," hoping to cash in on the pine's reputation for producing good wood. This conifer was given its surname to honor David Douglas, an envoy of the London Horticultural Society, who sent the tree's seeds to England while on an expedition to the Pacific Northwest in the 1820s. However it is classified, the Douglas fir is at least easy to identify, for its cones contain the so-called "hiding mice." These are the markings found under each dark-brown cone scale—two small, pale points on either side of a larger, central one: a mouse's hind legs and tail.

Growing as high as 300 feet, the Douglas fir probably ranks as the third tallest tree in the world, after the coast redwood and a type of Australian eucalyptus. If one century-old report is to be believed, though, the fir deserves first place. According to the story, when an extremely tall specimen was felled in 1895, the local sheriff was called out to measure the downed giant; it reputedly tipped the tape at 417 feet—a full 50 feet taller than the current record-holding redwood.

This story is not widely accepted, however, and the Douglas fir has gained its greatest fame not for its size but for its utility, having become the workhorse of the forest; it ranks as the most heavily cut tree in the country, serves as

the leading source of plywood, and also provides a popular type of Christmas tree. It was once put to a host of other uses, but many of these are neglected today: Indians made a tea from fir needles, which was used to treat tuberculosis and other lung ailments; they also burned boughs in a steamhouse as a remedy for rheumatism. The smoke from such smoldering branches also served as a good luck charm. Douglas fir roots were made into a thread used in basketry, and its branches provided the shafts for salmon spears. During World War II, Douglas fir plywood was used for everything from storage tanks to pontoon bridges to PT boats, since it tested, pound for pound, stronger than steel.

Woodland prairie

Each of the upland oak species prefers a particular setting. Canyon live oak favors rocky cliffsides, such as those along the middle section of the Grasshopper Trail and at the eastern end of Preacher Gulch Road. Oregon white oak and California black oak like less extreme hillslope topography; they often locate near one another. The lower section of Pole Line Road is an oak lover's paradise, while Gould Road, the Addie Johnson Grave Trail, Look Road, and Thornton Road also have groupings of these trees. Scrub oak sometimes grows close to its larger relatives, as it does along the middle section of Thornton Road.

The Bull Creek upcountry is speckled with spectacular prairies. Look for them: 1) along the middle part of Pole Line Road, 2) on the first part of Hanson Ridge Road, 3) on Gould Road near the Upper Gould Barn, 4) on Preacher Gulch Road east of its junction with Squaw Creek Ridge Road, 5) on the lower half of Look Prairie Road.

Small Creek Canyons:

Humboldt Redwoods' many narrow creek canyons are home to a host of water-loving plants. In these shaded settings, trees and ferns predominate: both bigleaf and vine maple overhang the rocky stream-beds, while red alder rises from the edge of the water; giant chain, five-fingered, and lady ferns are often abundant, and goldenback ferns sometimes perch on nearby banks. Among other plants, the stunning California spikenard and the striking giant horsetail are streamside favorites, and if there is enough sunlight, colorful seep-spring monkey flowers may grow along creek margins. The Matthews Creek crossing on the Five Allens Trail is rich in vegetation, as are the canyons of Decker and Mill creeks on the Burlington-Bull Creek Trail. The Grasshopper Road bridge over Squaw Creek offers a good view of the plants in the canyon below, as does the Bull Creek Road bridge over Burns Creek.

Riversides:

The riverbanks along the lower South Fork Eel are intermittently lined with a wall of shimmering, rustling vegetation. In these locations, the plant life climbs through a succession of reeds, bushes, and graceful trees, lead-ing the eye towards the towering, sen-tinel-like redwoods that rise from the higher bench-lands. Giant horsetail and scouring rush mingle with Pacific red elderberry and blackberry near the beaches, while ascending above them are willows, Oregon ash, red alder, bigleaf maple, and black cottonwood—their leaves and limbs woven into a vibrant, verdant tapestry. The riverside scenery chan-ges at rocky outcroppings like Eagle Point on the South Fork Eel and High

River region inhabitant—
great blue heron

Rock on the main Eel; here the boulder-studded banks host several cliff dwellers, including canyon live oak, toyon, Merten's saxifrage, and Indian paintbrush.

Riverside vegetation,
South Fork Eel

There are thousands of small settings within the Park where a collection of plants congregates in singular splendor. A pause at almost any point along either a road or trail will reveal some tree, fern, shrub, or flower that contains a spark of beauty which might otherwise be overlooked. Many prime plant-sighting sites are indicated in the following sections of the book.

CRITTERS GREAT AND SMALL

Morning sunlight warms the trail above the lazily flowing South Fork Eel. All is quiet, save the occasional hum of traffic from across the canyon. Suddenly the air is rent by a sound resembling a wildly spinning ratchet wrench; there is a flash of blue and white, and a kingfisher darts over the river and into the willows on the far bank . . . .

The road down from Look Prairie lies empty, dappled by afternoon sunlight that filters through the overhanging oaks. Then a small, dark animal appears from around the next bend, padding its way uphill. Too distant to be recognized, it cocks its head and stares up the road. The creature turns away, and with a single fluid motion it vanishes over the roadbank, leaving behind the lingering image of its short, turned-up tail. In a moment the message comes — bobcat!

Kingfisher

*   *   *   *   *

Encounters with the Park's wildlife will often be brief and unexpected, for most of its creatures are cautious by nature and will avoid contact with humans. The chances of seeing the area's shy residents can be increased, however, with a little advance planning. Some recommended preparations include the following: 1) go out near dawn or dusk, when many species are active; 2) select a viewing area where habitats meet, like a prairie/woodland boundary; 3) wear inconspicuous clothing; 4) choose a position downwind from the viewing area; 5) wait quietly until something interesting comes by. Even without such preparation, there will probably be a few sightings — the occasional turkey vulture circling above a sunny prairie, the nearly immobile banana slug on its day's travel across a few feet of forest floor, or perhaps a pair of black-tailed deer grazing on a distant grassy hillside. And then there are those magical, lucky moments — when someone can eavesdrop on a kingfisher or share the roadbed with a bobcat.

Seen or unseen, a multitude of wildlife makes Humboldt Redwoods its home. Some of the Park's more intriguing inhabitants include the following:

Mammals

The local mammals are a diverse and diverting group. They range from the nearly frivolous, like the frolicsome river otters that splash among the Eel's riffles, to the sometimes fearsome, such as the black bears and mountain lions that roam over the slopes of Grasshopper Peak.

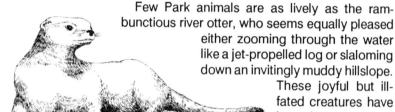

Few Park animals are as lively as the rambunctious river otter, who seems equally pleased either zooming through the water like a jet-propelled log or slaloming down an invitingly muddy hillslope. These joyful but ill-fated creatures have long been trapped and hunted in both Europe and America; in ancient China, however, otters were more valued alive than dead — they were captured by fishermen and trained to herd fish into nets.

river otter

Lumbering of gait, the deceptive black bear is actually agile as a linebacker and faster than a sprinter. Bears are the largest creatures found in the Park, and they maintain their size by eating nearly everything they encounter, including berries, grass, nuts, orchard fruit, tree sapwood, insects, small mammals, fish, and, when available, campers' food. Most black bears will depart quickly when they meet humans, but they should always be considered potentially dangerous and treated accordingly.

The most anyone can expect to see of a mountain lion are its tracks; sometimes called puma, panther, cougar, or catamount, this solitary predator was once the most widely found cat in the Western Hemisphere, but it has disappeared from most areas and now mainly inhabits mountain wilderness. Deer is the mountain lion's preferred food, although when necessary it will also consume other mammals and occasionally even birds and grasshoppers; it often covers the remains of large kills with branches and leaves; a hunting male sometimes travels as much as 25 miles in a single night.

While the elusive mountain lion may be known only by its prints, the coyote can often be located by its sounds; its mournful howls can be heard from Park ridges near Big Hill. This thick-tailed member of the dog family is the fastest moving predator in America; it prefers to eat small mammals and birds, but will subsist on everything from grasshoppers to fruit to winter-killed deer and elk, if necessary.

Less noisy, but more noisome, are the announcements of both the striped and spotted skunk; appropriately enough, these polecats like the prairies of Pole Line Road. Insects, mice, and shrews are main meals for both varieties of skunks, which themselves often fall prey to great horned owls. Although the striped skunk is the larger of the two, the spotted is the more eye-catching, especially when it performs a strange sort of handstand on its forelegs; the maneuver should be observed only at a distance, since it is often a prelude to spraying.

spotted skunk

The Park's most frequently seen large mammal is the black-tailed deer, which browses on the many upland prairies, cropping grass or plucking low-level leaves. Also called the mule deer, its dark tail and large, independently mobile ears justify its dual name. Unlike the white-tailed deer of the east, which is a graceful runner, the black-tail uses a stiff-legged, high-bounding gait, called "stotting," when moving at high speed. This bounding motion is well suited to the black-tail's often steep and rocky western environment.

An award for animal architecture should go to the dusky-footed woodrat. One of the so-called "pack rats," it delights in collecting odd objects, the shinier the better; these items are then incorporated into a large stickpile with multiple, interconnected rooms that serve as nests, food caches, and latrines. About a dozen of these stacked-stick structures line the southern part of Barkdull Ranch Road, making it the Park's highest density woodrat development.

The most visible, and audible, small mammal of the redwoods is doubtless the Douglas' squirrel; it is rendered conspicuous by both its orange belly and loud mouth. A barrage of angry chatter often assails those who enter the creature's domain, but this shrill scolding is usually quick to subside. More persistent is the squirrel's harvesting of Douglas fir cones, which it nips from the tree limbs at the rate of 12 per minute; the little cone-consumer eventually drops groundward and carries the fallen booty off to storage.

Although less obvious in its actions, the northern flying squirrel creates an impressive spectacle nonetheless. This small rodent is active only at twilight, when it glides from tree to tree through the forest; it begins its commute by spreading a set of lateral skin flaps, and it then descends at high speed, adjusting the flaps to dodge branches. The airborne acrobat finally raises its tail and brakes to a gentle stop, landing — as much as 150 feet from its launch site — with a soft thump on a tree trunk.

Northern flying squirrel

Another oddly constructed creature is the ringtail — an ambushing, pouncing predator that looks like a composite of three other animals; it has a foxlike face, a cat's lithe body, and a black and white, ringed tail more dazzling than that of any raccoon. The ringtail enjoys a varied diet that features small mammals, insects, birds, and fruits; it dens in rocky areas, hollow trees, stumps, or logs.

Although its tail may not be as impressive as the ringtail's, the raccoon has an unsurpassed mask — a black eye band dashingly outlined in white. Usually found feeding near water, these obstreperous omnivores will eat anything they can get their delicate paws on, often defying interruption with a variety of vocalizations that include growls, hisses, churrs, and purrs. A favorite den site is large, hollow trees.

Birds

One of the Park's most spectacular birds is the great blue heron, whose long legs and large bill are colored an arresting orange-yellow, a perfect contrast to its bluish gray plumage. Heron mealtimes are relaxed events; the bird merely stands motionless in shallow water until lunch (usually a small fish or frog) comes by, and then quickly spears the oblivious entree with its beak. When in flight, a doubly curved neck and huge, ponderously flapping wings make the great blue heron appear to be a creature from some long-forgotten time, an airborne antiquity looking for its lost epoch.

Far above the rivers, the osprey creates an imposing nest of interlaced sticks in the dead tops of tall redwood trees. Sometimes called the fish hawk, this remarkable raptor dives from great heights into only a few feet of water, where it will catch and retrieve fish that sometimes weigh as much as itself. Blackish above and white below, the osprey has distinctive black markings at its wing tips and wrists.

As comic as the osprey is heroic, the American dipper, or water ouzel, keeps constantly busy plucking small insects and other food from the fast-flowing water of rocky river riffles. The ouzel accomplishes this feat with a series of jerky, jivelike movements, dipping in strange syncopation to a beat heard by it alone.

While the water birds dazzle with their appearance and amuse with their antics, many of their forest-dwelling counterparts are seldom seen but often heard. The brown creeper, for example, is a small and inconspicuous creature which spends its life spiraling up the trunks of trees in search of insects. When it reaches the top of one tree, it plunges to the bottom of another and begins its long "creep" all over again. It sometimes enlivens this seemingly monotonous routine by emitting its call – a single high, thin note that drifts mysteriously through the forest.

Even tinier than the creeper is the stubby winter wren, whose frequently uptilted tail makes its body seem unnaturally short. Exhibiting small creature cleverness, it conceals its true home by building decoy nests and entryways. When singing, the winter wren creates a bubbling sequence of chatters and operatic trills – a wren-dition that would make Pavarotti proud.

A larger but less musical bird is the varied thrush, a reticent relative of the robin, whose dark breast band and muted orange chest give it a subdued appearance. Its call, a strange, hollow-sounding single note, may at first seem unremarkable, but after being repeated several times in the deep shadows of the damp forest, it assumes a haunting quality that leads the listener ever onward, hopeful of finding the sound's source within the gloaming. This thrush gained its name because the pitch of its calling note is often changed slightly, or "varied."

varied thrush

The hermit thrush is more musical, zipping through the scales like a runaway flutist, but hiding all the while in dense foliage, too shy to confront its audience. If the hermit does make an appearance, it will probably do so when scouring the ground for such delicacies as earthworms, insects, and berries.

Sounds of a different sort emanate from the ruffed grouse, a brownish, chicken-sized bird that conducts its courtship by drumming its wings to create an accelerating series of thumps. The vibration is so low-pitched as to seem nondirectional, making it nearly impossible to locate this phantomesque percussionist.

A sharp rattling noise often indicates that a woodpecker of some sort is working nearby, hammering its hard, pointed beak into a tree trunk in search of insects. While the hairy woodpecker and the northern flicker are more common, it is the pileated woodpecker that is most striking, with its large size and bright red crest making it conspicuous in any woodland setting; it produces a staccato, machine-gun-like burst of "kaks," to note the presence of an intruder.

Redwood snags may be worthless to the woodsman, but they are of great value to the Vaux's swift. This small and speedy bird uses the hollow interiors of burned or broken redwoods as sites to build its twig-and-needle nests. It spends each day zipping around the sky, often logging hundreds of miles in pursuit of insects; then, at twilight, vast flocks of Vaux's will congregate above a single redwood cavity, like commuters waiting to enter a subway. Suddenly a spiraling line of them will dive into the tree, where they roost in overlapping rows, clinging by their claws to the walls of their hollow home.

Pileated woodpecker

Like the swift, the Anna's hummingbird is a speedster; it has to be, for hummingbirds daily consume as much as half their body weight in sugar and must thus fly frantically about in search of food. The Anna's is a delicately colored creature with a metallic green back and sides, a reddish throat (the male's head is also red), and white underparts. The male is an active, if unsophisticated, vocalist, whose song has been described as "a jumble of high squeaks and raspy notes." His display flight is more polished and would awe a fighter pilot, for it features a high, heavenward climb, followed by a plummeting dive that only levels out at the last moment. A loud "peep!" concludes the performance.

THE SPOTTED OWL, THE MARBLED MURRELET, AND CHOON-TA-AHS-CHO

Humboldt Redwoods hosts two rare and elusive birds that require very specific — and rapidly disappearing — habitat. One, the dark-eyed spotted owl, has already cast a giant shadow over the remaining ancient forests of the Pacific Coast; to insure this endangered bird's survival, numerous tracts of old-growth land must be preserved, thereby slowing or halting logging in many areas. Environmental and timber interests have fought over the fate of this reclusive raptor for several years, in the process turning the spotted owl into the shyest celebrity since Howard Hughes.

The marbled murrelet may soon become the spotted owl's rival as an avian object of controversy. While it normally inhabits bays and coastal waters, during breeding season the murrelet travels inland into the coastal mountains, where it builds its nest in stands of mature trees. The bird's continued procreation thus depends on protecting yet more land that timber companies want to log.

Although attention has focused almost solely on the two embattled birds, the fate of many other creatures is at stake in the fight to save ancient forests. What may seem to be merely collections of old-growth trees are actually complex communities of many interdependent plants and animals — all of which will suffer as their homes are destroyed.

Long ago, Humboldt County was home to a bird that the local Lolangkok Indians called "Choon-ta-ahs-cho." Like the marbled murrelet and the spotted owl, it, too, became imperiled by the activities of man; today it sadly symbolizes the balance of nature gone awry. Our name for Choon-ta-ahs-cho? — the California condor.

Marbled murrelets above the river

Park prairielands are often scrutinized by soaring red-tailed hawks in search of their next meal. Slower than many birds of prey, they use a variety of strategies, ranging from stealth to stealing, for finding food. The red-tail's call, well described as a "descending scream," is imitated to perfection by the Steller's jay, a somewhat brazen and mischievous bird that often pesters campers and sports an appropriately punk-styled feather crest. More sober in appearance but equally brash in behavior is the scrub jay, a long-tailed but crestless blue and white omnivore that enjoys eating both insects and acorns.

Amphibians, Reptiles, Fishes, and Others:

The Pacific treefrog could as well be called a logfrog, since it likes secreting itself in the loose bark and wood of downed snags. A rambling

amphibian, it often shuns both trees and logs, spending much of its time in water or on the ground. The male treefrog possesses the quintessential frog croak, which it amplifies by enlarging its throat sac up to three times the size of its head.

An eye-catching amphibian is the northern roughskin newt, whose yellow-orange belly

Pacific treefrog

glows beneath the edges of its brown and black upper side. As if to enhance his attractiveness, the male's skin temporarily becomes smooth during mating season. Always smooth of skin, whether romancing or not, is the Pacific giant salamander, which has a mottled back and light underside. Unlike most salamanders, the Pacific giant has a voice, although it takes a catastrophe to activate it—a victim of amphibian anxiety, it produces a low yelp when captured.

Sometimes growing to more than a foot long, the northern alligator lizard mimics its namesake by possessing a strong, sharp bite. Two subspecies are found in the Park: the redundantly named northern northern has a light, lengthwise band in the middle of its back, while the Shasta northern's back is mottled with numerous dark blotches.

A colorful resident of the Park's uplands is the ringneck snake; its back and sides are a somewhat drab earthen tone — either olive, brown, black, or gray, but it has a bright orange, red, or yellow underside. For good measure, its neck usually features a cream, yellow, or orange ring.

King, or chinook, salmon and the smaller silver/coho salmon follow a pattern similar to the marbled murrelet, living most of their life at sea and then coming inland to spawn. This anadromous, or "up running" behavior is quite precise, with the female returning to the stream site where she was born and there giving birth to her offspring. She then covers her eggs with gravel and dies, thus missing both the trials and rewards of parenthood.

Steelhead are sea-running rainbow trout that make salmon-like returns to their home streams for spawning. They thrive in the ocean environment, growing much larger than freshwater trout while developing a silvery protein coating that obscures any coloring underneath.

Lastly, but only because of its extreme slowness, comes the often-ridiculed banana slug. This shell-less gastropod is essentially a nude snail, and squeamish observers seem offended by the exposure of its mustard- to olive-colored body. The banana slug compensates for its lack of speed by having a voracious appetite, abetted by a tongue that is covered with several thousand tiny teeth. Fetid adder's tongue flowers are a favorite food — sometimes a pair of slugs will attack the same plant, each munching on its own blossom.

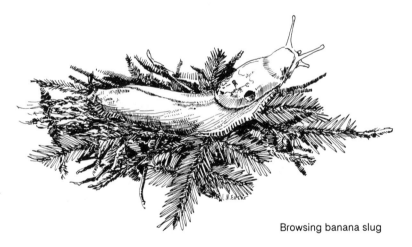

Browsing banana slug

From black bear to banana slug, from kingfisher to king salmon; slow or fast, large or small — in the region's realm of wildlife, Humboldt Redwoods (almost) has it all.

THE LAND OF THE LOLANGKOKS

The area within and around Humboldt Redwoods State Park was once the home of the Sinkyone Indians, one of several small tribes that inhabited the rugged mountains and river canyons of the region. There were two groups, or tribelets, of Sinkyones: the To-cho-be Ke-ah, or Shelter Cove Sinkyones, lived in an area that ran from the coast inland to the South Fork Eel and from the Miranda-Phillipsville area south to Leggett; the second group was called the Lolangkoks, after their name for Bull Creek. "Sinkyone" came from the tribe's word for the South Fork Eel, Sin-ke-kok.

Near the center of the Lolangkoks' land was Grasshopper Peak. From this high point, the group's territory stretched north to present-day Scotia, east along the main Eel River to Whitlow, south almost to Phillipsville and Ettersburg, and west nearly to Honeydew. The Lolangkoks controlled all of the main Eel and South Fork Eel rivers within those boundaries, as well as a small portion of the Mattole River and the entire drainages of Bull and Salmon creeks. The sites of over 50 Lolangkok villages have been identified in this area, about 15 of which are within Humboldt Redwoods. A much smaller portion of the Park, consisting of the Alexander, Lane, Holbrook, and Whittemore groves, was once the domain of the Shelter Cove Sinkyones.

Not much is known about the Lolangkoks; their numbers diminished quickly after the arrival of white settlers, and no one bothered to record much information about their way of life until only a few of them were left. In 1850, there were probably more than 2,000 Lolangkoks; by 1910, scarcely a hundred remained. When anthropologists and linguists belatedly visited the southern Humboldt region in the 1920s, they found just a handful of surviving Sinkyones. Two tribesmen who provided considerable information were George Burt, who had been born on a flat midway up the Bull Creek drainage, and Jack Woodman, who resided in the Briceland area.

Like most Indians of the region, the Lolangkoks lived in a tightly enclosed world, their movement restricted by the region's steep terrain, dense forests, and high winter waters. One perhaps-typical tribesman, who lived opposite the mouth of Bull Creek, reportedly spent his entire life without ever venturing more than 20 miles in any direction from his home village.

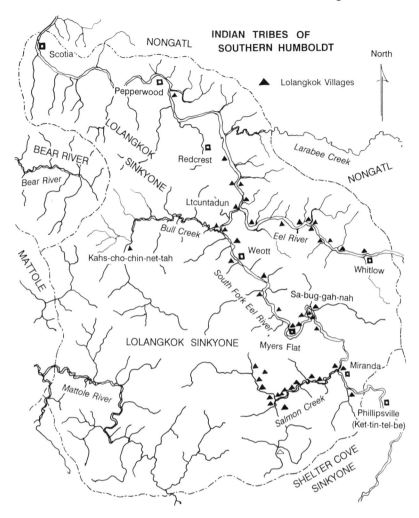

INDIAN TRIBES OF
SOUTHERN HUMBOLDT

North

▲ Lolangkok Villages

The Lolangkoks traveled extensively within their own territory, however, occupying at least three different seasonal locations during the year. The warm, dry months from late spring to early fall saw them roaming the upland slopes and prairies, moving their camps when necessary to follow their primary game animals, the black-tailed deer and the Roosevelt elk. During this time they also hunted bear, raccoon, rabbits, and game birds. Then, with the coming of the first rains of fall, the Lolangkoks migrated to the banks of the South Fork Eel and main Eel and began fishing for salmon and steelhead. When the storms had filled the rivers, the Indians moved up to permanent villages along the larger creeks; here they continued fishing until their annual return to the high country.

TWO DEER

A black-tailed deer, grazing on the grassy hillside, twitched his ears and looked up. Another deer had come out from the edge of the prairie and was slowly approaching. Only the head of the newcomer was visible above the tall grass; it was a buck, his antlers having two prongs. The first deer twitched his nose, but no scent came to him, for the wind was blowing from the wrong direction. After a few moments he resumed his grazing.

There was a singing sound in the air, and then the arrow hit the grazer, going deep into his chest. The deer's head jerked up, his eyes wide with surprise. He tried to flex his legs to bound away, but there was no strength in them. His body straightened only slightly, and then with a shudder he fell to the ground.

TWO DEER

The hunter stood up from the grass. Resting his bow upon the ground, he removed the stuffed deer head he'd been wearing. Some leaves and clumps of moss from the stuffing clung to his hair, and he now removed them, putting them back inside the head. It had been hot wearing the disguise, and the hunter's knees were sore from crawling through the grass. Now, however, he quickly forgot his discomfort; the buck he had killed was a large one, and there would be much meat left for smoking after his band had eaten from the animal that night.

In addition to the food provided by seasonal fish and game, the Lolangkoks gathered and ate a variety of seeds, roots, nuts, and berries. Acorns that had been ground into flour were a staple in their diet, and California buckeye nuts, called *lah-se*, were also very popular. Special delicacies included roasted grasshopper and *nah-tos* — slugs. The latter were dried and then stored; later they were cooked in hot ashes.

The center of Lolangkok life was the basic family unit — husband, wife, and children; sometimes a family associated with a larger, informal group of relatives that lived close to one another. Chiefs were recognized as leaders of tribal bands, and families were obligated more to the band and tribe than to their relatives. The land each band occupied was shared in common.

Strict rules governed certain family relationships. A sister and brother were allowed to speak directly to each other only in certain necessary situations. A woman could only communicate with her son-in-law through a third party, and she had to cover her face with her buckskin blanket when passing him. A young woman, however, could speak to her father-in-law, but only slowly, seriously, and briefly. She was never to laugh in his presence.

Most Lolangkok marriages were monogamous, but some men, especially those of importance, were allowed to have more than one wife. Brides were purchased; friends and family would often help the prospective groom accumulate enough money to wed a rich young woman; if the man was very poor, he might work for his in-laws to make payment. Divorce was common and well accepted. A wife could leave her husband for mistreatment, infidelity, or failure to provide for the family; a husband, on the other hand, could end the marriage if his wife was sterile, unfaithful, or ill humored. There were few illegitimate children, and abortion was practiced only when a wife became jealous of her husband. A woman would abort by hitting herself on the abdomen with rocks; often she died as well as the fetus.

*   *   *

MARRIAGE AND FAMILY:
TWO COYOTE STORIES

The figure of coyote is found in the myths of many Indian cultures. Frequently appearing as either trickster, benefactor, or dupe, he fills the latter role in this pair of Sinkyone stories.

The Fish Dam

Coyote, Shu-be, had a wife and many children. He made a dam on the river and placed a net in it to catch fish. He caught many fish, but he did not bring any home. He sat there and ate them. Then he went home. His wife told the children: "He looks swelled up. He doesn't look hungry." He would not eat acorn soup. He would not eat anything. Next day his wife went to the dam and found the fish. The children found the fish also. She did not tell Shu-be that she had found the fish, but she said to him: "Tomorrow night at sundown, go to your dam and catch fish and bring them home." That night he caught many fish, and at daybreak she took the children and went away because he did not bring any fish home to them. She took a deerskin blanket and put rocks in it in her place where she slept and covered it up. Shu-be came home with the fish and thought the rocks were the woman. He told her to get up, that he was hungry. He hit the rocks with his elbow and broke his arm. Then he lay down and was sick. He yelled for someone to come and told people to come in and have the fish. They told him he had better live on them himself. The woman left for good. He searched for her but never found her.

(as related by Jack Woodman)

COYOTE AND SHREWMOLE

Coyote and Shrewmole

Shu-be, the coyote, and Ske-cho, the shrewmole, made the world and the people. Ske-cho said that when people died they should come back to live again, but Shu-be said, "No, there would be too many; when they die they had better stay dead." Ske-cho agreed. After a while Shu-be's children took sick and died. He wanted them to come back to life, but Ske-cho said, "No, you said you wanted dead people to stay dead, so your children cannot come back." Then Shu-be cried.

(as related by George Burt)

The Lolangkoks built two types of permanent dwellings, a wedge-shaped lean-to and a conical building assembled around a center pole; both were made with slabs of redwood bark. They also constructed two types of circular houses, one for dancing and the other for sweat baths. Summer camp structures were temporary brush enclosures that were abandoned after the season and left to fall apart from weathering.

Sinkyone acorn buzzer toy

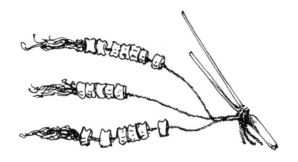

Sinkyone ring-and-pin game of salmon vertebrae

Few tools or other implements were used by the Lolangkoks. Among their most important possessions were bows and arrows, dugout canoes, and drills for starting fires — all made from wood — and spoons made of elkhorn. Baskets were woven of redwood fiber with designs made from five-finger fern and bark from red alder; household baskets were made by the women, while the men made most of the fishing baskets and all of those used for hunting. Deer and elk hides provided clothing and blankets. The Lolangkoks dressed with little adornment, although on ceremonial occasions the women wore fringed and beaded clothing. The adult women wore basketry hats.

A Lolangkok year had eight seasons — spring, summer, fall, and winter were each preceded by an onset, or "coming," season. Time was reckoned by the sun (or its absence), with the day divided into ten parts. Each part denoted a phase of the day's progress, rather than a fixed amount of time; the first three phases, for example, consisted of "before daylight," "daylight," and "before sunup."

The Sinkyone language spoken by the Lolangkoks is one of the Athapascan tongues; other Indians who share in this widespread linguistic family include the Apaches and Navajos of the Southwest, the Sarcees of the Great Plains, and numerous Canadian and Alaskan tribes. The Sinkyones were one of five "southern" Athapascan-speaking peoples that lived adjacent to each other; the Hupas of northern Humboldt County also speak a variety of Athapascan.

Apparently there was little warfare among the small tribes of the coastal mountain area. Each tribe was able to support itself on its own land, and thus had little need to conduct raids; in addition, the region's rugged terrain discouraged attacks. Nonetheless, the Sinkyones did have occasional skirmishes, usually with either the Mattole tribe to the west or the always-hated Wailiki to the south. Battles seem to have been somewhat ritualized: arrows were shot at the enemy's war leaders, who stood in the front rank and attempted to dodge the missiles. The unprotected lesser warriors could easily have been slaughtered, but they were usually not attacked.

Jack Woodman, one of the last full-blooded Sinkyones, reported that he had fought in five different battles, three times against other Indian tribes and twice against the whites. One of the latter fights took place downriver from Myers Flat, the other on the flats of Bull Creek.

Indian warrior
(Pedicularis densiflora)

The magenta flower spikes of Indian warriors are often seen rising from a sunny cliffside or clustered upon a warm, dry mountain slope. Delicate soft-green leaves, similar to fern fronds, surround the base of each plant, with several of the deep-hued petals rising higher on the stem. According to legend, one of the flowers will grow for each fallen Indian warrior, so it is sadly appropriate that the plant thrives in the land of the vanished, vanquished Lolangkok tribesmen. [blooms February-June]

There is little specific information about the conflicts between the Lolangkoks and the whites. According to one report, the tribelet's namesake stream, Lolangkok, received its white name of Bull Creek when some Indians took a bull from a homesteader and slaughtered it by the streambank; the Indians were followed by a group of settlers who attacked and killed them. Another account designates the flat beside lower Squaw Creek as the site of a more systematic assault; as many as 300 Lolangkoks may have been massacred. Both types of attacks were in keeping with the early history of northwestern California, when many of the whites pursued a policy of Indian genocide. Small bands of well-armed men and larger groups of "volunteers" combed the countryside in search of "Diggers," as all of the Indians were indiscriminately called. Those natives that were not killed outright were often kidnapped and then sometimes sold to other whites. From 1860 to 1863, numerous younger Indians were "indentured" to Humboldt County citizens under a state law that legalized this form of slavery. Federal troops sometimes attempted to "protect" the Indians from the settlers, but this usually meant taking the natives to a poorly run and dangerously unhealthy reservation.

* * *

" . . . NO INDIAN CAN SHOW HIS HEAD ANYWHERE . . ."

During the 1850s and 1860s, many of the local reports about the region's "Indian troubles" depicted the natives as ruthless aggressors, bent on creating mayhem among the settlers. A few accounts, however, told a different story. Colonel Francis L. Lippett, who for a time commanded the troops at Eureka's Fort Humboldt, wrote in 1862 that ". . . no Indian can show his head anywhere without being shot down like a wild beast. The women and children, even, are considered good game, . . ."

A few years earlier, special agent J. Ross Brown had investigated Indian conditions for the government. He concluded that:

> *It was found convenient to take possession of their country without recompense, rob them of their wives and children, kill them in every cowardly and barbarous manner that could be devised, and when that was impracticable, drive them as far as possible out of the way.*

When a group of whites massacred a band of Wiyots, mostly women and children, on an island in Humboldt Bay, a young newspaperman named Bret Harte wrote a scathing editorial in a local paper. As a result, he received numerous threats from outraged Indian haters and soon departed for San Francisco. Harte's protests, like those of Brown and Lippett, had little effect; the attacks on the Indians ceased only when the whites had gained control of the native lands and nearly obliterated most of the tribes.

* * *

Many of the Indians who survived the white attacks were removed from their homeland. Between 1854 and 1861, at least 74 Sinkyones were taken to the infamous Klamath Reservation, which one modern-day Indian author has termed a "concentration camp." When this site was closed, the Indians were relocated on the reservation at Hoopa. Some of the Sinkyones were sent to the Round Valley Reservation in northern Mendocino County.

Starvation also took its toll. Whites encroached on Indian hunting and gathering grounds, bringing in grazing animals and disrupting the natural plant life by introducing alien grasses onto the prairies. Other settlers built along the rivers and creeks, occupying the sites of Lolangkok fishing villages. Many tribal food sources were thus either diminished or eliminated. The ill-fated Indians who slaughtered the bull at Bull Creek may well have been desperate for the food.

Weakened by hunger and the stress of conflict, the natives were especially susceptible to illness, including many new ailments brought by the whites. In 1919, a laconic report in a local paper noted a "rumor" of smallpox among the Indians of Bull Creek. By then, there were few Lolangkoks left.

*   *   *

THE SINKYONES, WORLD RENEWAL, AND THE FLOOD

The Sinkyones' word for their highest divinity meant "the great traveler." The name was so sacred that it was seldom spoken aloud; instead the deity was usually called "That Man" or something similar. Shortly before he died, Jack Woodman told a story about this figure.

According to Woodman, each year That Man appeared to the Sinkyones' shaman and told him when and where to hold the tribe's dance for world renewal. The shaman then informed the chief, who in turn notified the rest of the people. When the time for the dance came, the village families moved to a campground outside a special brush enclosure. After some preliminary ceremonies inside the enclosure, the shaman told the story of That Man, who

> *. . . made this world and patted it down so that everything would stay in place. But bad men were not satisfied and tore it down, tore up the ocean banks, tore up the trees, tore down the mountains. Since that time we have had to sing and dance every year to make it right again.*

Then the songs and dances commenced, lasting three or four hours and resuming on each of the next few nights.

One time That Man visited Woodman. He told Jack that he had come over Elk Ridge, which lay southwest of Bull Creek, and had seen where the white men had peeled tanbark. "It looks just like my people lying around," That Man said, "lying around with all their skin cut off."

According to Jack, That Man "looked, he looked, he looked once more and he hung his head. He was sad, sad, and he would not look again, he felt so grieved." That Man also "saw men breaking rocks and plowing up grass. He saw all things leaving and going back to where they came from." Then That Man told Jack that he "wanted to make another freshet from the ocean — make everybody die so the world would come back as it used to be." Jack argued with That Man, telling him "don't do that," until finally nothing more was said about it.

Jack Woodman died in 1929. By then the Sinkyone world renewal dance was no longer danced. The white people who had taken over the tribe's territory continued plowing the grass and harvesting the tanbark. In 1937 a "freshet" swept the area, followed by even bigger ones in 1955 and 1964. They washed with a vengeance over the old Indian lands, wiping out much of what the whites had grown and built. The Sinkyones were long since gone; there wasn't anyone left to tell That Man not to bring the floods.

SETTLERS AND SAWYERS:
WHITES COME TO THE REDWOODS

The first whites to enter Sinkyone country were the four members of the L. K. Wood Party, who struggled up the valleys of the main Eel and South Fork Eel in the winter of 1850. The men were carrying news that would soon transform the entire region: a "lost" anchorage to the north had just been rediscovered, one that could provide easier access to the remote Trinity gold fields. The following April a fleet of more than 40 ships hastily departed San Francisco, their decks filled with shop-keepers, speculators, and soldiers of fortune – all bound for what would soon be named Humboldt Bay.

The new settlers congregated near the coast. Within four years they had organized the County of Humboldt, with its seat at the bayside seaport of Eureka, while other communities sprang up around the bay and along the lower Eel River. Almost no one had located in the rugged country to the south, however. By 1859, just one white was reported in residence on the South Fork Eel – probably Simon Phillips, who had married an Indian woman from the Sinkyone village of Ket-tin-tel-be, a location that would later be known as Phillipsville.

* * *

L. K. WOOD'S UN-BEARABLE TRIP

Although the only grizzly bears now seen in California are those adorning the state flag, they were once a common inhabitant of the North Coast region. L. K. Wood and his companions saw more than a dozen on their way through southern Humboldt County, and the men tangled with at least a couple too many.

The group had left the Eel River valley at what is now Scotia, climbing south onto the ridge near Monument Peak. Here they came upon a contingent of five grizzlies before being forced back to the Eel by winter snows.

Wood's party then followed the rivers south, travelling along Indian and game trails, until they reached the vicinity of present-day Miranda. From there they ventured west into the mountains and again met a pack of bruins – no less than eight this time. The men began shooting at the bears, killing one and wounding another; two of the grizzlies suddenly

80

counterattacked, mauling Wood severely. In great pain from a broken leg, the wounded leader managed to continue with the others until they reached the Mark West Ranch, north of Sonoma, where he was at last able to recuperate. To add insult to Wood's injuries, only the grizzlies received lasting recognition for the hilltop encounter, for the battle site has since become known as the Bear Buttes.

* * *

Two events in the early 1860s made the southern Humboldt region more hospitable to newcomers: the Homestead Act of 1862 offered settlers a way to acquire cheap property, while a series of attacks against the local Indians either killed or removed most of the area's original inhabitants. By 1870, there were almost 300 white residents in the southeastern part of the county, a number that nearly tripled during the next decade. The early arrivals included the Myers family, who were farming a sunny flat on a broad bend of the South Fork Eel; the Logans, who had settled at what later became Miranda, and Tosaldo and Addie Johnson, who had moved onto a prairie above the redwood groves of Bull Creek. Another surge of settlement ensued, spurred by the continued sale of 160-acre homesteads for $1.25 per acre. By the turn of the century, ranches and farms dotted the prairies and riverside flats, producing meat, dairy goods, fruits, and vegetables. Much of the food was floated downriver to market in shallow-draught boats; for a short time, Grant Myers's *Great Maria* was one of them.

* * *

NAUTICAL DISASTERS ON THE EEL:
#1 – THE <u>GREAT</u> <u>MARIA</u>

In 1900, it was reported that "the river schooner <u>Great</u> <u>Maria</u> is on the dock at Phillipsville, undergoing thorough cleaning and overhauling, after which she will make regular trips up the South Fork from Scotia." Brave words, but ones that soon proved to be overly optimistic.

The so-called "schooner" was actually an ungainly, square-ended vessel whose makeshift sails were used only for upriver travel. The main source of power was a three-man crew that pushed the craft along with long poles they stuck in the riverbottom. When more help was needed, horses were harnessed to the boat.

Grant Myers rented the <u>Great</u> <u>Maria</u> to Joe Stockel, who used her to carry cargoes between Scotia and Phillipsville; the boat also journeyed up the main Eel to Camp Grant and McCann. All too soon, however, these wide-ranging voyages came to an end.

On the evening of December 18, 1901, the vessel left Dyerville, bound downriver; its decks were laden with 200 boxes of Camp Grant's finest apples. Within minutes the craft hit rough water, and waves up to three feet high began splashing aboard. The Great Maria quickly filled with water. Captain Nelson, at the helm, was washed off his feet, but made his way back to the boat by clutching a box of apples.

The crew of Stockel, Victor Pedrotti, and a man named Martin weren't doing as well; the three men, along with most of the apples, were being pushed under the water by the turbulent current. A boat was sent out from shore, but it was unable to reach the struggling crewmen.

A dugout canoe was then dispatched, and it succeeded in reaching Captain Nelson, who had jumped from the Great Maria with a towline. When the dugout brought the Captain ashore, however, it was found that the towline had not been attached to the boat. In the meantime, crewman Martin had also leapt into the water, and he now struggled up the riverbank.

That left Stockel and Pedrotti still on board; they waited helplessly as the beleaguered boat was swept down the river. Finally, about half a mile farther on, the Great Maria lodged in a drift of logs and the two crewmen scrambled to safety.

The boat was hopelessly mired beneath the wood, but Stockel attempted to salvage some of the apples that were caught nearby. The remainder of the waterborne fruit floated away on the Eel, arriving downriver just in time to provide the local children with some holiday season apple bobbing—a Christmas gift, of sorts, from the late, Great Maria.

*   *   *

By 1900, the only community of any size between Garberville and Scotia was the crossroads center of Dyerville, located where the wagon road along the main Eel met routes from Bull Creek and the South Fork Eel. There was a hotel and store in Pepperwood, and overnight accommodations, called "stopping places," on ranches at Pepperwood, Englewood, Myers, and Phillipsville. So long as travel was limited to rough dirt roadways and the unpredictable river, the region reposed in sleepy serenity; early in the new century, however, "progress" arrived, coming southward on the glinting steel tracks of the Northwestern Pacific Railroad. In 1908 the line was advancing up the east side of the Eel from Scotia; meanwhile, down in Mendocino County, the northbound route had reached Willits, and work crews were busy at both ends closing the 60-mile gap. Strangely enough, it was the construction of the railroad which brought about another of the Eel's great boating adventures.

NAUTICAL DISASTERS ON THE EEL:
#2 — THE *POISON OAK*

The construction firm of Klippel & McLean had a problem. They were supposed to be building a section of the railroad south of Scotia, but their pack mules were unable to do any hauling; the animals' hides had become infected from nearly constant contact with poison oak. Another method of transportation was needed, for without supplies, work on the railbed would slow to a halt.

McLean had a plan, however, and as a result, the aptly named Poison Oak *was born. Constructed on short notice by a Eureka boatbuilder, she was a paddle-wheel steamer, as big as a barn, with a 75-horse-power diesel engine to propel her. Captain Joshua Elder of Sacramento was recruited to command the vessel; his crew arrived at the Eel River launch site straight from a four-day binge among the saloons of Eureka.*

The *Poison Oak*

The Poison Oak *lay moored by the riverside, her decks loaded with goods. Nothing was tied down, for a smooth voyage was anticipated. A. D. North, the boat's construction engineer, whacked her bow with a bottle of river water. The engine roared, lines were cast off, Captain*

Elder shouted orders that no one could hear, and the <u>Poison Oak</u> slipped into the Eel.

The river's current was immediately noticeable. Elder turned the wheel hard to port to head the boat upstream.

Nothing happened.

The puzzled captain then swung the wheel sharply starboard, hoping this would have some effect.

Again, nothing.

By now the Eel had caught <u>Poison Oak</u> and was moving her downriver at a leisurely pace. In the pilot house, Elder at last realized what had happened: the bleary-eyed crew had attached the steering ropes incorrectly and there was no way to bring the boat under control. Elder and the errant crewmen exchanged curses as the vessel continued on its runaway trip. Finally, after a maiden voyage of some ten miles, the <u>Poison Oak</u> struck a sandbar and caught fast; as she listed to one side, her unsecured cargo slid gently into the river.

The railroad project had suffered another setback, but the ever-inventive McLean was undaunted. He would bring in a barge with a steam engine and a winch on it . . . the winch would be used to pull the <u>Poison Oak</u> off the sandbar . . . they'd then reload the boat with supplies, and winch her slowly up the river . . . the barge would, of course, be called the <u>Poison Ivy</u> . . .

* * *

With the railroad came the loggers. Spur lines bridged the Eel at Elinor and Holmes, providing access to the great timber stands southwest of the river. Tie camps sprang up along the county road, their products hauled across the Eel to line the newly constructed sections of the railbed.

By 1912, the Northwestern Pacific had crossed the main Eel opposite Dyerville and built a large switching yard and depot on the flats there. A new town, called South Fork, grew up around the stop; it would become the shipping point for a wealth of ranch products, tanbark, and redwood that had earlier been beyond the railroad's reach. As the NWP pushed south through the Eel's rugged gorge, expenses skyrocketed, with track being laid at a cost of $25 per inch, but the rail line was finally finished in late 1914. Soon passengers and goods were rolling between the two great bays — San Francisco and Humboldt. That wasn't all; the county wagon road was being converted into a thoroughfare fit (or nearly so) for the up-and-coming automobile. The reconstructed route was rousingly called the "Redwood Highway," but slowed by both World War I and difficult terrain, it was not completed until 1922.

Spur line crossing the Eel from Holmes Flat

The tall trees of the South Fork Eel could now be reached by either car or train; bolstered by the development of the State Park, the region attracted redwood admirers from the Bay Area and beyond. The small communities along the highway grew to accommodate the influx of tourists, with Weott supplanting Dyerville as the major town in the area. Since much of the canyon corridor was protected as parkland, logging and tanbark operations often had to locate away from the river; up-country, Bull Creek was a bustle of activity, at times having as many as three mills in operation. During Prohibition, the thickly timbered forestlands furthered another commercial activity, conveniently shrouding numerous streamside stills.

Logging activity slowed during the Depression, and fewer tourists came to visit the Park; some of the locals relied on hunting, trapping, and fishing to see them through the difficult times. A Civilian Conservation Corps camp was opened at Dyerville, near Park headquarters, and was later moved to Burlington. Members of the Corps often worked on Park projects during the thirties, offsetting some of the effects of the reduced state budget. A CCC work camp operated for a time out of Look Prairie.

Humboldt Redwoods closed during World War II, but logging near the Park continued. Starting in 1947, the first local cutting of Douglas fir began, providing a new source of employment while ravaging the forests of upper Bull Creek.

Tourism along the Redwood Highway revived following the war, and by mid-century most of the small communities along the road boasted a collection of motels, auto courts, cafes, and gas stations, all bent on relieving tired travellers of their cares—as well as a few of their dollars. Park users were lured to Humboldt Redwoods by the low fees: 50 cents per car per day for camping and 25 cents for picnicking. After the lean depression and war years, the prospects for the region at last appeared rosy.

Pepperwood, 1949

But then the great 1955 Christmas-time flood hit, and the prosperity that had seemed just around the corner instead went around the bend, washed down the Eel along with the hopes and homes of hundreds of canyon dwellers. In Weott and Pepperwood, residents found their houses piled up against huge redwood trees; tiny Elinor became tinier still, as all but one dwelling was destroyed. The community of Bull Creek lost many of its buildings and even saw its cemetery swept away. Some of the town's structures were rebuilt, only to be torn down a decade later when the area became part of the Park.

Most of the region's communities bounced back after the washout, but just nine years later another holiday season flood struck; the 1964 deluge was even more destructive than its predecessor, with water rising as much as 33 feet above the Avenue of the Giants. Pepperwood was virtually wiped out, and the other low-lying towns never fully recovered.

Added to the effects of the two great floods was the construction of the 101 Freeway, which began in 1957. The course of the new thoroughfare often ran high above the rivers, and it bypassed or merely skirted the towns that had straddled the Redwood Highway. This could have dealt the already-reeling communities a final, fatal blow, had it not been for the conversion of the old road into the "Avenue of the Giants"; it became a well-marked "scenic alternate" that provided sightseers with a leisurely route through the heart of the redwood forests. No more would through traffic rumble past the stores of Weott, Phillipsville, and the other towns, but it was replaced by enough sempervirens-seeking excursionists to keep many of the locals in business. The redwoods that had been saved from the ax 20, 30, or even 40 years earlier were now saving the communities that had grown up around them. Because the trees had endured, so did the towns.

By the end of the 1960s, the region had assumed much of its present-day form. Nearly all of the Bull Creek watershed had become Park property; the town had been levelled and its residents had relocated. The sections of the 101 Freeway which ran through the Park were completed, and the Save-the-Redwoods League acquired a corridor of land along the northern Avenue. From the 1970s onward, the pace of change has slowed to a crawl. There have been some gains and losses—the Park has added more property, the mill in Myers Flat has closed, the Dyerville Giant has dropped to the ground—but overall, the land has regained a stability it had not enjoyed since the days of the Sinkyone Indians more than a century ago. While the ever-changing world whizzes by on all sides, Humboldt Redwoods has become one of those rare places where time, remarkably, has circled back closer to the past.

TAKING THE "AVENUE":
A RIDE THROUGH THE REDWOODS

The Avenue of the Giants was once part of the Redwood Highway, a winding, two-lane road that connected the remote North Coast with the San Francisco Bay Area. Today, the Avenue is a 31.5-mile "scenic alternate," officially designated as State Highway 254, which stretches from the junction hamlet of Sylvandale to the now-obliterated farm community of Elinor. Much of the route travels through the great riverside redwood groves of Humboldt Redwoods State Park, providing access to campgrounds, day use areas, numerous trails, and the Park's Visitor Center. Small rustic towns dot the Avenue at intervals a few miles apart, while an occasional side road leads into the southern Humboldt hinterlands. One such route, Mattole Road, enters the towering stands of the famed Rockefeller Forest and then follows scenic Bull Creek to connect with a network of trails and primitive roads in the Park's backcountry.

The Avenue can conveniently be divided into three sections — south, central, and north. Each segment has its own unique character, each is filled with its share of attractions, and all have easy freeway access. South of the Avenue are a pair of redwood groves that also belong to the Park; a side trip to visit them can conveniently include stops at Garberville and Redway, the two largest communities in southern Humboldt County.

GATEWAY TO THE GIANTS: GARBERVILLE AND REDWAY

A good place for northbound travellers to prepare for both the Avenue and the rest of the Park is the Garberville-Redway area, which provides the most extensive services in the region; the next stop with as much to offer is Fortuna, 50 miles north. Near Redway are two detached units of the Park, the Whittemore and Holbrook groves, whose shaded confines offer river access and cool summer picnic spots.

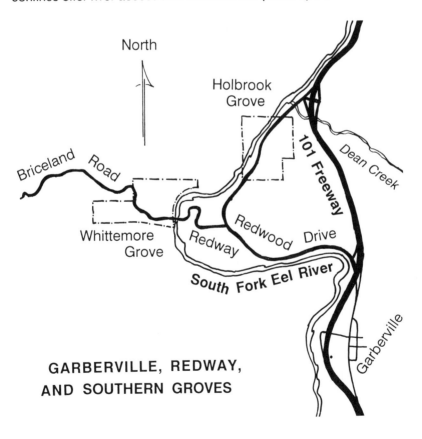

GARBERVILLE, REDWAY,
AND SOUTHERN GROVES

Four miles north of the Humboldt County line, Highway 101 twists through the darkened depths of Richardson Grove State Park, a small but intense collection of large redwoods; the route then becomes freeway, arriving at the open valley of Benbow Lake State Recreation Area five miles later. From the hilltop north of Benbow, an offramp leads to Garberville, pop. 1,350, elev. 528, the business center of southern Humboldt County. The offramp becomes the south end of Garberville's main street, Redwood Drive, which runs north through the heart of town. The compact community, situated on a gently sloping tableland above the South Fork Eel River, offers a complete range of services. Part of the business district lies east of Redwood Drive on short side streets; here will be found the town's hospital, library, and DMV office.

* * *

WHEN GETTING TO GARBERVILLE TOOK GUMPTION

In 1868 Jacob C. Garber built the "South Fork Trading Post" on the site of the town that later took his name. To stock his shelves, Garber relied on huge pack trains of between 100 and 150 mules to bring supplies from Shelter Cove, more than 20 miles distant on the coast. It wasn't until 1879 that Chinese laborers finally built a wagon road to replace this pack trail, and for years afterward there was still no direct route north to Eureka. The circuitous, 88-mile trip took eight days, longer if the rivers were up.

If the town's isolation didn't dissuade travellers from paying a visit, its reputation did. One early observer called the community "the great resort of this sheep country and a rough place. Knives are universally worn by all frequenters of its saloons and hotels."

Despite these difficulties, Garberville had grown by 1907 to include not one but two hotels, a confectionery, a dealer in a "fine line of Studebaker buggies and wagons," and an undertaker. The town remained a remote outpost, although its residents could now bravely claim that "we are in touch with the outside world by telephone."

Reaching Garberville was still difficult in 1911 when author Jack London and his wife Charmian arrived in town. The Londons were en route to Oregon from their estate in Sonoma County, and Jack made the trip especially tough by using the occasion to learn the intricacies of driving a four-horse team and buggy. Charmian also tried her hand at navigating the grades and turns of the rugged coastal mountains and did at least as well as her novice-teamster husband.

When Jack subsequently wrote an account of the trip for <u>Sunset</u> magazine, his description of the sights of southern Humboldt required just a single sentence, although it was a long one:

From Garberville, where we ate eels to repletion and got acquainted with the aborigines, we drove down the Eel river valley for two days through the most unthinkably glorious body of redwood timber to be seen anywhere.

A decade later, after the Redwood Highway was completed, tourists by the thousands began passing through the once-isolated town. Gone were the days of plodding pack trains and harrowing buggy rides; the auto had arrived, and to reach Garberville you no longer needed gumption — just a full tank of gas.

Governor Stephens at the opening
of the Redwood Highway, Garberville

Redwood Drive crosses the 101 Freeway at the north end of town; travellers who wish to bypass both Redway and the Whittemore and Holbrook redwood groves can resume the freeway here and connect with the Avenue of the Giants turnoff six miles ahead.

Following Redwood Drive north, the route soon drops closer to the South Fork Eel, passing beneath the tall, tan bluffs east of the river and then crossing a lightly wooded benchland. At 2.6 miles the road rises and enters Redway, pop. 1,400, elev. 528. The business district, which is strung out along Redwood Drive, includes gas stations, motels, cafes, market, liquor store, and laundromat. Near the north end of town, mile 3.0, Briceland Road branches left; this paved, two-lane route leads west to Shelter Cove, the King Range, Sinkyone State Park, and the Whittemore Grove, which is the southernmost unit of Humboldt Redwoods.

Side trip to Whittemore Grove:

From its junction with Redwood Drive, Briceland Road proceeds gradually downhill, twists through several curves, and then crosses the South Fork Eel at mile 1.0. A dirt road exits right, mile 1.2, into the Whittemore Grove. Beneath medium-large redwoods are a small parking area, restrooms, and a varied understory and ground-cover that includes California hazel, Pacific starflower, milkmaids, redwood sorrel, trillium, and fetid adder's tongue. The grove honors Harris Whittemore, a Connecticut philanthropist who pioneered reforestation work in his native state.

*   *   *

Returning to Redway, Redwood Drive continues north out of town, descending at mile 3.8 into a stand of tall redwoods. At 4.1 miles an unmarked gravel road exits left into the Holbrook Grove, passing a gate as it cuts back sharply into the forest. The access road winds through the grove for 0.3 mile, where it reaches a second gate and a small parking area. Below is a gravel bar beside the South Fork Eel that provides opportunities for sunbathing, swimming, and boating. Either or both gates may be locked.

Redwood Drive soon exits the eastern end of the grove; after passing briefly through mixed woodlands, the route crosses Dean Creek at mile 4.8. Immediately the road turns right to go under the 101 Freeway; the onramp for northbound traffic is on the left just beyond the underpass. There were once two Indian villages near the stream here, which was known as Tahs-ki-kok, "white flag creek."

Now the route rejoins the northbound 101 Freeway, heading towards the Avenue of the Giants. A pullout, right at milepost 15.25, features a map of the Avenue. The freeway then curves above the open, rocky channel of the South Fork; the surrounding hills are covered with a mixture of grassy prairies and woodlands of oak, madrone, and Douglas fir.

The exit for the Avenue of the Giants comes at freeway milepost 17.76; a short distance down the offramp is another interpretive map for the Avenue, accompanied by a distribution box for "Avenue of the Giants Auto Tour" pamphlets. This publication describes nine locations along the route, all marked with Auto Tour signs, which feature some of the more interesting roadside attractions of Humboldt Redwoods State Park. The offramp then continues downhill to a junction with the Avenue.

THE SOUTHERN AVENUE:
SUNSHINE BY THE RIVERSIDE

Along its southern section, the Avenue of the Giants winds above the eastern side of the South Fork Eel; the canyon is generally broad and open, with large, sandy flats often extending into the floodplain. Redwoods cover the narrow benchlands beside the river, while mixed forests and an occasional prairie rise up the adjacent ridgeslopes. In earlier times, the region was home to both sub-tribes of Sinkyone Indians — the Shelter Cove group to the south and the Lolangkoks to the north. The riverside is dotted with the sites of their fishing villages.

Today, this stretch of the Avenue serves as a transition zone, where small enclaves of giant redwoods prepare travellers for the great groves that lie ahead. Several short hiking trails provide introductions to the plant life of the area and also offer cooling respites from the sunnier sections of the road. When the heavier forests are reached north of Myers Flat, those who have studied the southern approach will qualify as old hands at appreciating redwood habitat.

Red-tailed hawk above the redwoods

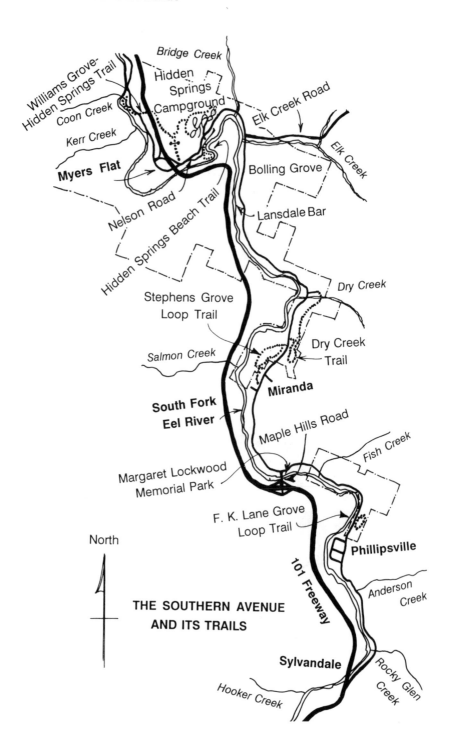

North

THE SOUTHERN AVENUE
AND ITS TRAILS

The northbound Avenue starts at the base of the 101 Freeway offramp, where a right turn begins the route. A left turn here leads onto a short southerly continuation of the Avenue that passes tiny Sylvandale before ending at a freeway onramp. Hooker Creek Road branches right just before the onramp; a gravel track exits, right, from the road's start and leads to boating access for the South Fork Eel.

* * *

A JEWEL AMONG THE REDWOODS

When Lucille Hull opened the "Redwood Jewel Box" in 1953, she had no idea that a decade later she would be saving trees instead of selling them. Operating the Sylvandale nursery and gift shop was supposed to allow Lucille and her husband Leo to drift into semi-retirement beside the languid South Fork Eel, but events didn't work out that way.

For one thing, Lucille couldn't do anything halfway, so she headed full speed into running the business, engaging tourists with her friendly talk, alerting them to the region's attractions, and generally amusing anyone who happened to be within earshot. Few could resist Lucille's animated chitchat, and many of her audience would purchase a redwood seedling or carved burl sculpture while they listened.

All went well until the 1955 flood, when Leo Hull suffered a heart attack after working all night to protect their possessions from the rising water. Leo never fully regained his health, and he died in the summer of 1959, just two months after the couple had sold the Redwood Jewel Box.

Not long afterward, much of Sylvandale was plowed under when the new freeway was built. One victim of the project was a 150-foot-tall redwood that the irrepressible Lucille had once climbed nearly to its top. It had been planted in 1902 by Walt and Voreh Sinclair to commemorate their marriage; when the couple sold the property to the Hulls, Lucille had promised to maintain the tree, but she'd been powerless to stop the highway department from dropping it.

Lucille eventually remarried and moved north to Trinidad; her new husband was Bill Vinyard, a professor at Humboldt State University. The couple soon learned that the highway developers were at it again, this time planning a route through the redwoods of Prairie Creek State Park. Lucille had lost one prize tree to the road builders, and she was determined not to let it happen again. She and Bill joined the growing fight to stop the proposed highway.

The issue soon expanded, for there was a chance of including the threatened trees in the plan for a "Redwood National Park." The

Vinyards became active in the local Sierra Club, and over the next 15 years worked first to help create the new park and then to expand it. Since that time, Lucille has remained a driving force within both the local and regional branches of the Club.

Helping save 300-foot redwoods has given Lucille Vinyard much pleasure, but her time spent selling 12-inch seedlings was satisfying, too. "The world came to my door," she says of her years at the Jewel Box. "I loved every minute of it."

*   *   *

Heading north from the 101 Freeway exit, the Avenue hugs the bank above the South Fork Eel. At mile 0.9 it arrives at the Chimney Tree, part of a privately owned tourist attraction; its owners levy no admission charge for entering the relic. The bottom portion of this 78-foot hollow redwood was once a gift shop, but is now merely an empty shell in which visitors may crane their necks skyward in the hope of seeing a small bit of daylight. A marker on the tree's interior more than four feet above floor level indicates "high water" during the little-remembered 1986 flood.

The sunny flatlands of Phillipsville, pop. 250, elev. 280, open west of the roadway at 2.3 miles. Paved, one-lane Phillipsville Road exits left here; in 0.2 mile it makes a right turn opposite a dirt spur road, left, that gives access to the South Fork Eel. Northward along the Avenue is the town's business district — a small collection of arcadian tourist accommodations and several vintage establishments for food, drink, and gifts. The grocery store dates from the 1920s, when it was part of the neighboring Deerhorn Lodge. In the previous century, the Shelter Cove Sinkyones had a large village, Ket-tin-tel-be, on the flat.

At the north end of town, mile 2.7, is a small red building, about the size and shape of a gypsy wagon, which houses the Phillipsville Post Office. The land just beyond it was once the ranch of an early postmaster, Jacob Combs, and his wife Margaret. When the mail would arrive from Eureka, rancher Combs would grumblingly trudge in from his fields to sort the letters and place them in the post office's nine mailboxes. The spot soon became a stopping place for travellers, including Jack and Charmian London when they made their 1911 trip through the region. Jack, a long-time socialist, was nevertheless careful to inform Margaret Combs that the London's servant, Nakata, was to be fed separately in the kitchen. Except for a sagging barn, little now remains of the Combses' once popular way station. A champion-size black walnut tree that at one time graced the property has long since died, although one of its descendants still spreads vastly over the untended fields.

Haying time on the Combs Ranch

Just past the ranch is the entrance, right, to the Franklin K. Lane Grove, 2.9 miles, one of the Park's earliest acquisitions; beside the paved parking area are restrooms and a pair of picnic tables. A trail heads northeast to enter a deeply shaded stand of redwoods, wherein lies an abandoned section of the original Redwood Highway [p. 110]. The Avenue soon bends left to regain the river, revealing a view, mile 3.5, of the cottonwood-covered flats north of Phillipsville; in fall, the tall trees glow above the riverbank, their leaves a mass of soft, shimmering gold.

A stark stone chimney on the hillside at mile 4.0, right, announces the Charles B. Alexander Grove. Departing left from the middle of the Grove is a dirt road that drops to a gravel bar/boat launch site. At mile 4.2 the Avenue passes over Fish Creek, once known as Ka-kes-kok, which descends from the right. This stream probably formed the boundary between the two Sinkyone Indian sub-tribes. The Lolangkoks occupied the area which the Avenue now enters, while the Shelter Cove group held the lands back towards Phillipsville; the latter's northernmost village, Kekestci, was near the mouth of the creek. Beyond the stream crossing, right at mile 4.3, are the ruins of the Forest of Arden, a once-popular river canyon resort.

The paved Maple Hills Road exits left at mile 4.8; it crosses the South Fork Eel and connects with the 101 Freeway. This is the only interchange between the southern end of the Avenue and Myers Flat, 7.5 miles ahead. Just before this side road reaches the river bridge, a dirt track exits left; it leads downhill to Margaret Lockwood Memorial Park, an undeveloped county facility that provides river access at a large gravel bar. Opposite the Maple Hills Road turnoff is a modest building that once housed the Fir Haven Co-Op, an exercise in countercultural commerce that failed to survive the 1980s.

Now the route turns north, rising higher above the river. A pullout at mile 5.2 offers a chance to examine California black oak, Oregon white oak, California buckeye, and toyon on the roadbanks; the latter colors the hillsides with its spectacular red berries in winter. Across the river to the southwest rise the Bear Buttes, site of the 1850 encounter between the L. K. Wood party and a band of grizzlies; north of the rocky ridgetop is the Salmon Creek drainage, a watershed once filled with more than a dozen Lolangkok villages.

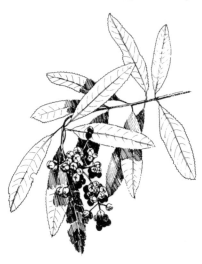

toyon, Christmasberry
(Heteromeles arbutifolia)
[blooms June-July]

More toyon and buckeye line the roadway as it approaches Miranda, pop. 350, elev. 330, at mile 6.0. The region's only junior and senior high schools cover much of the eastern side of town, while motor courts, eating establishments, grocery store, post office, gas station, and souvenir shop line the Avenue.

The area was called Jacobson's Valley by the early settlers; it became *Miranda* in 1903 when over-zealous postal authorities responded to a request that they establish a post office called *Mirada*. Well-travelled visitors of today should not confuse the community with a more recently named Miranda—the innermost satellite of the planet Uranus.

At the north end of town, mile 6.5, an unmarked trail leaves the left side of the Avenue, opposite the north end of the high school parking lot. This spur route connects with the Stephens Grove Loop Trail, which departs from the Avenue a half mile to the north.

The road then drops down a shaded grade, coming to a junction with Logan Road, right, at mile 6.7. The Logans were a pioneer family in the area, arriving from Illinois in 1874. For many years a later Logan, Jane, served as Miranda's postmistress. She was a kindhearted but spirited woman who in old age could be found barreling along the roadways in a war surplus jeep.

Near the bottom of the grade is a sign, mile 6.9, announcing the entrance to Humboldt Redwoods State Park. Beyond here, the Avenue will run through an almost uninterrupted corridor of parklands until it reaches its northern terminus, nearly 25 miles ahead.

Presently the route levels in the middle of a thick grove of redwoods, mile 7.0; a turnout, left, provides access to the unmarked but historic Stephens Grove. Acquired by Humboldt Redwoods in 1922, the 148-acre stand was named for California Governor William D. Stephens, whose tenure saw the approval of an early bill to fund land purchases for the Park. Stephens almost refused to sign the measure, claiming that the money was needed for schools, but Congressman (and Save-the-Redwoods League member) William Kent roared at him, "Hell, Bill! Close the schools. The kids would love it, and they'd make up the work in a couple of years. If we lose these trees, it will take 2,000 years to make *them* up!"

The Stephens Grove Loop Trail circuits the fertile benchland south of the turnout [p. 116]. Immediately ahead on the Avenue at mile 7.1 is a pullout, left, that offers parking for a southern approach to the Dry Creek Trail [p. 108]. This undesignated route leaves the opposite side of the roadway from a point marked by a phone cable sign.

Shaggy redwoods shade the Frank and Delphine Belotti Grove, mile 7.4; they blend into the Pioneer Grove at mile 7.6, a stand of especially statuesque roadside giants. The Avenue then crosses often-wet Dry Creek; just to the north are two side routes. To the right, an unmarked dirt road provides northern access to the Dry Creek Trail a hundred yards up the canyon. On the left, beyond a metal gate, is an old road remnant that soon shrinks to a trail. The route leads 0.2 miles west to a gravel bar at the edge of the South Fork Eel. Growing atop the bar are a few California poppies and a striking specimen of smallflower tamarisk, an exotic shrub that often colonizes along river courses; numerous clusters of petite pink flowers explode from its branches in spring. To the southeast, the deep channelling of Dry Creek has exposed a cross section of compactly mixed silts and gravels—a perfect display of benchland alluvium.

Paved Cathey Road exits to the right at 8.0 miles. It climbs a mile to a prairie-checkered hillslope where members of the pioneer Cathey family still reside. John and Jane Cathey moved to the area in 1886 and, like most homesteaders, were nearly self-sufficient. Once a year, however, John travelled north to Springville (modern-day Fortuna) for provisions; it took him five days to complete the round trip—today the journey requires about three hours.

West of the Avenue at 8.9 miles is the Uriah T. Albee and Cornelia T. Albee Grove. At the grove's parking area, mile 9.0, is a short path to the bluffs above the river; it passes false Solomon's seal, California hazel, and trail plant before meeting a wall of poison oak that discourages all but the foolhardy from proceeding farther. The north end of the parking area is marked by a circular stone fountain, no longer operating, that was long a place of refreshment for thirsty, and thrifty, travellers.

Mile 9.1 brings the Blair Grove, marked by a large hollow log, left. A bridge built west of here in the early twenties crossed the river at a location the Lolangkoks called Ni-te-te El-lah-te — "dog drowned."

The Lansdale Grove, mile 9.2, was dedicated in 1932 to both Philip Van Horne Lansdale and Sidney M. Smith, but now seems known by only the former's name. Beneath the grove's medium-size redwoods are a cluster of clintonias and a covering of redwood sorrel.

After passing some bankside sticky monkey flowers, mile 9.5, right, the route comes to a gravel road, left at mile 9.7, that leads down the riverbank to Lansdale Bar. Only vehicles with four-wheel drive can be expected to negotiate the patch of sand at the bottom of the road. The gravelly bar is a launch site for boats and canoes, and there is a fishing hole about 0.2 mile downriver. Across the South Fork was Sentelcelin-dun, or "rock flat flows out place," a Lolangkok village.

A sign, left at mile 10.3, indicates a grand vista of the Griffin Grove across the river. Immediately before the Elk Creek Bridge is a small parking area, right, mile 10.4. From here, a short but scenic path follows the south bank of the creek upstream, passing through lush vegetation that includes California spikenard, vanilla leaf, five-fingered fern, smooth yellow violet, and dogwood. The trail ends in 0.1 mile at a creekside overlook; on the right are several lovely bushes of flowering currant.

flowering currant
(Ribes sanguineum var. glutinosum)

When currently flowering, the flowering currant is a delight to eye and nose. Clusters of small pink flowers dangle from leafy stalks, their delicate fragrance wafted by the slightest wind. In summer, the flowers mature into clusters of small black, edible berries that exude a whitish powder. Unlike the related gooseberry, the currant's fruit lacks bristles. Indians mixed the dried berries with animal fat and saved the concoction for future consumption. [blooms February-April]

Griffin Grove
from Bolling Grove

The Avenue then spans Elk Creek, called Sol-te-kok in the Sinkyone language, on a small but stately concrete bridge that dates from 1940. Immediately north is a parking area for the historic Bolling Grove, which honors an Army officer killed in World War I; it was the first memorial grove purchased for the Park. Across the roadway from the parking area, a pair of redwoods have formed an improbable alliance, their trunks growing into each other at two separate locations. A third tree, left to its solitary devices, has sprouted a number of eye-catching burls.

Directly past the grove, mile 10.5, is a junction with Elk Creek Road (two-lane, paved) which leads northeast to Mail Ridge. The ridge, which sits between the South Fork Eel and main Eel rivers, was traversed by an early postal route. The road forms the start of an invigorating loop trip for intrepid travellers.

Bolling Grove double tree

Side trip to Fruitland, McCann,
Camp Grant, and South Fork

(This route rejoins the Avenue of the Giants in 13.5 miles at the Founders Grove. The road features a 12-foot low clearance and one section of narrow, steep dirt surface; it is not recommended for use in wet weather or by large vehicles.)

Elk Creek Road climbs a steep, forested hillside to reach the top of Mail Ridge and a junction with Dyerville Loop Road at mile 2.8. A right turn here leads to Fort Seward, Alderpoint, and other destinations in southeastern Humboldt County. Straight ahead, a dirt road drops quickly to the site of Whitlow, a.k.a. Sequoia, a ranching area that was once a stop on the railroad. Left, along paved Dyerville Loop Road, is the route for the side trip; it immediately passes through the ridgetop prairies of Fruitland, offering a pleasant view eastward of several mountains, including the cone-shaped Lassic peaks.

The road narrows to one lane at mile 3.9, and then reaches a junction, 4.0 miles, with a second, steeper descent to Whitlow, which forks right. The main route curves left and soon turns to dirt. After running along the side of Mail Ridge, the road drops towards the main Eel, at mile 6.8 winding around Devil's Elbow, described in an early account as "a bold turn on the mountainside . . . that alarms the timid," and one that still bedevils drivers. The route enters the all-but-vanished precincts of McCann, mile 7.0, another erstwhile rail stop; the floods have reduced the town to a solitary concrete foundation. Here McCann Road (dirt, impassable at high water) branches right to cross the Eel on a low bridge that is frequently submerged during stormy weather. Residents of the river's east bank, a hardy band indeed, must brave the winter waters in the McCann ferry, a small county-operated motorboat; its launch site is located just below a pullout, right, at mile 7.5.

Dyerville Loop Road then rises briefly along Thompson Bluffs before dropping to cross the railroad at 9.5 miles. The route becomes paved soon afterward, passing through second-growth redwood until it turns west at mile 10.2; here it enters the open bottomlands of Camp Grant, a military installation during the previous century's Indian conflicts. Since those earlier times, the soldiers' swords have truly been turned into plowshares, for the site is now known for its tomatoes, cantaloupes, and other produce. The road leaves this fertile floodplain at mile 11.1, crossing under a railroad viaduct notorious for its niggardly 12-foot clearance.

After climbing up a tree-filled hillslope, the route descends to the ruins of South Fork, mile 12.5, once the region's main rail connection but now marked only by a few faded trailers and a lone, long-empty boxcar. Ahead at mile 13.3 is the Park's famed Founders Grove, followed, mile 13.5, by the return to the Avenue of the Giants.

*   *   *

Past Elk Creek Road, the Avenue runs close beside the South Fork Eel, forced there by a steep hillside to the east. A turnout, left at mile 10.8, overlooks the river; on the opposite side of the roadway, several soap roots cling to the hillside.

The Avenue then bridges Bridge Creek, a small waterway that was nonetheless given the large name of Tub-bel-chin-tah Cha-gel-kok by the local Lolangkoks. What appears to be a concrete railing is actually made of carved, heavily weathered redwood timbers.

Now the road makes a wide arc around a northward bend in the river. Left at mile 10.9 is a striking view of the Felton Grove on the far bank. At the grove's dedication, in 1927, there was an afternoon performance of a pageant entitled "Ersa of the Redwoods."

A parking area, left at mile 11.5, features a carved redwood trough that in earlier times held water piped from across the Avenue. Immediately ahead is a crosswalk (watch for pedestrians) followed by a paved road, right, to the Hidden Springs Campground. Across the Avenue on the left is the start of the Hidden Springs Beach Trail [p. 112].

soap root, amole
(Chlorogalum pomeridianum)

Soap root is one of the few plants that can be used as both a cleaning agent and a food. Indians and Hispanic settlers crushed its uncooked bulbs and worked them into a lather to make either shampoo or soap, the Hispanics calling the root *amole*. Indians reportedly used the shampoo not only on their own heads but also to wash the scalps of enemies taken in battle. Early-day gold miners used the fibrous outer parts of the bulb as mattress stuffing. The bulbs lose their soapiness when baked; Indians ate them as if they were potatoes. Soap root grows in dry areas, and is most easily identified by its cluster of long, wavy, light green leaves that spread outwards and upwards from its base. It has small white flowers on the ends of its tall stems; they open only at dusk or on overcast days. [blooms May-August]

The access road to the campground turns back sharply northward, first passing several clusters of giant chain fern and then a large patch of western bleeding heart, right, before reaching the entrance station.

Hidden Springs Campground is built upon a rapidly rising hillside that is covered by a second-growth mixed forest. Several loop roads wind up the slopes, linking the terraced, railing-enclosed campsites. Imaginative campers may envision themselves inhabiting a sort of Nob Hill of the forest, where thickets of tanoak shelter their steeply sided, open-air estates. The action-oriented may depart these cliff-hanging confines by the Williams Grove-Hidden Springs Trail [p. 117]. A cozy amphitheater nestles in a collection of young redwoods and old stumps near the campground's reclusive springs; a hollow, burned

western bleeding heart
(Dicentra formosa)
[blooms March-July]

Amphitheater,
Hidden Springs Campground

stump serves as an entrance portal to the theater. Within the campground are 154 sites, each with picnic table, food cupboard, and fire
ring. There is piped water, and the wheelchair-accessible restrooms
are equipped with showers and laundry tubs. The campsites will each
accommodate 24-foot trailers and motorhomes up to 33 feet in length.

From the entrance to Hidden Springs Campground, the Avenue
proceeds south to the turnoff, left, mile 12.0, for unmarked Nelson Road.
Sites both historic and scenic await along this abbreviated byway.

Side trip on Nelson Road:

One of two remnants of the original Redwood Highway, Nelson
Road now provides access to Hidden Springs Beach and nearby
sections of the South Fork Eel. From its start, the route runs to the
northeast between the Avenue and the river. The road crosses a
redwood-covered benchland, mile 0.1; to the left is the retaining wall
for the Myers Flat Sidehill Viaduct, over which the Avenue of the
Giants passes. The cribbing for the viaduct is a striking construction

of huge redwood sections that are stacked one upon another, as if made from a gigantic set of Lincoln Logs. For decades, motorists have whizzed by overhead, unaware that they owe their passage to this moss-covered, rot-resistant horizontal forest—composed of the only trees that could be trusted to such an enduring task.

At 0.2 mile the route cuts through a low ridge that runs east to picturesque Eagle Point. Trails descend each side of the ridge slope, leading to Hidden Springs Beach. The river area near the beach offers swimming and several medium-size fishing holes. The road then reaches the William P. and Elizabeth Nelson Grove, mile 0.4; the Hidden Springs Beach Trail intersects here. Nelson Road continues to a log barricade and turnaround, mile 0.6, beyond which hikers may continue a short distance.

*   *   *

Resuming the Avenue from the side route, West Road exits right at mile 12.2. It reaches a locked gate at 0.1 mile, after which its paved surface turns to dirt. The rutted track continues uphill past the half-hidden Myers Flat Cemetery before coming to a second locked gate, 0.3 mile, where it meets the Hidden Springs-Williams Grove Trail.

*   *   *

THE GRAVES ON THE GREEN HILLSIDE

They are almost all here now, those people with the wonderful given names who gave their family's name to the flat below. The trees have grown up around their resting place, and the road that passed nearby has become only a rutted track, but there is still a sheen to some of the headstones, and the words upon the markers seem to reverberate through the woods:

"Ulysses S. Grant Myers — 'Pap' — 1864 - 1937" . . . named for a recent hero of the Civil War . . . came to the flat with his family when still a small child . . . schooled in San Francisco . . . sailed in '97 for the Klondike and returned with enough money to make Mattie Smith his bride . . . built the Myers Hotel with part of his gold dust and told tall tales in its parlor as he grew into old age . . . called "Grant" until his sixties, when his new daughter-in-law, Geraldine, nicknamed him "Pap," claiming she didn't know what else to call him. . . .

"Leslie R. Myers — 1910 - 1935" . . . even in death they could not get his name right . . . actually born "Lesser Roosevelt," a reflection of his father Grant's admiration for Teddy the Roughrider, who'd recently been President. . . .

"Nevada C. Jennings — 'Vada' — 1902 - 1987" . . . Lesser's older sister . . . her birthday was September 9, California Admission Day . . . her parents had a friend named for the state just east . . . the little girl became "Nevada California Myers" as a result. . . .

Myers Flat cemetery

*And the other, less spectacular names are here, too: "Sarah Myers,"
Grant's mother . . . "Andrew Fay Myers," another of Grant and Mattie's
sons . . . "Clifford Myers" . . . "Mary Myers" . . . "H. G. Myers" . . . almost
everyone a part of the family by either birth or marriage. . . .*

*Near the cemetery gate there are, however, a few markers that bear
other names. Here the bushes grow taller and the graves show greater
signs of neglect. One headstone may easily be overlooked; it is simply
a piece of grey river rock, worn smooth by the ages and bearing only
the hand-lettered inscription: "Tom."*

*Was Tom perhaps an Indian , known, as so many of them were to the
whites, by only a single name? It is far past the time to tell. His grave
lies within the silent shade, holding fast to its secret — it is only at the
sunny center of the cemetery that the inscriptions reveal great stories,
commemorating a century of famous people and events.*

*Yet the trees and grass grow next to Tom's grave as they do near the
others, taking no notice of the surface of their surroundings. The plants
are only concerned with finding fertile soil, and here, within the hillside
graveyard, one spot is as good as the next.*

TRAILS OF THE SOUTHERN AVENUE

[for map showing trails, see p. 94]

DRY CREEK TRAIL

Summary: Hikers will find few people but lots of plants on this secluded hillside pathway — it's used mostly by the cross-country team from nearby South Fork High School.

Distance: 2.5 miles as a north to south loop; 2.0 miles, one way, from its north end to its southerly connection with the Avenue

Elevation Change: 300-foot gain and loss

Location: The recommended trailhead is on the north side of Dry Creek, 100 yards east from an unmarked, dirt turnoff at mile 7.7 of the Avenue; the southern approach starts abruptly at the east side of the Avenue, mile 7.1.

Warning: *Although designated by the Park as a horse trail, the route cannot be recommended as such; it has a difficult stream crossing near its northern terminus and a potentially dangerous exit onto the Avenue at its southern end.*

**Pacific starflower,
woodland star**
(Trientalis latifolia)
[blooms April-July]

Description: After dropping from the dirt roadway, the trail crosses Dry Creek on a small wooden bridge. The path then switchbacks uphill through mixed forest; the steep slopes support California hazel, thimbleberry, milkwort, and a profusion of Pacific starflowers.

The route continues to rise southward, encountering bedstraw, vanilla leaf, wood rose, and hairy honeysuckle before arriving on top of a ridge shoulder at 0.6 mile. As the trail bends left, several coastal wood ferns repose beside the pathway.

A small bridge at mile 0.9 spans a tiny streamlet, after which the route descends from the ridge shoulder, coming to a fork at mile 1.0 that is appropriately marked by several trail plants. The way to the left makes a short loop southward; among the many pathside plants are yerba buena, bedstraw, California hazel, and raspberry. After rising and falling across the hillside, the trail turns right and then reaches another junction at 1.5 miles. A right turn here leads 50 yards uphill to the beginning of the loop; the spur route to the left winds downhill towards the Avenue.

coastal wood fern
(Dryopteris arguta)

The spur crosses through a long stretch of fetid adder's tongue, wanders by some wood rose, and then passes beneath bigleaf maple and California hazel before reaching an abrupt junction with the Avenue just north of the Stephens Grove.

fetid adder's tongue
(Scoliopus bigelovii)

Few forest plants will so startle the unwary as fetid adder's tongue. Its large basal leaves are mottled with plaguelike purple blotches, while thin, wine-colored veins mark its narrow, strangely pretty petals. The flowers exude a striking smell, similar to that of dead starfish, which proves attractive only to flies and slugs. The plant's stem commences to droop after the flower reaches maturity, leading to the nickname "slinkpod," and also accounting for the scientific name of Scoliopus, which means "crooked foot." Fetid adder's tongue blooms early, so that by high spring it is often reduced to a few wilted leaves and a chewed-off stem, the petals and sepals having already served as some banana slug's banquet. [blooms February-March]

F. K. LANE GROVE LOOP TRAIL

Summary: Lots of shade, a stretch of old highway, and masses of smooth yellow violets make this short loop an amicable amble through the southernmost grove along the Avenue.

Distance: 0.5 mile, round trip

Elevation Change: negligible

Location: The trail starts to the left of the restrooms at the F. K. Lane Grove's parking lot, mile 2.9 of the Avenue.

Description: The pathway immediately plunges into a shadowy stand of tall redwoods, reaching a fork at mile 0.1. The way left winds around several large logs before climbing to a low terrace, mile 0.2; a large rock, left, holds a plaque honoring Franklin K. Lane, Secretary of the Interior during the Wilson administration and first president of the Save-the-Redwoods League. The route then crosses a tattered remnant of the original Redwood Highway.

*   *   *

REDWOOD RESCUE ALONG THE HIGHWAY

Early one morning in 1932, highway worker Mel Martin got an urgent call from his boss; a big windstorm had swept through southern Humboldt the night before, dropping 32 full-size redwoods between Miranda and Stafford. It was up to Mel and his crew to clear the route.

Soon Martin and his cohorts were proceeding along the highway, hauling their huge Wade drag saw with them. This mechanized monster was the state-of-the-art power saw for its day—over 400 pounds of engine and blade, about as easy to move as a grand piano. When the workers reached a downed tree, they would wrestle the Wade into place and then "let 'er buck"; it would saw a chunk out of each log, which was then removed by truck. Chunk by chunk, tree by tree, Mel and his workmates reopened the highway.

The highway supervisors tried to anticipate such problems by periodically removing "leaners"—the out-of-balance redwoods that tilted ominously towards the road. One year Martin's crew took out 114 of the tipsy trees, which would have been left standing had they not grown so close to the highway.

By the late 1930s, many more roadside redwoods were placed in jeopardy when the state began to bring the aging highway up to modern standards. Numerous curves were eliminated—209 of them in one stretch of just nine miles—and the roadbed was widened; the project required the removal of any inconveniently placed trees.

Everyone agreed that the narrow, twisting highway needed improvement, but the Save-the-Redwoods League complained about the cost; the League beseeched the state to reroute the road around prized stands of threatened trees. In two cases the highway commissioners acquiesced, sparing the redwoods of the F. K. Lane Grove and also those in the Nelson Grove, near Hidden Springs Beach; both bypassed sections of the old roadway were retained as grove access routes.

Today, more than 50 years later, the Lane Grove's roadbed lies covered with the litter of long abandonment; Nelson Road is still open for the southern half of its distance. Thanks to the League, both remnants still offer spectacular scenery—a border of twice-saved redwoods.

Widening the Redwood Highway

The trail moves through a covering of ferns and flowers until it nears a steep hillside and bends right, mile 0.3; another right turn brings it back to the old highway at mile 0.4—the relict roadbed runs through a dark corridor framed by tall, elderly redwoods. To the right a weathered but still white milepost displays its now-useless number: B 622-50. Beyond the marker, the abandoned highway runs north towards the

Lane monument; a wave of smooth yellow violets now washes over much of the time-ravaged roadway.

**smooth yellow violet,
stream violet, pioneer violet**
(Viola glabella)

A denizen of moist, wooded areas, the smooth yellow violet grows on slender stalks that rise as much as a foot above ground level. Its heart-shaped leaves look somewhat like a frailer version of wild ginger, but they lack the latter's heavy veining and dark coloration. In addition to its main flowers, this colorful violet also produces a secondary type of blossom lower on its stem; these are self-pollinating and thus provide the plant with a sure source of seeds. [blooms March-June]

From the second highway crossing, the trail descends briefly to the start of the loop. The route then returns to the parking area, mile 0.5.

HIDDEN SPRINGS BEACH TRAIL

Summary: This short loop offers something for everyone—a pair of Lolangkok village sites, enough plant species to bedazzle the most blase botanist, a ruggedly scenic rocky point, pleasant summertime swimming, and a marvel of hillside highway engineering.

Distance: 1.1 miles, round trip, via the loop circling Eagle Point

Elevation Change: 150-foot loss and 150-foot gain

Location: The trailhead is opposite the entrance to Hidden Springs Beach Campground, mile 11.5 on the Avenue; there is parking on the Avenue a short distance to the north.

Warning: *The rocky scramble around the eastern end of Eagle Point can be difficult—it can be avoided by turning right at the first trail fork and looping over the ridge to reach Hidden Springs Beach.*

Description: A Park trail sign and an old wooden railing mark the start of the route, which immediately drops down the bank below the Avenue, zigzagging through medium-size redwoods and small tanoaks. The trail then crosses the aging pavement of Nelson Road [p. 105], a remnant of the original Redwood Highway, at 0.1 mile. It exits the far side of the road about 50 feet to the right, descending to a riverside benchland through fetid adder's tongue, two-eyed violet, and thimbleberry. At mile 0.3 the path bends right to pass above the South Fork Eel; bigleaf maple and California hazel join the forest mix. The trail then runs up against the base of Eagle Point, a rock-strewn ridge spur that projects from the hillside into the river channel. The course splits here to encircle the point.

Turning left, the route hugs the base of the cliff, soon crossing a jumble of large rocks that have fallen down the eastern side of Eagle Point; the river splashes by a few feet to the left. Clumps of Humboldt County fuchsia cover the rocks below the trail, their striking red flowers aglow during the late summer.

Humboldt County fuchsia
(Epilobium canum
ssp. septentrionale)

This bright, late-blooming flower is found only in northwestern California. It is one of several fuchsias with nectar-filled, tubular red flowers, a characteristic that has earned them the shared nickname of "hummingbird's trumpet." This subspecies is being monitored as a potential rare and endangered plant. [blooms August-September]

On the opposite side of the path, the boulder-embedded cliff face sports a springtime covering of tightly clinging Merten's saxifrage.

Merten's saxifrage
(Saxifraga mertensiana)

This spindly stemmed saxifrage seems to ignore any need for fertility as it relentlessly pursues moisture, even climbing across almost-barren rock so long as the surface is wet enough. A cluster of nearly circular leaves surrounds the Merten's base, while tiny whitish flowers dangle from antennaelike stems above. Some of the blossoms are later replaced by bulbs that may produce new plants after they fall to the ground. The plant was named for Karl Heinrich Mertens, who discovered it on Alaska's Sitka Island in the late 1820s. [blooms March-May]

Across the river from the point is a tall, burned snag — the beach area to the left was the site of a Lolangkok village called Sekontcobandun. Eagle Point itself was known as Sa-bug-gah-nah, "rock around," and a village just downstream at Hidden Springs Beach apparently also went by this name. George Burt, the last known full-blooded Lolangkok, lived

Sekontcobandun,
from Eagle Point

there for a time before returning to his homeland at Bull Creek. A third village, Sestcicbandun, was a short distance downstream from the beach; it was situated beside an river eddy that provided good fishing. The nearby hillside oaks added to the site's abundant food supply.

Hidden Springs Beach comes into view as the trail rounds the point; to the right, canyon live oaks crown the top of the promontory, supported by a scattering of Douglas firs. The cliffside is covered with a tapestry of toyon, California black oak, and California laurel that is augmented in summer by the blooms of Indian paintbrush, Douglas iris, cream bush, and Pacific ninebark.

The South Fork Eel bends around the beach to head west. The water here is comfortably warm in summertime, and there are pools deep enough to allow swimming. Those who paddle to the river's southern shore will find several Oregon ashes growing by the riverside and may also encounter a troop of turtles sunning themselves on nearby logs.

Pacific ninebark
(Physocarpus capitatus)
[blooms May-July]

High across the canyon, the 101 Freeway appears to hang from the hillside as it passes across the Eagle Point Viaduct, a scaffoldlike construction of green-painted steel and gray concrete whose pilings were driven into bedrock 40 feet below ground surface. The viaduct was built to bypass a proposed route upslope that would have taken out many redwoods.

The beach extends downriver, but the trail soon climbs into the woodlands just west of Eagle Point. On the shaded bank, right, are several kinds of ferns: licorice, goldenback, coastal wood, and, rarest of all in the Park, a California maidenhair.

California maidenhair fern
(Adiantum jordanii)

For some, this delicate, black-stemmed fern displays a maidenly propriety as is seeks out secluded spots within the woodlands; others note the cascades of scallop-shaped leaflets that sway like tresses in the breeze. Yet despite the suitability of its name, the maidenhair fern was once contrarily connected with recently widowed Indian women. As a sign of mourning, they would first burn off their hair at the neckline and then don a special cap decorated with the fern's dark stems.

To the left of the trail is a benchland covered with large redwoods; the route rises along the hillside and at mile 0.7 connects with Nelson Road. The loop curves over the top of the ridge and drops down the eastern slope. Here the bank is covered with flowering plants — vanilla leaf, smooth yellow violet, redwood sorrel, wood rose, trillium, and Pacific starflower among them. The circuit of Eagle Point is completed at mile 0.8; a left turn retraces the first part of the trail back to the Avenue, ending at 1.1 miles.

STEPHENS GROVE LOOP TRAIL

Summary: A short saunter across a redwood-covered benchland, this route circles through the site of an early Park campground.

Distance: 0.7 mile for the basic loop; 1.3 miles including the spur trail

Elevation change: negligible for basic loop; a 100-foot gain and loss on the spur trail

Location: The loop starts at the north end of the unmarked Stephens Grove, on the west side of the Avenue at mile 7.0; the spur trail starts in Miranda, mile 6.5 of the Avenue, across from South Fork High School.

Description: The Stephens Grove, acquired in 1922, is one of the earliest units in Humboldt Redwoods. A Park campground was built here in the mid-twenties, but the spot had served travellers since about 1883, when freight wagons would stop over on their trips between Shelter Cove and the Eel River valley. The campground was damaged by the 1955 flood and destroyed by the 1964 washout.

The unmarked trail heads south from a small parking area, twisting around a large fallen redwood and then reaching a fork. Both branches meander across a low benchland that is filled with monumental but somewhat-faded redwoods; ferns and a few forest flowers poke above a litter of duff. Along the eastern section of trail, the stonework of two bridge remnants recalls the grove's earlier days as a campground. At the far end of the loop, amid the stumps of trees cut long ago, a spur trail continues south. It climbs the hillside on an old roadbed, passing two wild cucumber patches; the route bends left at the hillcrest to meet the Avenue at the north end of Miranda.

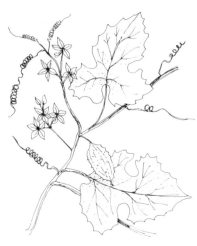

wild cucumber
manroot, bigroot
(*Marah oreganus*)

Wild cucumber is probably the best hitchhiker in the coastal forest, climbing onto neighboring plants by means of its numerous spring-shaped tendrils; often its large, five-pointed leaves will then cover the host plant. In spring, the ends of its vine stems sprout small white flowers that are dwarfed by the wild cucumber's large leaves. The plant is also known as "bigroot" or "manroot," references to its large and sometimes person-shaped roots. Another name for it, which seems to defy explanation, is "chilicothe." Wild cucumber seeds were sometimes eaten to relieve kidney disorders. [blooms March-June]

WILLIAMS GROVE-HIDDEN SPRINGS TRAIL

Summary: The route offers an exhilarating excursion that connects two of the Park's prime activity areas, the Hidden Springs Campground and the Williams Grove day and group use site.

Distance: either 2.4 or 2.9 miles, one way, depending on which fork of the trail is used at its eastern end

Elevation Change: 300-foot gain and 600 foot-loss, east to west

Location: The eastern end of the trail offers a choice of two starting points—at either campsite 75 or campsite 134 in the Hidden Springs Campground, which is located at mile 11.5 of the Avenue. The trail's western end leaves the Avenue at mile 13.5, just opposite the entrance to the Williams Grove.

Description: Both branches leave Hidden Springs Campground by climbing through mixed second-growth forest; the two routes join at 0.4 mile from the campsite 134 trailhead and 0.9 mile from the one at campsite 75. (Subsequent distances along the route will be calculated from the site 75 trailhead.) Black huckleberry abounds along both routes.

From the junction, the trail heads west toward the Williams Grove on an old roadbed; stumps from earlier logging repose beneath adolescent redwood and Douglas fir.

black huckleberry
(Vaccinium ovatum)
[blooms April-August]

Left at mile 1.1 are a dozen young redwoods that surround an opening once inhabited by an enormous ancestor. The trail then descends gradually, and at mile 1.2 it leaves the roadbed by dropping left over the hillside. (A sign marks this departure; those who miss it and continue along the roadbed will presently reach West Road, where a second sign conveniently points downgrade towards another junction with the trail.)

After switchbacking downhill, the trail crosses West Road at mile 1.4. This deeply rutted route begins at the Avenue east of Myers Flat, passes the town cemetery, and then rises northward into obscurity.

As the trail leaves the intersection, it encounters the rusted hulk of an auto that apparently challenged West Road and lost. The route drops down the hillside and then undulates through shadowy forest.

The damp ground of a small stream crossing, mile 1.7, supports trillium, fairybell, fat false Solomon's seal, giant horsetail, Pacific starflower, various ferns, and some lovely clusters of trail plant.

trail plant
(Adenocaulon bicolor)

Few people notice the trail plant for its tiny, greenish white flowers. Instead it is the spade-shaped leaves which attract attention; they show their bright green tops when undisturbed, but turn over to expose their whitish undersides when something brushes against them, thus marking the path of whatever has passed. Trail plant favors moist evergreen forests, sometimes growing in large colonies. [blooms May-September]

After leaving the creek, the route runs past redwood sorrel, bedstraw, calypso orchid, and both Smith's and Hooker's fairybell; it then climbs via a single switchback to a roadbank terrace that offers an overlook, mile 2.0. In the distance, the South Fork Eel loops lazily around Myers Flat. Directly below is the 101 Freeway.

Now the trail returns to forest, crossing along the hillside through thick tanoak before descending several switchbacks to enter, at mile 2.6, a tunnel under the freeway. The route then winds downhill past an increasingly rich array of plants that includes Himalaya berry, yerba de selva, hairy honeysuckle, redwood violet, and redwood inside-out flower. At the bottom of the descent, mile 2.8, mature redwoods shelter bigleaf maple, thimbleberry, wild ginger, vanilla leaf, and their benchland cohorts. The trail concludes at the Avenue, opposite the entrance to the Williams Grove, mile 2.9.

THE CENTRAL AVENUE:
GREAT GROVES BELOW GRASSHOPPER

The middle section of the Avenue travels through the heart of Humboldt Redwoods State Park, passing along a corridor of stunning riverside redwoods before reaching the climax of many tours, the world-famous Founders Grove. North of Myers Flat, a succession of summer bridges spans the South Fork Eel, offering easy access to the Children's Forest, Canoe Creek, Grasshopper Peak, and the sublime Rockefeller Forest. The Park's Visitor Center, located at Burlington, offers posters, books, interpretive displays, and a wonderful wide-angle map of Humboldt Redwoods. Even the most time-bound tourist will want to include a drive along the superlative central Avenue.

* * * * *

From West Road, the Avenue runs west a short distance to an interchange with the 101 Freeway, mile 12.3. Just beyond the underpass an unmarked paved road exits left, soon turning to rutted gravel. It proceeds south 0.2 mile to a beach beside the South Fork where boaters can launch or take out their vessels.

Now the Avenue enters downtown Myers Flat, pop. 200, elev. 196, a small but colorful village built at the north end of a large, open point of riverside benchland. Known as Kunteltcobi to the Lolangkoks, the flat was purchased by Elias and Andrew Myers in 1867 from a pair of earlier settlers for $1,000. The flat's humus-rich silt was tilled and tended by the Myerses and soon their ranch boasted bountiful orchards and lush truck and flower gardens. Elias's son, Ulysses S. Grant Myers, eventually took over the property with his wife, Mattie, and under their care the ranch continued to prosper. In 1915, a hundred acres were being cultivated, and the orchards contained 700 apple and 300 pear trees. Among the ranch's prized crops were its sweet potatoes and corn, while hogs, chickens, and dairy products added to the diversified output. At about this time, travel was increasing through "Myers," as the spot was then called, and the family proceeded to build a hotel to serve as a resort and way station; by the late twenties a store had been added. After Grant Myers died in 1937, Mattie subdivided part of the ranch and the stopping place grew into a more complete community.

THE CENTRAL AVENUE AND ITS TRAILS

In the mid-1940s, two pairs of brothers started the Morrison and Jackson Mill on the northwest corner of the flat. The operation came to employ 125 workers; its products, which included both redwood siding and cooling towers, were shipped by rail from the station at the town of South Fork. Near the end of the decade, two sea captains purchased the motor court and "Shrine" tree that were located near the mill. "The sea's no place for a family man," Captain Gillette explained, "so we decided to sail a motor court for a change and take our families along!"

Much of the flat itself went sailing when the 1955 flood struck. Carol Morrison was a small child at the time, living south of the mill co-owned by her father, Duke. She and her family had to evacuate their home when the rising river threatened to engulf it. As they left, Mrs. Morrison made all her children join hands for their trek across the flood-swept flat, an act which probably kept Carol from being washed away when the swirling, tugging torrent quickly closed around the little girl, rising up to her armpits.

Although the community was severely damaged in both the 1955 and 1964 floods, the mill stayed in operation until 1978, being supervised during its last few years by Lucille Arnott, a rare female mill manager. Since the mill's closure, Myers Flat has struggled for survival. The business district was put up for sale in 1990; although the asking price was only $2,600,000, it's been a slow market for used towns, and there have been no takers.

Myers Flat today offers the services of a gas station, gift shop, restaurant, cider shop, cafe, RV park, motel, market, saloon, laundromat, and hardware store, along with not one, but two, beauty parlors. A pair of businesses require additional comment:

The Myers Inn, located across from the grocery store in the center of town, is a recent restoration of Grant Myers's original hotel. This striking, shingle-sided building combines the squarish solidity of a frontier blockhouse with a Southern plantation's airy verandas, an unusual architectural alliance that creates a surprisingly charming effect. Inside, the cozy lobby displays not only a wedding portrait of Grant and Mattie Myers, but also a scroll from the Mechanics Institute of San Francisco, dated 1887, that acknowledges the ranch's "Display of Fruitland Vegetables." Gone are the dual parlors—one for the ladies, one for gentlemen—that graced the hotel's downstairs in earlier days.

At the north end of town, a 10-foot-tall redwood grizzly bear greets visitors to the Shrine Drive-Thru Tree, where, for a small fee, adroit motorists may maneuver their vehicles through an opening cut in the bottom of a blasted but still living Sequoia sempervirens—the long-suffering redwood conveniently providing the Avenue with a sort of lumberman's tunnel of love. The tree derives its name from having once been owned by a member of the Shriners fraternal organization, during which time all proceeds from the attraction were reportedly donated to Shriner charitable activities.

The Myers Inn

The town's one side street, appropriately called Myers Road, proceeds left off the Avenue opposite the Myers Inn. The paved county route runs 0.4 mile southwest across the flat before coming to a dead end at a riverside RV park. Along the way, the road passes the remains of the Myers Flat drive-in theater, whose decaying superstructure is now nearly covered by a clutch of willows. Several rusting cars stare vacantly towards the screen from the parking area, perhaps abandoned there by viewers of the theater's final movie.

Returning to the Avenue of the Giants, the route exits Myers Flat at mile 12.7 to wind above the South Fork until, at mile 13.3, it enters a shadowy grove of mixed-size redwoods. The road then passes beneath a sylvan canopy that will succor the sun-weary on bright summer days. Left at 13.5 miles is the entrance to the Williams Grove; this riverside stand of redwoods honors Solon H. Williams, who, as Deputy State

Forester in the 1920s, became the acting superintendent of the new Humboldt State Redwood Park. The site features facilities for family picnicking and for large group campouts and picnics. Opposite the grove's entrance is the western terminus of the Hidden Springs-Williams Grove Trail [p. 117].

The Grove's access road runs southwest, first passing family picnic sites, left, before reaching an intersection with a spur road, right, that leads to the group picnic and camping areas. To the left is a sanitary dump station (use fee charged) and a parking area. A row of tall, fragrant California laurels slants northwest from the parking lot, while to their left a sandy track makes its way riverward.

California laurel, Oregon myrtle, bay tree, pepperwood
(Umbellularia californica)

The pungent aroma of its leaves makes this tree easy to identify; the difficulty comes in deciding what to call it. The name California laurel is often used, for the species grows mainly in California and is indeed a member of the laurel family. To some, it is known as California bay, or simply bay tree, in reference to its berry, which was called "baye" in Old English. Folks in Oregon proudly call it Oregon myrtle, perhaps because its leaves resemble those of the wax myrtle (which itself is sometimes confusingly called Pacific bayberry); its wood is often marketed as Oregon myrtle when sculpted into ornamental objects. In some places, people prefer to emphasize the peppery taste of the tree's leaves, calling the species pepperwood. It also has a host of less frequently used names: spice-bush, balm of heaven, sassafras laurel, cajeput, California olive, and mountain laurel; this last name is also used in the East for a small tree of the heath family. Regardless of what it is called, the tree is a useful and distinctive part of North Coast forests and is pretty enough to be used as an ornamental in yards and for lining city streets.

Dried California bay leaf has become a common spice in the U.S., replacing the more expensive European variety. Indians ate the tree's thin-shelled nuts and also found many medicinal purposes for the leaves, using them as a disinfectant, wound cleanser, headache remedy, and for rheumatism-reducing rubdowns. The leaves also served as a flea repellent, a use which is regaining popularity among toxics-conscious pet owners. While the tree itself has a multiplicity of names, there at least seems to be agreement that its odoriferous leaves should be called bay. But, to paraphrase Shakespeare, by any other name they would still smell as strong.

At the group picnic parking area, another trail heads towards the South Fork Eel to connect with a summer bridge. Across the river is access to the Children's Forest and other destinations via the southern portion of the South Fork Eel Trail [p. 156]. There is a good swimming area near the bridge and a small fishing hole. The Williams Grove group camping area can accommodate either one or two large parties and has a total capacity of 125 people. The area offers picnic tables, barbecues, and showerless restrooms.

The Avenue travels north among the rubicund columns of Williams Grove redwoods until mile 13.7, where it emerges for a short spell into open riverside. Soon the forest returns to shade the roadway, intensifying at the Hammond Grove, mile 14.2, where clusters of Indian warriors stand sentinel. The forested benchland then widens, and at mile 14.7 the entrance to the Garden Club of America Grove appears on the left.

An access road leads northwest 200 yards to the grove's parking area; restrooms and picnic tables are nearby. The forest here is a collection of stumps, second-growth, and some larger redwoods; the prize part of the grove lies across the river. At the north end of the parking area, a marked path climbs the hillside and then wanders through a ground cover of greenery to connect with the Kent Grove Loop Trail [p. 152]. Another trail leaves the parking lot farther west; it descends to the river, passing through a bower of Oregon ash, willow, California laurel, and black cottonwood. A matting of grape leaves covers much of the trees' lower foliage.

black cottonwood
(Populus trichocarpa)

The region's tallest native hardwood and an extremely fast-growing tree, the black cottonwood is able to reach a height of a hundred feet in just 20 years. In summer, the cottonwood's heart-shaped leaves sough sibilantly in the afternoon breeze, their color changing from deep green to silvery white as they twist from side to side; the foliage later turns a luminous soft yellow, so that the trees glow like pale torches beneath the gray fall skies. It is one of several species named for the cotton fluff that covers their seeds; more noticeable is the tree's sweet, springtime scent, which infuses whole stretches of the warming riverbanks and justifies the black cottonwood's membership in a tree group known as the "balsam poplars." [blooms February-April]

The path soon comes to a summer bridge that connects with the South Fork Eel Trail [p. 156]. There, on the far side of the river, one can walk the edge of the Garden Club's giant grove, which comprises almost 10% of the Park's total acreage. Also available is a secluded side trail to the misty lower reaches of Canoe Creek [p. 142]. Downstream from the bridge lies another of the river's swimming and fishing holes.

Black cottonwood

Continuing through heavy woods, the Avenue soon encounters a pair of groves dedicated to noted members of the Save-the-Redwoods League. The first, at mile 15.0, honors William Kent, the conservationist/congressman who donated the land for Muir Woods National Monument; the short, verdant Kent Grove Loop Trail exits from the parking area, left [p. 152]. Immediately north is the Mather Grove, named for Stephen Tyng Mather, first Chief of the National Park Service.

The start of the Fleischmann Grove is followed shortly by a parking area and trailhead at mile 16.0, left [p 143]. Here the Avenue runs beneath sheltering redwoods across a widening benchland.

Mile 16.2 brings a junction with Pesula Road, a narrow right-of-way that alternates between gravel and pavement while climbing eastward. This route passes over the 101 Freeway on its way to several hillside houses that lie just beyond the Park boundary.

An opening in the redwoods announces Burlington, mile 16.5, formerly a small community and now the site of Park headquarters. A paved entryway, right, leads to the Park's office; it is open weekdays, except holidays, from 8 a.m. to 5 p.m; phone (707) 946-2311.

Just north of the headquarters entrance, a row of bigleaf maples runs along the right side of the Avenue, shading both an expanse of grass and the parking area for the Park's Visitor Center. Although the trees here were planted, bigleaf maple is also a native resident of the region.

The Visitor Center is housed in a long, rustic building which rests among the surrounding trees like an enormous, square-hewn log; its entryway is decorated by a small circular garden that encloses a collection of the Park's native plants. A walkway to the left of the entrance leads to the restrooms of adjacent Burlington Campground.

bigleaf maple
(Acer macrophyllum)

Its leaves *are* big; they can reach a foot in both length and width, a size that gives pause to any hiker who encounters them fallen upon the trail. Their color is also arresting, be it the bright, glowing green of summer or the pale gold of fall. In either season, the bigleaf maple's foliage brings a delightful diversity to a conifer-filled forest, but it is spring when the tree is perhaps most charming of all. It then sprouts clusters of yellow-green flowers that soon ripen into oddly beautiful, double-winged fruits called "keys" in prosaic language and "samaras" by those who love the sound of a wonderful word. During the ensuing months, the fruits rustle soothingly in the wind as the maple leaves grow towards bigness beside them. The samaras reach maturity in the fall, when they detach from the tree's limbs and twirl gracefully to the ground.

Bigleaf maples often grow where rockslides have tumbled across river or stream terraces; since conifers have difficulty surviving in such locations, there are usually gaps in the forest canopy that allow the maples to thrive. The tree is one of the few Western hardwoods that produces good lumber, the wood sometimes containing "curly" and "bird's eye" configurations. Northwest Indian tribes made maple utensils, cradle boards, and canoe paddles. Today, the wood is used in boatbuilding and also for cabinets, furniture, interior finish, and flooring. [blooms March-May]

The Center offers several fact-filled presentations about the Park: a short slide show describing Humboldt Redwoods and its key features, video programs about the region's history, a collection of stuffed birds and animals representing indigenous species, history exhibits that include photos and artifacts, and an aerial perspective map of the Park, painted by local artist Larry Eifert. Many Park-related items are offered for sale, including books, cards, posters, and maps. The Center's friendly staff is ready to answer questions and provide further information. The Center is open daily during the summer from 9 a.m. to 5 p.m. and on a reduced schedule the rest of the year; phone (707) 946-2263.

Across the Avenue from the Visitor Center's parking lot, a path enters the Gould Grove; it soon leads to both the Nature Loop Trail [p. 155]. and the Fleischmann Grove Trail [p. 144]. The former route connects with an access path to the Burlington summer bridge.

The Burlington area was first settled in 1878 by Jimmy Carothers. He was a strange but colorful character who brightened the forested surroundings for many years.

* * *

POOR MAN, RICH MAN: JIMMY CAROTHERS INSULATES HIS SHACK

When calling on neighbors near his homestead at Burlington, Jimmy Carothers cut a strange figure. His battered hat had lost all sense of shape, and the faded shirt he wore was so big it had to be tucked into folds and pinned together; his baggy, oversized trousers hung precariously by one strap of his suspenders. On his feet were a pair of mismatched shoes, one black, one tan, each a different size and both too large. It wasn't surprising that during his visits, Carothers would claim any discard in sight: old baling wire, frayed rope, dusty bottles, rusty tin cans and buckets, and especially pieces of string. He would carry off any and all such objects, muttering to himself that they were " . . . valuable, very valuable."

Jimmy removed these discards to his property, where he stored them in and around a weatherbeaten hut that was nearly obscured by a thicket of brush and young redwoods. The shelter was a patchwork of boards and flattened tin cans; its dirt floor was covered by the debris he'd collected.

The locals must have smiled when a sketch of Carothers appeared in a history book about Humboldt County. It was the kind of vanity publication that charged a fee for printing the biographies, and there, amazingly, was a story about Jimmy, complete with a photo of him in a coat and tie, casting a bewildered look at the camera. What a tale he had told the author, something about coming from a prominent family and being heir to a fortune; the most surprising thing of all was that he'd somehow found enough money to have the account included in the book.

It was only much later that the skeptics got their comeuppance. When Jimmy eventually passed away, someone got to searching around the old man's shack; hidden among its nooks and crannies were hundreds of gold pieces—$5, $10, and $20 coins. The hoard amounted to over $60,000, all of it sharing space with the "valuable" string and tin cans. It turned out that Carothers's reclusive sister had died in her Eureka mansion two years earlier, leaving him to inherit the entire fortune of what had indeed been a notable family. Jimmy had died far richer than anyone thought, poor only in the esteem of his friends.

*   *   *

When the highway came through Burlington in the 1910s, some of the adjacent redwoods were cut for split products; the stumps that were left can still be seen along the Nature Loop Trail and in the campground. By 1917, a butcher shop and a pool hall occupied the site of the present Park headquarters, while just to the north were a general store and a stage stop. The community was called Tighe and Green's Camp in the 1920s, when it lost out to neighboring Weott in a contest for the local post office. Later the government did come to the area; first a state highway yard was built, and after the 1937 flood, the CCC camp was relocated here from Dyerville. In 1955, following the next big flood, the Park headquarters also made the same switch; today it is the only operation remaining in Burlington.

Directly north of the Visitors Center, mile 16.6 of the Avenue, is the Burlington Campground; its 56 campsites are situated among a collection of large stumps and second-growth redwoods. The nearly level, sparsely covered ground creates a setting sharply different from the tanoak-screened hillsides found at Hidden Springs; campers here will soon get to know their neighbors. Each campsite has a picnic table, food cupboard, and fire ring. The sites accept trailers up to 24 feet in length and motorhomes up to 33 feet. There are wheelchair-accessible restrooms and showers, laundry tubs, and piped water. The campground offers handy trail access to Weott [p. 140], the South Fork Eel, and, via a summer bridge across the river, to the hiking routes below Grasshopper Peak [p. 156].

From Burlington, the Avenue continues northward through thick redwoods; at mile 16.9 a paved service road exits right, and a dirt road departs left; the latter is blocked by a wooden gate and leads to the summer bridge at the river.

The flats then end, and the Avenue runs close to the South Fork Eel near the base of a steep hillside. A string of bigleaf maples at mile 17.1 brightens the way in spring, summer, and fall, while a stunning stand of

Burlington Campground bulletin board

redwoods is visible across the river at mile 17.3; sticky monkey flowers stick to the steep roadbank beyond the viewpoint. A dirt road, left at mile 17.5, leads down to Gould Bar, a location that offers a small fishing hole, a nice riffle, and boating access. The turnoff is marked by a large, bumpy-burled redwood.

Across the Avenue just north of the Gould Bar turnoff, an unmarked path climbs 150 yards up the hillside to connect with the Burlington-Weott Trail. The route follows what was once the driveway to the Gould house, whose owners were major landholders in upper Bull Creek.

Emerging from the woods, the roadway passes beneath a hillside, right, where sweet pea provides summertime color. The Avenue then re-enters forest at the Native Daughters of the Golden West Grove, mile 17.9. At the parking area, left, a plaque commemorates the various Native Daughters chapters, or "parlors," that contributed to the grove's

Burl tree above Gould Bar

acquisition. Several narrow pathways wind westward towards the bluffs above the South Fork Eel; the trail on the far left provides the only easy route down to the river. The grove itself is a charming collection of full-size redwoods, beneath which California laurel, sword and bracken fern, fairybell, poison oak, and redwood sorrel all grow in shaded seclusion. At the riverbank are bigleaf maple, willow, and scouring rush.

North of the grove, at mile 18.1, the Avenue enters a wide opening in the forest. The roadway expands also, revealing the remnants of concrete curbing to either side. This is the former "downtown" section of Weott, population 450, elevation 160.   Soon an explanation is provided for the business district's demise; a post rises 33 feet above the roadway to show the high water mark of the 1964 flood.   Buildings which had survived in 1955—when the water merely came up to the second story—were swept away nine years later, leaving only strips of gray cement behind.   Just one business relocated along the Avenue after the second deluge, the Parkway Burger Bar, operated by the incongruously named "Hot Dog" Harry Metaxes.   The trailer which housed his diner still reposes by the roadside, and, until recently, a faded sign beseeched southbound motorists to "Eat Or We Both Starve."   Although it has been a long while since the Parkway served any food, Hot Dog Harry is still happily alive in Weott, apparently unaffected by his famine-fearing prophecy.

A tie-cutting outfit, called Helm's Camp, occupied the townsite in the 1910s; it supplied the Northwestern Pacific Railroad, which was then under construction to the east.   The area subsequently became known as McKee's Mill, after a split-stuff layout that located here.   In 1917, J. E. Johnson opened the town's first store, which operated from a tent

McKee's Mill, on the Redwood Highway

on the main roadway; Johnson also drove a peddler's wagon to outlying areas. The local market is still run by his descendants. After the highway came through in 1918, the community grew rapidly; an application for a post office was accepted in the 1920s, bringing with it the new name of Weott. This is a variant of *Wiyot*, an Indian tribe that has long lived in the area around Humboldt Bay. The choice of this distant tribe to be the town's namesake is somewhat baffling, since the Wiyots' relations with the local Lolangkok Indians were almost always hostile.

Pictures of old Weott show a sizable town; during the twenties and thirties there were two butcher shops, a grocery store, a general store, three gas station/garages, a dress shop, an ice cream parlor, a trucking company, two barbershops, and one and a half bars. The fractional drinking establishment was the tiny Loma Vista; it had only six stools from which patrons could imbibe. Ed Davis, the owner, compensated for the bar's small size by recruiting the most attractive waitresses to be found in Eureka.

Weott in the 1940s

The biggest attraction in town, though, was Walter Bell's Maribel Theater, which he had named for his wife Mary. Bell was somehow able to get the latest films from Hollywood, attracting moviegoers from as far away as Scotia as a result. Since even these hits had their occasional dull moments, a young local named Harold Fisher would sometimes enliven the proceedings by loosing a bagful of bats into the darkened room — the creatures would then careen between the screen and projector, to the delight of at least part of the audience.

*   *   *

HAROLD FISHER'S HILLSIDE HIGH JINKS

"Harold!" The cry was followed by a string of curses.

Harold Fisher looked down the hillside towards the noise. There, waving his arms wildly, was Harold's boss, "Pegleg" Bill Fraser. The boy scrambled down to the gesticulating figure.

Fraser was seated on the ground, his wooden leg missing.

"It's down there, somewhere," he said, motioning towards a large huckleberry thicket. "Damned thing caught on a rock and went sliding the hell and gone . . . can't go nowhere without it."

Harold surveyed the slope. They were near a spring on the side of Grasshopper Peak, inspecting the pipeline that ran down to Weott's water works, and the surrounding topography tilted at a sharp angle. If Fraser were to try moving around much, he would likely go tumbling all the way to the river.

"Harold." The boy turned to see Pegleg looking at him.

"You'll have to find it, son," Fraser said, and Harold thought he saw a flicker of wariness, or perhaps even fear, in the man's eyes.

Harold knew what his boss was thinking. Young Fisher's reputation as a hardened prankster was known up and down the river. Wherever there was a chance for entertainment, Harold would find it, and the woebegone Fraser had just offered him a golden opportunity.

The boy's face betrayed nothing. "Right, Bill," was all he answered before moving down to look in the bushes.

The huckleberries formed a dense tangle; Harold realized it would be easy to claim that his search had been a failure. Still, Fraser had been good to him, giving Fisher a job while he was still just a teenager. . . . It was a dilemma . . .

After what seemed like hours, Harold poked his head out of the thicket. Fraser stared down at the boy, and his heart sank. Fisher wore the most hangdog expression the man had ever seen.

"Found your leg, Bill," the boy finally said, holding the missing limb aloft. "Thought I wasn't going to for a while there." He began the long trudge uphill.

For Harold, deciding to retrieve the leg had been a tradeoff. He had given up his chance for an amusing day . . . but at least he would sleep well that night.

What remains of Weott is reached by turning right at the high water marker, mile 18.2, onto Newton Road; this route climbs uphill and soon passes a turnoff, left, to the town store and post office. On the right at mile 0.2 is the unmarked northern end of the Burlington-Weott Trail, which ascends the bank just behind a section of mottled, gray-white guardrail [p. 140]. Newton Road then enters "uptown" Weott, passing a gas station and motel just before arriving, mile 0.5, at a 101 Freeway interchange.

North of its junction with Newton Road, the Avenue completes its run through the lower townsite. Left at mile 18.4 is a gravel road whose locked gate blocks motor vehicle access; the route leads west a hundred yards to the Marin Garden Club Grove Hike and Bike Camp. Near a small central clearing are restrooms, a sheltered eating area, poison-oak-lined paths to the river, and several campsites; the overnight use fee is payable at the entrance gate.

The Avenue bends left after departing Weott and passes through an open area, mile 18.6; visible across the river is a stand of high-rise redwoods. The roadway then enters its own collection of large trees, including several nice specimens at the Dungan Grove, 19.2 miles.

Now the route turns right, cutting across an ever-widening flat filled with large redwoods. At mile 19.7, the Avenue intersects the Big Cut Trail; a paved road then exits left, mile 19.8, and enters the California Federation of Women's Clubs Grove, often called simply the Federation Grove.

The grove's access road passes a fee collection site and then winds among towering redwoods; the trees rise from verdant beds of vegetation — redwood sorrel, sugar scoop, Siberian candyflower, trail plant, thin false Solomon's seal, milkmaids, smooth yellow violet, and poison oak predominate, while sword fern, elderberry, and California hazel fill in above. One of the Park's tallest redwoods grows near the roadside; simply called "Tree #5," it is designated only by a tiny metal tag attached to its enormous trunk. Soon the route passes a turnout, left at 0.2 mile, from where the Big Cut Trail departs south [p. 138]; the road then bends right to reach the Hearthstone picnic and parking areas, ending in a small loop above the South Fork at 0.4 mile. Another branch of the Big Cut Trail leaves from the parking area.

The Hearthstone, otherwise known as the "Four Fireplaces," features a quartet of cooking areas arranged around a common central chimney. Made of cut rock, the eye-catching edifice was designed by noted San Francisco architect Julia Morgan; it also offers a motto carved above each fireplace, the most arresting of which states:

WOULD THAT WE WERE GREAT AS THESE,

AND MEN AS BROTHERLY AS TREES.

The "Four Fireplaces,"
Federation Grove

Nearby are huge picnic tables and benches, their 20-foot lengths cut from redwood and worn smooth, respectively, by the dinnerware and posteriors of countless picnickers. For refreshment, a handsome stone fountain gurgles water near the roadside. Exiting from the picnic area is a trail which drops quickly to a gravel-littered beach beside the South Fork Eel; the water here provides the Park's most popular swimming area. A summer bridge crosses to the Rockefeller Forest, where a short trail circles part of the elevated benchland west of the river [p. 223]. Upstream from the crossing was Lah-sa-cho-te, a straight stretch of river where the Lolangkoks found many lampreys in spring.

Just north of the Federation Grove, the Avenue passes over the 101 Freeway. For a short distance the two roadways run parallel to each other, separated only by a chain link fence. Above the Avenue on the right, mile 20.0, are the steep terraces of "Big Cut," which rise 480 feet up the mountainside—when Duckett Bluff was shaved off for the new freeway in 1958, it became the highest cut ever made on a California highway. The bluff had more poetically been called Sa-es-kuk, "on top rock," by the Lolangkoks.

Federation Grove fountain

Leaving the stark hillslope, the route enters a stand of tall redwoods at the Rolph Grove, mile 20.2. Almost immediately, a trail leaves the roadway from a small turnout, right. A barely-visible sign announces this to be the Mahan Plaque Trail, a short loop that combines stunning beauty with stirring history [p. 153].

The Avenue next encounters the Canfield Grove, passing a parking area, left at mile 20.5, where a marked trail exits through a cut in a large redwood log. Soon this pathway begins a short loop, notable for its profusion of forest flowers and for the goosepen tree which was fashioned into a small home [p. 145].

At mile 20.6, the Avenue intersects Dyerville Loop Road:

1) A left turn leads to southbound access for the 101 Freeway. At the start of this route, a gravel road exits right and runs northwest, crossing under the freeway before ending on a gravelly beach beside the South Fork Eel. This is Leatherwood Bar, a fishing area with a long, deep run, and also a swimming spot and take-out point for kayaks and canoes.

2) A right turn begins Dyerville Loop Road, a scenic byway of historical significance [p. 102]. At 0.2 mile along this route is the famed Founders Grove Nature Trail [p. 144]; picnic tables and restrooms are located at a small parking lot across the road from the trailhead. For many tourists, a visit to the Founders Tree is a requisite part of their Park experience; the now-fallen Dyerville Giant is also on the short loop, its 1991 toppling having transformed it into the Dyerville Log. Just east of the grove, Dyerville Loop Road exits the Park; two miles ahead is a railroad viaduct with an RV-wrecking 12-foot clearance.

3) The Avenue continues straight through the intersection, passing another "high water" marker, left, that records a 1964 flood height some 15 feet above the roadway. The route then leaves the north end of the Dyerville Flats, crossing the South Fork Eel at 20.7 miles. To the right is a view of the river's confluence with the main Eel. On the left is the 101 Freeway's Leatherwood Bridge; at the height of the '64 flood, a log jam formed against the bridge, threatening to carry the structure away. While the bridge deck was "visibly lifting and shifting on its supports," three intrepid highway workers were lowered onto the logs, where they placed charges of dynamite. A few moments later, the charges blew out the jam, the bridge was saved, and the dynamiting trio went back to less demanding work.

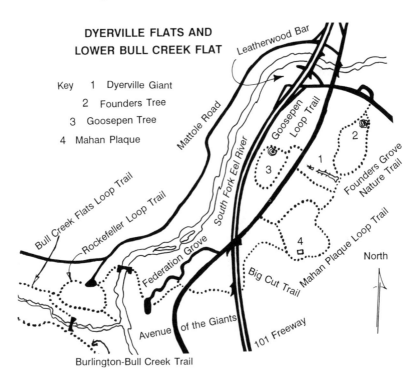

DYERVILLE FLATS AND
LOWER BULL CREEK FLAT

Key   1   Dyerville Giant
      2   Founders Tree
      3   Goosepen Tree
      4   Mahan Plaque

TRAILS OF THE CENTRAL AVENUE

[for map showing trails, see p. 120]

BIG CUT TRAIL

Summary: Short but wide-ranging, this route passes along the side of the 101 Freeway's "Big Cut" while connecting the Federation Grove with the Founders Grove area.

Distance: 1.0 mile, one way

Elevation Change: 120-foot gain and 70-foot loss, south to north

Location: The trail's southern end starts in the Federation Grove, reached by an access road at mile 19.7 of the Avenue; the northern end branches from the Mahan Plaque Trail, which leaves the Avenue at mile 20.2 [see detail map, p. 137].

Description: There are two approaches at the southern end of the trail. One route leaves the Federation Grove access road 0.2 mile in from the Avenue, while the second departs from the parking area at the end of the access road; both trailheads are marked. The paths soon meet in the midst of a lush stand of exceptionally large redwoods. The route then heads east; a surrounding carpet of redwood sorrel gradually diminishes into patches the size of mere throw rugs. The trail rises slightly at mile 0.2 and then crosses the Avenue; signs mark the path on both sides of the roadway.

A tunnel soon takes the route under the 101 Freeway. After ascending several switchbacks, the trail levels somewhat and proceeds north to reach a terrace midway up the side of Big Cut at mile 0.6. In order to make room for the freeway, this engineering extravaganza removed a huge section of hillside, creating an extremely steep, multi-terraced roadbank higher than the tallest redwood. Crossing the cut on one of the wide terraces, the route passes through trail-clotting stands of broom; the sunny opening also features Bolander's phacelia, western wax myrtle, and rattlesnake grass as part of an unusual melange of plants. A stunning vista opens to the left: a row of towering redwoods rise from the benchland above the South Fork Eel, their tall trunks bracketing the mouth of Bull Creek.

After encountering an unexpected hillside cottonwood, the trail leaves Big Cut and enters the hillside edge of the Rolph Grove, mile 0.8,

Near the Big Cut trailhead,
Federation Grove

bending right to pass around the end of the bluff and then moving down
the shaded slope among a growing array of redwood flora. Spread
below is the edge of South Dyerville Flat, where a sun-dappled blanket
of redwood sorrel is engraved with the thin, twisting brown lines of
narrow pathways.

As a series of switchbacks takes the route downward towards the
benchland floor, a quartet of plants display their distinctive leaves:
western coltsfoot, California spikenard, vanilla leaf, and wild ginger. The
trail levels at mile 1.0, passes a bed of thin false Solomon's seal, and
arrives at a junction with the Mahan Plaque Loop Trail. The Avenue is
a hundred yards to the left, while the Founders Grove can be reached
via either branch of the Mahan trail [p. 153].

long-tailed wild ginger
(Asarum caudatum)

Wild ginger is an unobtrusive but triply attractive plant. When noticed on a darkened forest floor, it appears as a sprawling collection of leathery, heart-shaped, dark green leaves. A search under the foliage reveals bizarre, brownish maroon flowers, their indented centers surrounded by three triangular-shaped petals that taper off into long points like the twisted ends of a waxed moustache. Deeper probing will uncover sweet smelling stems and roots; these were ground and dried by early settlers and used as a substitute for tropical ginger. [blooms March-July]

BURLINGTON-WEOTT TRAIL

Summary: Hillside plant life is the highlight of this easily accessible route which runs between the Burlington Campground and the town of Weott.

Distance: 1.6 miles, one way

Elevation Change: 150-foot gain and 100-foot loss, south to north

Location: The southern end of the trail leaves the Burlington Campground between sites 24 and 25; the northern end exits from Newton Road in Weott 0.2 mile east of the Avenue.

Description: Fifty feet north of its start, the trail drops to cross Robinson Creek; on the far side of the stream, a side route forks left on its way to the Burlington summer bridge. The main trail branches right, rising onto a stump-studded flat of mixed-size redwoods. Red huckleberry, wood rose, and vanilla leaf are prominent among the many plants. The path crosses a Park access road at mile 0.1 and then moves up the hillslope east of the flats.

The wide trailbed is bordered by trillium, Pacific dogwood, redwood inside-out flower, and fat false Solomon's seal. In spring the delicate white blossoms of a row of windflowers brighten the deeply shaded pathside.

At 0.4 mile the route levels, continuing to follow the curving contour of the hillside; upslope a short distance is the often-audible 101 Freeway. A leaning, four-trunked redwood at mile 0.6 marks a spectacular plant-sighting site: the trailside offers an array of fat false Solomon's seals and several stunning redwood lilies.

Columbia windflower
(Anemone deltoidea)

This demure plant dwells on shaded forest floors, sending up a solitary shoot less than a foot in height. A whorl of three oval leaflets surrounds the lower stem, while above, each stalk is surmounted by a pale white flower. Oddly, the Columbia windflower has no petals; its sepals, which are white instead of the usual green, give the flower its color. A folklore belief maintains that this anemone opens only when the wind is blowing. [blooms April-July]

After rounding a bend, the trail crosses a cascading stream on a picturesque bridge fashioned from part of a redwood trunk. Yerba de selva and hairy honeysuckle enjoy a bankside habitat as the route rambles on to an intersection at 0.9 mile. To the left, the remains of an old driveway lead to the Avenue at a point just opposite the turnoff to Gould Bar. A right turn follows the driveway uphill to the rock and concrete ruins of a home once belonging to the Gould family, who were major landowners in upper Bull Creek. The main trail proceeds straight ahead, crossing a small stream at mile 1.0.

redwood lily
(Lilium rubescens)

The redwood lily, which grows in brushy or wooded areas, is often noticed for its tall, dark green stalks and multiple whorls of leaves. The upright, funnel-shaped flowers are initially white with a sprinkling of purple spots but turn entirely purple with age. Also called lilac lily, chaparral lily, and chamise lily, the plant is reputed to be the most fragrant member of its family. One champion specimen reportedly grew to be nine feet tall, with 36 separate flowers. [blooms June-July]

The trail forks at mile 1.1; right leads to the Weott school playground and the upper town, while left continues the main route. A boggy patch of pathway, mile 1.4, is surrounded by tall bracken ferns. Unless recently trimmed, poison oak frequently encroaches on the trail here. The route then winds through a stand of tanoaks and redwoods, and meets Newton Road at 1.6 miles. This junction may be difficult to detect when approached from the north;

it occurs at the second road bend up from the Avenue. The trail commences by climbing a low bank just behind a weathered guardrail.

CANOE CREEK TRAIL

Summary: This semi-circuit of a charming creek canyon passes Pacific yews and the "log of the five ferns."

Distance: 0.9 mile, one way

Elevation change: negligible

Location: The southern end of the trail branches west from the Garden Club-Burlington Trail at mile 0.4; the northern end leaves the same trail at mile 0.6.

Description: From its southern terminus, the Canoe Creek Trail moves across a verdant terrace beneath large, attractive redwoods. The route climbs gently over a low ridge, regaining the flats at mile 0.2.

A short descent at 0.4 mile leads to a pleasantly situated wooden bench with an overlook of the forthcoming creek crossing. Dogwoods overhang the resting place while California spikenard, Pacific yew, and tarweed grow nearby. Two logs serve as the creek's bridge; willow and alder line the streambed. On the bank north of the crossing is an unusual array of plant life: giant horsetail, milkwort, and red huckleberry. The route then proceeds east through thick forest; a moss-covered Pacific yew appears on the right at mile 0.5, looking somewhat like a sickly, low-limbed redwood.

Pacific yew, western yew
(Taxus brevifolia)

Over 600 years ago the English yew *(Taxus baccata)* helped change the course of medieval warfare; longbows made from its stiff but springy wood allowed the English archers of King Edward III to decimate the French army at the Battle of Crecy. The new bow was accurate at a range of up to 250 yards and could be fired five to six times as quickly as the cumbersome crossbows then used by the French. Today, the Pacific yew is proving as valuable as its historic European cousin, though in a less sanguinary way. A potent anti-cancer drug called taxol is derived from the tree's bark, offering an impressive weapon to modern-day physicians, much as the English yew once did for military strategists.

The Pacific yew has long languished obscurely in the forests of the West; seldom growing more than 50 feet tall, it is the only conifer that when mature does not reach the forest canopy. Ungainly in appearance, with a twisted trunk and drooping limbs, the tree adds to its dishevelment by often trailing tendrils of wispy lichen. Its suddenly valuable bark has a broken, peeling texture, but on closer inspection reveals a madrone-like beauty, with purplish exterior scales curling away from a rosy interior. The tree's yellow-green needles resemble those of its great forest-mate, the coast redwood, but the yew's needles are green on both sides and ridged on top, while redwood needles have a white stripe on their underside and are grooved. Female yews produce a red, berry-like fruit, technically termed an "aril," that contrasts strikingly with the needles. Within the arils are pleasant-tasting seeds so high in poisonous alkaloids that, for humans, they can literally be heart stopping.

The route then moves away from the creek, entering a fern-filled swale at mile 0.6. A hospitable trailside log, left, serves as the home for five different varieties of ferns: five-finger, bracken, lady, sword, and deer. A sixth species, giant chain fern, grows in exile just across the path.

Continuing across the fertile flatland, the route reaches the southern spur of the Grasshopper Trail, which heads up the hillside on the left. Here the Canoe Creek Trail turns right and passes between a pair of goosepen redwoods; in a few yards the route ends at the Garden Club-Burlington Trail, mile 0.9.

deer fern
(Blechnum spicant)

FLEISCHMANN GROVE TRAIL

Summary: Benchland redwoods and a bit of highway history flavor this conveniently located path.

Distance: 1.3 miles, round trip

Elevation Change: negligible

Location: The route's northern end is reached by a short approach trail that exits the Avenue at mile 16.5, opposite the parking lot for the

Burlington Visitor Center; the southern end leaves a parking area on the west side of the Avenue, mile 16.0.

Description: Fifty yards from its start at the Avenue, the approach path divides; right is the Nature Loop Trail, left is the Fleischmann Grove Trail. The latter route immediately runs between several patches of redwood violets as it heads southward.

The trail turns left at mile 0.1 to cross a stream gorge; the bank to the south is covered with masses of five-fingered ferns, along with sword, lady, and giant chain ferns. A small wooden bridge spans the creek, as patches of wild ginger, California spikenard, and redwood sorrel spread above the streambed. The creek issues from a culvert, left, that crosses under the Avenue; the concrete conduit bears the date "1915," indicating that it was set during the construction of the Redwood Highway.

Beyond the bridge, the trail regains the benchland, passing a vista of the South Fork Eel at mile 0.3. Continuing south past patches of scouring rush, the route reaches a fork at 0.6 mile. The way left meets mile 16.0 of the Avenue at a small paved parking area, from where it then continues south, soon curving right to complete a small loop. The return retraces the first stages of the route.

FOUNDERS GROVE NATURE TRAIL

Summary: This short stroll is the most heavily hiked trail in the Park; it circles past the towering Founders Tree and the fallen Dyerville Giant.

Distance: 0.4 mile, round trip

Elevation Change: negligible

Location: The trail starts across Dyerville Loop Road from the Grove's parking lot, just east of an intersection with mile 20.6 of the Avenue [see detail map, p. 137].

Warning: *Be alert for traffic when crossing Dyerville Loop Road.*

Description: A wide, sawdust-strewn path leads 50 yards to the Founders Tree, a stately sempervirens specimen more than a thousand years old. It was considered the world's tallest tree until a storm unceremoniously took off its top; the thus-reduced redwood has added new height since the accident and now measures in at about 357 feet, which is good enough for seventh place in the current rankings. Aware of another vulnerability, the Park has placed a protective railing around the back of the tree in an attempt to prevent admirers from trampling the Founders' fragile root system. Serving the same purpose is a boardwalk that runs halfway around the tree's massive trunk. The main trail forks in front of the boardwalk; a nearby box dispenses returnable brochures for the self-guided nature tour that follows the route.

Following the course described by the brochure, the route turns left, looping beneath sky-scratching redwoods as it passes the numbered locations described in the trail guide. Redwood inside-out flower, lady fern, giant chain fern, and California spike-nard rise above vast beds of redwood sorrel to mingle with the many pathside milkmaids.

milkmaids, California toothwort
(Dentaria californica)

One of the earliest wildflowers to bloom in spring, milkmaids sends up a small white or pink flower whose four petals are formed into the shape of a cross. During fall and winter, a single fleshy, rounded leaf marks the position of the plant. Milkmaids's rootstock has a toothed appearance, giving the plant its other common name, "tooth-wort," while the pungent taste of its small root tubers accounts for it occasionally being called "pep-perroot." This multi-named flower is also some-times known as "lady's smocks" or "spring blossoms." [blooms February-June]

At 0.2 mile the loop comes to a series of large fallen redwoods, the most spectacular of which is the shattered Dyerville Giant, the massive and memorably shaped tree that toppled in March of 1991. At the base of this downed behemoth is a side trail, left, which twists around a large log on its way south to join the lovely Mahan Plaque Trail [p. 153]. The main route makes a right turn directly in front of the Giant's exposed roots and runs next to part of the tree's tremendous trunk; it then veers right to cut through several large neighboring logs. The trail winds its way back north to the Founders Tree and concludes at mile 0.4.

GOOSEPEN TREE LOOP TRAIL

Summary: A delightful little jaunt through lush redwood forest, this trail encounters several striking scenes.

Distance: 0.4 mile, round trip

Elevation Change: negligible

Location: The trailhead is at a paved parking area on the west side of the Avenue, mile 20.5 [see detail map, p. 137].

Description: The marked route exits the parking area by passing between two sections of a huge log; a large redwood to the left immediately claims attention with a beautiful burl that projects from its trunk about 30 feet above the ground. Like a planter pot, the burl hosts a small tanoak tree. The forest floor is a mass of greenery: poison oak, redwood sorrel, lady fern, elderberry, and trail plant support a host of Hooker's and Smith's fairybells.

Smith's fairybell
(Disporum smithii)

The flowers which give these plants their names hang, almost hidden, from beneath dark green, oval-shaped leaves at the end of branching, crooked stems. Perhaps an inch long, the blooms often cluster in pairs or trios, creamy white in color. Only a close examination of the flowers will distinguish between the species: the Smith's has a slightly longer, cylindrical "bell," with a three-part stigma dropping from its center; because of its size, it is sometimes called "large-flowered fairybell." The Hooker's flower bell is shorter and more funnel-like, and its stigma is entire, with no divisions. The Hooker's also has hairs upon its style and upper leaf surfaces, leading to its alternate name of "hairy fairybell," which does have a certain ring to it. [both bloom March-May]

Hooker's fairybell
(Disporum hookeri)

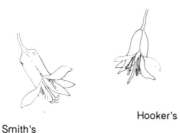

Hooker's

Smith's

Fifty yards from the parking area the trail divides; a sign indicates that the loop should be commenced to the right. Presently a large, double-trunked redwood comes into view, noticeable for its pronounced southerly lean and for the twin openings at its base. The tree proves to be a classic "goose-pen," its burned-out base the result of some long-past lightning strike. In this case, the pen served not geese but a human inhabitant; the small interior shows the remains of shelving that was once nailed to the walls, and a rusted metal awning still hangs over the northern "door." The tree, in fact, may have served as the residence of "Goosepen Charlie," an Englishman otherwise known as Charles Edison, who derived his income from selling salal cuttings and other foliage to city florists.

Beyond the abandoned dwelling, the route turns left to run through a huge bed of redwood sorrel; the grove's thick vegetation insulates the trail from the 101 Freeway, which passes a hundred yards to the right.

An unlikely quartet of plants adorns the southern end of the trail: wood rose, California laurel, scouring rush, and milkmaids. The route turns left here, mile 0.2, and begins its return, running beside a long, foliage-bedecked log. Ahead, a patch of redwood sorrel covers the gently rolling landscape like a ground fog; smooth yellow violet, fairybells, and vanilla leaf poke above the green cloud like tiny trees. All too soon the trail completes its loop, returning to the parking area at 0.4 mile.

A home for more than geese

GRASSHOPPER TRAIL

Summary: One of Humboldt Redwood's longest and most scenic routes, it offers thick forests, a string of steeply sloped prairies, and a dozen different wildflowers; the trail ends atop Grasshopper Peak, the highest point in the Park.

Distance: 6.1 miles using the southern approach; 6.3 miles via the northern approach

Elevation Change: gain of 3,100 feet

Location: The trail has two approaches: the southern one is reached by crossing the summer bridge at the Garden Club of America Grove, then turning north on the Garden Club-Burlington Trail and proceeding to the second junction with the Canoe Creek Trail; the Grasshopper approach is the middle of the three trails at this intersection. The northern approach leaves the Garden Club-Burlington Trail one mile south of the Burlington summer bridge crossing. The upper end of the trail meets Grasshopper Road at the summit of the peak.

Warning: *A round trip day hike to Grasshopper Peak via this trail is long and time consuming; connecting routes at the start add a minimum of 0.6 mile each way. The shortest total distance from the Avenue is thus 13.4 miles. There is no reliable water source anywhere along the route, although the fire lookout maintains a water supply when open.*

Description: The Grasshopper Trail is one of the classic hikes in the Park; a delightful array of trees and wildflowers will be found en route.

The trail's southern approach is 0.3 mile long; the northern approach is 0.5 mile. Both rise through mixed forest to meet on a nearly flat ridge spur. The route then proceeds west up a very gradual grade. (Note: mileages listed for the rest of the trail are from the start of the southern approach; distances from the northern approach are 0.2 mile greater.)

Black huckleberry is plentiful early in the route; a mass of milkmaids, mile 0.7, and some wood rose, mile 0.9, also beautify the trailside. At mile 1.1 the pale shoots of phantom orchid poke through the pathway. Upgrades and level stretches then alternate as madrones add to the forest mix. At mile 1.5 a short, triangular wooden trail sign marks the junction with an abandoned side route, left, that once connected with the Canoe Creek Trail. After a set of switchbacks, the main route moves through a dense stand of diminutive Douglas fir, 1.8 miles.

A small stream sometimes flows under the trail at mile 2.0; it should not be counted on as a year-round source of water; giant chain fern and wild ginger grow in the damp creekbed. The route then rises steeply, levelling at mile 2.2 near two large redwoods, right.

Three shade-loving plants grow here beside the pathway: spotted coral root and a pair of look-alikes, white-veined wintergreen and rattlesnake orchid. The latter can usually be distinguished by a more checkered pattern to its veining and sharper points to its leaves.

Continuing its climb, the route enters a thicket of small Douglas fir and tanoak at mile 2.3; this somber sequence is relieved briefly, mile 2.7, by a flower-filled opening. The path levels and then drops to a saddle, mile 2.9, where it joins with a dirt road. A right turn here leads downhill to end at Mill Creek, some 1,100 feet below in the canyon to the north. The Grasshopper Trail follows the roadbed to the left.

**white-veined wintergreen,
white-veined shinleaf**
(Pyrola picta)
[blooms June-August]

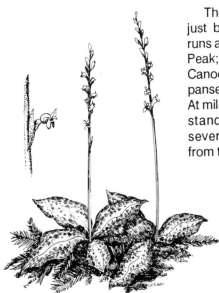

**rattlesnake orchid,
rattlesnake plantain**
(Goodyera oblongifolia)
[blooms July-September]

The now-widened route passes just below a ridgeline, right, that runs all the way up to Grasshopper Peak; to the left is a view of the Canoe Creek drainage, a huge expanse of unlogged, pathless forest. At mile 3.3 the trail winds through a stand of mature Douglas fir — several striking specimens rise from the downhill slope, left.

Redwood inside-out flower, Douglas iris, and heart-leaved twayblade grow at the trailside near the end of the fir grove. The route then crosses a rolling hillside prairie where, in springtime, miniature lupine and true baby stars speckle the grass. To the right, the bleached boards of some long-forgotten structure lie in scattered neglect.

The trail rises through a mix of forest and grassland, still parallelling the ridgeline that runs upslope on the right. A road remnant drops downslope, left, near where two tall madrones loom in the woods. At 3.6 miles a pair of canyon live oaks stretch their dark limbs far down the hillside to hang over the road; it seems that the trees have overextended themselves and should soon go tumbling into the canyon below, but they remain firmly in place, rooted to rock.

canyon live oak
(Quercus chrysolepis)

From Greeks to Slavs to Celtic Druids, many peoples have worshipped oaks, and it takes but one glance at a contorted chrysolepis, perched high on some rocky hillside, to understand why. Although canyon live oaks locate in habitats of seemingly inhospitable ruggedness, they grow tenaciously, gnarling into shapes that widen the eyes and quicken the spirit. Their stout trunks and twisted limbs exude strength, yet the trees appear strangely soft in their coverings of dark, velvetlike bark. Stand beneath an oak's spreading

mantle of leaves and the space seems protected; some might sense it is sacred.

The tree's acorns sit in thick, scaly cups, covered with a golden yellow "wool" that explains the nickname "golden cup" oak; its leaves can range from smooth to sharply toothed, usually with fuzzy golden undersides; hence another name, "goldenleaf" oak. Producing a wood so hard that it was used for splitting redwood, the tree has also been called the "maul" oak, as woodsmen, like worshippers, honor the canyon live oak for its strength.

As the trail continues its climb, scrub oak and California laurel seek the shaded areas, while California poppy, blue dicks, and bracken fern bask in the sunlight. Starting at mile 4.1 the way is lined with a profusion of flowers: first spotted coral root and two-eyed violet, then hounds-tongue and pussy ears, and finally winecup clarkia, gentian, and both blue *and* white baby blue eyes. One after another, swatches of prairie swoop down from the ridgetop, the grass often riddled with rocks; by June the openings are filled with wildflowers. A small dripping spring, mile 4.9, waters houndstongue, wild strawberry and miner's lettuce.

At 5.4 miles, the trail rises to a saddle on the ridgecrest, gaining a view north into Decker Creek's dark watershed. The route then returns to the southern side of the ridge, entering a stand of Douglas fir before looping around an entire colony of spotted coral root, mile 5.5.

spotted coral root
(Corallorhiza maculata)

This strange plant grows only in the darkest forest, sending up small stems that resemble reddish asparagus stalks; these culminate in a collection of branching, lesser stemlets. Small flowers hang from the stemlets, each with two tiny white petals whose centers are stained a deep red-purple. Despite its name, the spotted coral root lacks true roots or even root hairs; like the phantom orchid, it is an epiparasite, interacting with soil-based fungi to gain its nutrients. [blooms May-July]

After crossing yet another prairie, the route climbs to an intersection with Grieg Road, mile 5.6. Grasshopper Trail Camp spreads along the narrow ridge spine to the right; it consists of a pit toilet and a level, shaded camping area. Water can be a problem; it is available at the Grasshopper Peak lookout when staff is present during the fire season, but at other times the closest source is an intermittent stream 0.2 mile south on the downhill side of Grieg Road.

A continuation of the trail ascends the hillside southwest of the road, zigzagging through more prairies and forest while passing, among other plants, scarlet larkspur and woodland star. The trail ends at the fire lookout on the top of Grasshopper Peak, mile 6.1. The view from this wind-swept promontory is the most extensive to be found in the Park. Distant mountains, including the Lassics and the often snow-capped Yolla Bollys, are visible to the east, while the serrated ridge of the King

Range lies to the southwest. Closer at hand are the drainages of Cuneo, Squaw, and Bull creeks, their grasslands and forests covering the folded westerly landscape like a quilt of green and gold. The patient eye can play over a host of details: the thin brown tracings of Preacher Gulch Road on the ridge below, the remnants of John Cuneo's orchard on its lonely point, the lush forest near Whiskey Flat — all this rewards the persevering hiker who at last perches atop the peak.

*   *   *

THE "WILDCAT" WHO LIVED ON GRASSHOPPER

During the 1930s, Grasshopper Peak Lookout was staffed by Charley "Wildcat" Kenney, described as "a large person with long fingernails and a big red beard." His companion was Seymour, an imposing, chowlike dog. Kenney would while away the summer hours letting his fingernails and beard grow and then descend to Weott for the winter. There he would settle in at Monty's Bar, spending his days telling stories. If this placid avocation was disturbed by another bar patron, Charlie would merely reach over and rake the offender's neck with his inch-long fingernails. He wasn't called "Wildcat" for nothing.

KENT GROVE LOOP TRAIL

Summary: This brief route circles a beautiful riverside benchland.

Distance: 0.5 mile for the loop; 0.8 including the spur to the Garden Club Grove

Elevation Change: negligible

Location: The loop begins at the parking lot for the Kent Grove, mile 15.0 of the Avenue; the spur starts at the north end of the Garden Club of America Grove parking lot, reached from mile 14.7 of the Avenue.

Description: The marked trail travels 75 feet towards a large, leaning redwood, whereupon the route forks; the way right moves across a heavily foliaged flat where bracken fern and redwood sorrel form the main ground covers. At mile 0.1 the trail turns left; behind a broken log, right, an informal path leads into the neighboring Mather Grove.

Soon the trail approaches the banks above the South Fork Eel; paths branch right to reach somewhat-precarious river overlooks. The loop route then undulates over a lovely, rolling forest landscape, reaching a thicket of thin false Solomon's seal at mile 0.2.

At mile 0.3 the path briefly runs above the alder-fringed river before bending left to reach the spur trail, right at mile 0.4, that connects with the Garden Club of America Grove. The loop continues northeast to its return at the Kent Grove parking lot.

MAHAN PLAQUE LOOP TRAIL

Summary: Ranking among the loveliest — and most historic — trails in the Park, this loop offers hillside dogwoods, a wonderful covering of redwood sorrel, and a stirring monument in the deep woods.

Distance: 0.5 mile, round trip

Elevation Change: negligible

Location: The obscurely marked trail leaves from a pullout on the east side of the Avenue, mile 20.2 [see detail map, p. 137].

Mahan Plaque Loop

Description: The trail enters a stand of massive, stately redwoods that rises from a lush covering of redwood sorrel. The narrow pathway seems about to be engulfed by the greenery.

redwood sorrel
(Oxalis oregana)

If the coast redwoods are "the pillars of nature's grandest temple," then redwood sorrel is the temple's carpet, for it spreads its soft green, cloverlike leaves across vast stretches of the forest floor, thriving in the darkness that is anathema to most other plants. Direct sunlight is in fact devastating to the delicate oxalis, causing it to protectively fold down its leaves as if they were off-season cafe umbrellas; the rich-hued foliage forms the background for a display of small white flowers that deepen into pinkness with age. Despite the presence of oxalic acid, both the plant's leaves and stems may be eaten in moderation, either raw in salads or fermented as a dessert. [blooms March-August]

The path divides about 100 feet from the roadway, with the right branch moving towards the hillside to meet the Big Cut Trail as it descends from the right; a side trip up to the first switchback along this route will provide a stunning view of the forested flat below.

Proceeding along the loop trail from the Big Cut junction, thickets of lady fern soon crowd the ground, with smooth yellow violet, milkmaids, bracken fern, and sword fern vying for space. Shortly past mile 0.1, a pair of Pacific dogwoods spread their delicate limbs over the hillslope.

Ahead on the left are a pair of large stumps; between them sits a large rock, inset with a plaque whose inscription reads:

Laura Perrot Mahan 1867-1937
James P. Mahan 1867-1937

Pioneers in the Save-the-Redwoods League. The California State Parks Commission has dedicated to their memory this site, where, on November 19, 1924, Mr. and Mrs. Mahan discovered that logging had begun, and led the movement that led to the saving of this grove.

A glance around the grove testifies to the effectiveness of the Mahans' work; only three or four large stumps are visible, but the grove is thick with the towering trunks of the trees they helped save.

The trail turns left just beyond this historic site, and then zigzags through more lush forest. A marker at mile 0.4 indicates a connecting route, right, which leads to another fork in 150 feet. At the second fork, the route left meets the Avenue at a point slightly north of the entrance to the Mahan Loop. The branch right arrives at the Dyerville Giant in 0.2 mile, where it joins the Founders Grove Nature Trail [p. 144].

Continuing to the left on the Mahan Loop, the route now moves through another thick bed of redwood sorrel. The circuit ends at mile 0.5; the Avenue is a hundred feet along the entrance trail to the right.

Pacific dogwood
(Cornus nuttallii)

Twice a year this small tree displays its ethereal beauty within the redwood forest. In spring, it dazzles the eye with a profusion of creamy white "bracts" — flowerlike leaves that surround the tiny, greenish white true flowers. In late summer or early fall, the tree may again produce these pseudo-flowers; the leaves then take on their autumnal hues — subtle shades of red, orange, pink, and yellow that often still bear streaks of summer green. The Pacific dogwood may grow to 50 feet in height, invariably choosing a graceful shape. [blooms April-July]

NATURE LOOP TRAIL

Summary: A little loop through large redwoods, this path is close to both the Burlington Campground and the Visitor Center.

Distance: 0.7 mile, round trip

Elevation Change: negligible

Location: The route starts opposite the Visitor Center parking lot at mile 16.5 of the Avenue.

Description: A short approach trail leaves the west side of the Avenue, immediately entering the shadowy Gould Grove. In 50 yards the route reaches a fork: the Fleischmann Grove Trail branches left, while the Nature Loop Trail commences to the right and proceeds north to mile 0.1; here, directly in front of a large redwood, the path divides. Bearing left, the trail proceeds along the redwood-shaded, duff-covered flat; a few sword ferns initially provide the main plant cover, but redwood sorrel and smooth yellow violet soon become plentiful. Intermittently placed interpretive signs provide information about important features of the forest. At mile 0.2 the trail twists downhill towards the South Fork

Eel, turns right, and soon crosses a small bridge. A side trail to the river forks left, mile 0.3, while the loop turns right. A second side route, this one leading to the Burlington Campground, branches left at mile 0.4, while the main trail again turns right. After crossing another bridge, the path bends sharp left, mile 0.5, and passes a plentitude of sugar scoops. The loop then wanders its way back to its start, finishing at mile 0.7.

sugar scoop
(Tiarella unifoliata)

A small and fragile-looking plant that prefers the dark forest floor of redwood flats, it is named for the scooplike appearance of the small capsules which form from the mature flowers. A member of the Saxifrage family, sugar scoop closely resembles several related flowers, including brookfoam and fringe cups. [blooms April-July]

SOUTH FORK EEL TRAIL ("RIVER" TRAIL)

This lengthy trail runs along the western bank of the South Fork Eel, stretching from the Myers Grove in the south to the Rockefeller Forest in the north. Three summer bridges connect the route with the Avenue of the Giants, dividing the trail into the four segments described below.

CHILDREN'S FOREST LOOP TRAIL

Summary: A short loop to the southern end of the River Trail, the parklike Children's Forest grove glows with greenery.

Distance: 1.7 miles, round trip; 2.1 miles with the Myers Grove spur

Elevation Change: 120-foot gain and loss

Location: From the Williams Grove, mile 13.5 on the Avenue, a summer bridge across the South Fork Eel leads to the route's start.

Description: The trail turns left from its junction with the bridge access trail; it proceeds through mixed forest, soon climbing to cross a small stream and then dropping to run along a narrow riverside terrace. Small redwoods gather somberly about large stumps as the route winds south. Beyond a second creek , mile 0.3, another thicket of young trees encroaches on the pathway. Soon redwoods begin to appear, and by mile 0.5 mature redwoods rise high above a scattering of sugar scoop and smooth yellow violet. California hazel, trail plant, and many small wood rose bushes join the trailside plant life at mile 0.6.

wood rose
(Rosa gymnocarpa)

The branching limbs and small leaves of this deep-forest dweller are enhanced twice annually: first by the small pink and white petals of its springtime blossoms and then by the reddish hips that form in late summer. The plant's species name, *gymnocarpa*, means "naked fruit" in Latin, a reference to the early loss of sepals from the wood rose's hips. Several Indian tribes ate the raw outer rinds of the hips, but rejected the seeds. [blooms May-July]

A tall sign announcing the Children's Forest, mile 0.7, stands at the beginning of the trail loop. The way right moves through a patch of vanilla leaf and then passes the dedication plaque, right, for the forest. Now the route wanders across a rolling bed of redwood sorrel as stately redwoods tower overhead. A small bridge spans Kerr Creek at mile 0.8; the course then turns left and soon arrives at the spur route to the Myers Plaque, which branches right. This short path runs through shadowy second-growth to reach a large stump at 0.2 mile. A monument here dedicates the logged-over grove to Ulysses S. Grant Myers's mother, Sarah, and one of his sons, Lessor (although the inscription mistakenly names him "Leslie"). The spur soon peters out, requiring hikers to retrace their steps to the loop trail.

From the spur junction, the loop turns left, recrossing Kerr Creek at 0.9 mile and then passing the *National Geographic World* Redwood Grove, purchased with donations from the magazine's young subscribers. The loop ends at 1.0 mile, and a return along the first section of the trail reaches the summer bridge connection at mile 1.7.

WILLIAMS GROVE-GARDEN CLUB TRAIL

Summary: A meandering path above the South Fork Eel, it encounters redwood inside-out flowers in abundance on its way between the Park's two southernmost summer bridges.

Distance: 1.6 miles, one way

Elevation Change: 120-foot gain and loss

Location: The trail's south end starts across the summer bridge from the Williams Grove (Avenue mile 13.5); the north end is across the bridge from the Garden Club of America Grove (mile 14.7 on the Avenue).

Description: Turning right from the summer bridge access trail, the route climbs northward through young redwoods, soon levelling on top of a benchland. California laurel, bigleaf maple, and Douglas fir dot sections of the woodland. At 0.1 mile the trail drops to cross the rocky, eroded gorge of Coon Creek on an aging wooden bridge. Black cottonwood, five-finger fern, California spikenard, western coltsfoot, pearly everlasting, red alder, and milkwort crowd the canyonsides. A faint path, left at the top of the northern bank, leads to an artifact for automobile aficionados — a rusting car hulk reposes peacefully near Pacific starflower and yerba de selva.

California milkwort
(Polygala californica)

The little but long-blooming milkwort remains reclusive during the showy blossom time of early spring, waiting until many of the flashier forest flowers have faded. Then, lacking much competition, it garners attention with the pleasing rosy purple flowers that bloom from its short, small-leaved stem. The pealike blossoms produce a notched capsule, which then splits open along its margin to release its store of small seeds. *Polygala* means "much milk," an indication that the plant was thought to stimulate milk flow in cows. [blooms April-July]

The main route cuts through a thicket of young Douglas firs and encounters a summertime display of ladies' tresses, a flamboyant flower seldom seen in the Park. An orchard remnant appears on the right at mile 0.2; the shadowing stumps and small redwoods of an old logging site subsequently surround the trail, the darkness brightened by the green luminescence of an occasional bigleaf maple. Switchbacks at mile 0.5 take the path to a higher terrace.

Following a bridgeless stream crossing, mile 0.7, the uncut redwoods of the Hammond Grove shelter sugar scoop, Pacific starflower, and many of their deep forest friends. A rustic bridge spans a debris-choked stream, and the trail soon drops towards the river, passing wild ginger and scouring rush at mile 1.0.

A thick patch of salal, 1.2 miles, precedes a split-log bench that overlooks the South Fork Eel. Giant horsetail, willow, and red alder are visible near the riverside. Another bridge, mile 1.3, crosses a deep, vegetation-rich ravine. The way is now along a narrow benchland that is punctuated by a pair of additional streams; a short distance beyond a rail-guarded river overlook, the upper trailbank abounds with such plants as goldenback fern, coast boykinia, hairy honeysuckle, and most noticeable of all, large clusters of redwood inside-out flower. The route then concludes at the access trail to the Garden Club of America Grove summer bridge, mile 1.6.

GARDEN CLUB-BURLINGTON TRAIL

Summary: This connecting route offers access to the Canoe Creek and Grasshopper trails; the crossing at Canoe Creek plunges past banks full of beautiful greenery.

redwood inside-out flower, redwood ivy
(Vancouveria planipetala)
[blooms April-June]

Distance: 2.6 miles, one way

Elevation Change: 520-foot gain and 480-foot loss, south to north

Location: The trail's southern end is across the summer bridge from the Garden Club of America Grove (mile 14.7 of the Avenue); the northern end is across the summer bridge from the Burlington Campground (Avenue mile 16.6).

Description: A right turn from the summer bridge access trail begins this section of the River Trail, which proceeds northward along the cliffs above the river. The smell of white sweet clover permeates the summer air as largish redwoods provide partial shade. California harebell reposes beneath both bigleaf maple and California laurel at 0.2 mile; the path here offers a stunning view of the river while descending on switchbacks to a narrow terrace. The trail meanders across the benchland until mile 0.3, where it turns left to run above the channel of Canoe Creek. Thimbleberry and red elderberry now spread near the pathside, as several varieties of ferns and flowers thrive in the increased dampness; a large log, left, is festooned with tendrils of poison oak.

The southern end of the Canoe Creek Trail branches left at mile 0.4, as the main route bends right and then drops towards the creek. The streambank is covered with seasonal verdure, most notably an eye-catching collection of California spikenard.

At the creek crossing is a view, left, of a high bank of alluvium; the stream has cut through the benchland here, exposing a striking soil profile — multiple layers of the rich, compacted gray gravels that nourish redwoods like no other substance. The trail ascends to a redwood- and fern-covered flat, meeting the northern end of the Canoe Creek Trail, left, at mile 0.6. Thirty feet along this route is the southern approach to the Grasshopper Trail.

California spikenard, elk clover
(Aralia californica)

If ever a plant was worth a second look, albeit after an interval of several months, it's the California spikenard. In summer, this wide-spreading streamside shrub is already spectacular, with masses of multiple, bright green leaves and numerous puffs of small, creamy white flowers that rise like spray from a fountain. But come fall, the spikenard outdoes even this display; its leaves turn a pale gold, like the lightest honey, while its flowers transform into clusters of deep purple berries that surmount the foliage in stunning, deeply harmonious contrast. Nature never shows a better eye for color than this. [blooms June-August]

As the path moves northward, the benchland gradually narrows, forcing the trail to turn left and head northwest. Goldenback fern at mile 0.8 and sticky monkey flower at 0.9 mile enliven the route, which rises to pass a scattering of coastal wood ferns at mile 1.1. The trail climbs past California harebell, mile 1.4, and enters a hillside mixed forest. At mile 1.6 the northern approach of the Grasshopper Trail exits to the left; the main trail now drops downhill, reaching a wooden bench, mile 1.9, that offers a prospect of the South Fork Eel. Then, at the Harold and Kathryn Black Grove, a large patch of vanilla leaf spreads along both sides of the path.

Twice more the route drops closer to the river to run along foliage-filled terraces. After passing through a dark thicket of small redwoods, mile 2.1, the trail climbs briefly, twists between a pair of picturesque logs, and then drops again. A rude wooden bridge spans a small creek at 2.3 miles; California hazels spread above the streambanks to the left while large redwoods rise downstream to the right. A thicket of smaller redwoods and a collection of aging stumps precede the conclusion of the trail, which comes at the Burlington summer bridge spur, mile 2.6.

vanilla leaf
(Achlys triphylla)

The vanilla leaf looks like two separate plants joined together by mischance. First, there is a stalk with a large, bright green leaf that consists of three closely set leaflets. The two side leaflets resemble elephant ears or moose antlers; in either case, they surround a central, facelike leaf section. Rising above this, like a stick of incense, is a second stalk that supports an end spike of tiny, cream-colored flowers. Despite their differences, the vanilla leaf's two parts manage to reach a sort of uneasy equilibrium, much like a delicate maiden perched atop a stolid beast. The plant gains its common name from the smell of its dried leaves, which were used by pioneer women to freshen linen closets. [blooms April-June]

BURLINGTON-BULL CREEK TRAIL

Summary: A stump house, the remains of a riverside retreat, and deeply shaded Decker Creek highlight the northernmost section of the River Trail.

Distance: 3.5 miles, one way

Elevation Change: 240-foot gain and 240-foot loss

Location: The segment's southern end is across the summer bridge from the Burlington Campground (Avenue mile 16.6); the northern end is at the Bull Creek Flats Loop Trail, just south of Bull Creek.

Description: From its start at the Burlington summer bridge approach, the trail forks right, moving along the hillside above the river. On the left at mile 0.1, a large, shaded stump looms above the path; the top of this redwood remnant is covered by a weathered roof from which a small stovepipe sprouts. At the stump's base is a low doorway; inside are the remains of some shelving. Whoever once lived here has long departed, and the erstwhile home is slowly returning to the woods.

A switchback brings the route down into a dark gorge where a long, jutting log serves as a bridge. The trail next crosses a benchland, climbs uphill, and then winds its way to a grassy clearing, left at mile 0.3, that is dotted with fruit trees. To the right, half-hidden behind a mock orange tree, the stark form of a chimney rises from a mass of sweet pea.

These are the ruins of Forest Lodge, the riverside retreat of the Perrotts, longtime ranchers in central Humboldt County. Laura Mahan, the activist President of the Humboldt Women's Save-the-Redwoods League, was a member of the family; she willed her interest in Forest Lodge to the Park, an arrangement that did not sit well with some of her relatives. The state acquired full title to the property in the 1970s and the lodge's four houses were all eventually razed. Gone now are the open-air sleeping porches that were built atop the huge redwood stumps west of the lodge; gone, too, are all but a few of the orchard's 200 trees, although some of the survivors still bear sweet apples in fall. Little else, except for the monument-like chimney, is left.

Stumps and living redwoods of various sizes mark the next section of the route, which crosses a terrace above the river. At mile 0.8 the trail rises and then drops steeply to a bridgeless crossing of Mill Creek. The small canyon overflows with streamside vegetation—giant horsetail, giant chain fern, California spikenard, and western coltsfoot are among the larger plants. On the north bank a spur trail exits right; it leads a hundred yards to an river overlook opposite Gould Bar.

The main trail then moves through more stumps and second-growth, arriving at a deep creek gorge, mile 1.3, whose crossing is made difficult by the lack of a bridge; cream bush, fringe cup, and bigleaf maple add variety to the scene. More logged-over land follows; an especially dark thicket of second-growth precedes Corner Creek, 2.0 miles, which is spanned by a log bridge. The route then rises to a higher benchland area, moving through several memorial groves of mature redwoods and passing over a small creek, mile 2.5, on another log crossing.

five-finger fern
*(Adiantum pedatum
var. aleuticum)*

A bend left at 2.7 miles leads downhill into a large, heavily shaded stream canyon. The steep creekbanks are covered with masses of five-finger ferns, their pale green fronds forming the perfectly repeated pattern of a woodland wallpaper.

At the bottom of the slope, the trail turns right to cross delightful Decker Creek, a lovely, lilting brook spanned by yet another log bridge. Leafy vine maples spread their limbs over several downed redwoods, shading the limpid waters of the rock-strewn stream.

More memorial groves line the way, their boundaries sometimes designated by low wooden posts bearing enigmatic inscriptions like "H-58." This is the only section of the Park where such markers are found.

vine maple
(Acer circinatum)

Although seldom seen in the Park, the vine maple is one of the most colorful characters in the red-wood forest's cast of plants. In mid-spring, its purple and white flowers dance above bright green leaves; by summer, showy red fruit has made its appearance.

While these early performances are impressive enough, the vine maple has actually been biding its time until the seasons' final act, for with the coming of fall its leaves turn a dramatic orange-red, causing the shrublike trees to glow within the forest fastness like small bonfires, their rich hues complementing the golds and yellows of their cousins, the bigleaf maples. Look for these moisture lovers along forested creek canyons and on mountain slopes. [blooms April-May]

A bench at the Buell Hammet Grove, mile 3.0, sits beside a covering of smooth yellow violets. The trail soon starts climbing the hillslope, coming to a view, mile 3.2, of the confluence of the South Fork Eel and Bull Creek; traffic noise from across the river canyon adds its obbligato to the tramp of tired hikers' feet. After crossing two small bridges, the route drops via switchbacks towards the lower Bull Creek Flats, passing windflower and Siberian candyflower before arriving at a grove of large redwoods. The route ends at its junction with the Bull Creek Loop Trail, mile 3.5. To the north, via a summer bridge, is a connection with the Rockefeller Loop Trail. West up the creek canyon is the Big Trees Area.

THE NORTHERN AVENUE:
LOST TOWNS AND LAST TREES

Nowhere along the Avenue have the effects of floods and freeway been greater than on its northernmost segment; of the towns that once stood along the roadway, only waterproof Redcrest, high and dry atop its hill, has survived as a complete community. Not far from the northern Avenue are the remnants of other vanquished villages — Holmes, Larabee, Shively, and Elinor — that can be reached by brief side routes.

This final section of the Avenue provides more than haunts for history buffs, however. Several short trails lead to some of the Park's most striking settings — a hushed, hillside stand of redwoods; a rocky riverside promontory with a view of the main Eel; the verdant, fern-filled grove honoring the park district's first superintendent. A return to the freeway is not far ahead, and such attractions offer a last chance to linger within the great forest landscape before leaving both the Avenue and Humboldt Redwoods State Park.

*   *   *   *   *

Immediately after crossing the South Fork Eel, the Avenue arrives at a junction with Mattole Road, which exits left beneath the 101 Freeway overpass at mile 20.8. This often-winding, paved route leads first to the Rockefeller Forest and then to the rest of the Park's Bull Creek watershed, offering access to a wonderland of trails, wildflowers, and historic sites [p. 198]. West of the Park's boundary, the road descends to Honeydew, in the lovely Mattole Valley, where it turns north to connect with Petrolia, Capetown, and Ferndale.

North of the Mattole Road turnoff, the Avenue bends right, passing over the site of Dyerville, an erstwhile crossroads community that was the area's supply center at the turn of the century. Floods in 1937 and 1955 each extracted portions of the town, and the subsequent construction of the 101 Freeway covered over any remaining traces. Thanks to the local staging of biannual marathons, Dyerville now experiences a sort of periodic resurrection as a score of portable restrooms rise, Phoenix-like, from the roadside to serve the many runners who come to race beneath the redwoods. The painted numerals that adorn the central Avenue and Mattole Road are the mile markers for these runs.

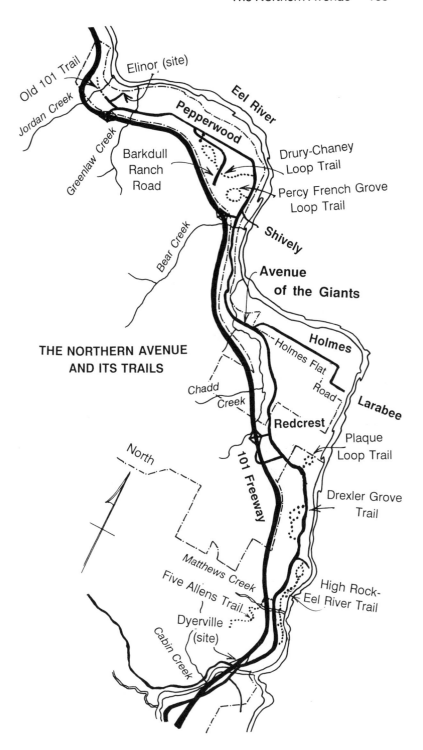

Old 101 Trail

Jordan Creek

Elinor (site)

Eel River

Pepperwood

Greenlaw Creek

Barkdull
Ranch
Road

Drury-Chaney
Loop Trail

Percy French Grove
Loop Trail

Bear Creek

Shively

Avenue
of the Giants

**THE NORTHERN AVENUE
AND ITS TRAILS**

Holmes

Holmes Flat

Road

Larabee

Chadd

Creek

Redcrest

Plaque
Loop Trail

North

Drexler Grove
Trail

101 Freeway

Matthews Creek

Five Allens Trail

Dyerville
(site)

Cabin Creek

High Rock-
Eel River Trail

TWO VANISHED TOWNS

White settlers came late to southern Humboldt County, but they were quick to change the area after their arrival. When the wagon road from Eureka reached the mouth of the South Fork Eel in 1876, a ferry was set up at the crossing, and soon a hotel was built on the nearby bluffs above the river. Within two years a store had opened, serving the home-steaders who were steadily moving into the locale. Two other impor-tant businesses followed: a livery stable to board trail-weary horses and a saloon for quenching their riders' thirst. The budding community had grown enough by 1890 that it required both a post office and a name. The citizens chose to honor the oldest resident, "Dad" Dyer, by calling the place Dyerville.

Overland stage fording
South Fork Eel near Dyerville, c. 1900

The town prospered as it served the region's growing population. The saloon, as might be expected, garnered its share of attention, gaining special notoriety for its unique, sieve-like ceiling. This ar-chitectural refinement was the result of the patrons' dissatisfaction with bartender "Pap" Townsend's occasional attempts to close up. When-ever Pap suggested shutting down for the night, a few of the more disgruntled drinkers would pull out their revolvers and fire roofward, thus persuading Townsend to extend the curfew and also adding to the bar's perforated decor.

Dyerville remained a busy community until the early 1930s, when the state bought up much of the town and relocated the headquarters for Humboldt Redwoods there. A state forestry fire station and CCC camp came next, but they moved to Burlington after the 1937 flood. The Park people held out until 1955, when Superintendent James Warren watched the Eel rise an incredible 19 feet in one hour as it left its banks to wash over Dyerville. This time the water proved too much; the Park headquarters finally joined the exodus to Burlington. The battered town's few surviving buildings were bulldozed away, and a couple of years later much of the townsite was covered with the concrete and pavement of the new freeway.

Today no sign remains of Dyerville, which has disappeared as completely as the other community which once occupied the same spot. Before the arrival of the white settlers, a Lolangkok Indian village was located on this land, just where the Dyerville store and the saloon of the holey ceiling were later built.

The Indians would have spoken of their village as Ltcuntadun; it sat upon the long benchland they called Chin-tah-tah. Below the village, their square-ended dugout canoes once plied the nearby river channels, and their wicker baskets, staked close to shore, caught a plentitude of lampreys. But there have been no Lolangkoks for more than 50 years, and the names they spoke have been all but lost. Now there is only the splashing of the rivers below the bluffs, where Sin-ke-kok, the South Fork Eel, rushes into Tah-cho, the main Eel; they meet in a mingling of the waters that was Len-lin Teg-o-be.

The stream sound rises, sometimes as a murmur, sometimes as a roar. Either way, it must speak for all those, white or red, who once lived at this spot. The vanished villages have long been silent; now only the river's voice remains.

★   ★   ★

An onramp for the northbound freeway exits left from the townsite, while ahead on the right, mile 20.9, a viewpoint overlooks the rivers' confluence. The railroad bridge spanning the main Eel is visible to the east. A dirt road adjacent to the overlook leads down to Dyerville Bar, which offers a fishing hole of moderate size.

After leaving Dyerville, the Avenue runs a narrow course between the 101 Freeway and the Eel; the bank to the road's left is seasonally filled with wild fennel, stonecrop, and sticky monkey flower. Across the river are tall second-growth redwoods that have replaced trees logged by the Pacific Lumber Company around 1920. At mile 21.1 there is access down the steep bank, right, to Piling Hole—a long, deep fishing spot. As the Avenue approaches a stand of old-growth forest, mile 21.4, a dirt road exits sharply to the right; it leads down to the Upper High Rock gravel bar and its large fishing hole.

On the right at mile 21.7, just past the C. F. Krauss Grove, is an unmarked path that cuts through an old log; this is the southernmost entrance to the High Rock-Eel River Trail, a lovely, rambling route that falls and rises for more than a mile beside the Eel [p. 189]. The Avenue then begins climbing, passing a parking area, right at mile 21.9, for the Arbor Day Grove. Here a marker indicates additional access to the High Rock-Eel River Trail. Appropriately enough, the neighboring stand of redwoods is the J. Sterling Morton Grove, which honors the Nebraskan credited with originating Arbor Day in 1872. Morton later served as Secretary of Agriculture during the administration of President Grover Cleveland.

Now the route rises to reach the Maria McKean Allen Grove at mile 22.1. A turnout here, left, is the starting point for the Five Allens Trail, which ascends the steep slope en route to a peaceful grove of hillside redwoods [p. 188].

The road crests a small ridge at 22.3 miles. At a narrow pullout, right, an unmarked path cuts up the bank, connecting immediately with the middle of the High Rock-Eel River Trail. The northern and southern sections of the trail descend the ridge from this junction, while between them, a short spur route climbs east to the top of High Rock; the craggy overlook, called Sa-cho-te by the Lolangkoks, indeed rises high above the Eel, providing vertiginous views of the river far below. On the banks of this promontory perch both sticky monkey flower and toyon.

Another Avenue parking area, immediately ahead on the right, also provides an unmarked connecting path to the High Rock-Eel River Trail. To the north, a paved road exits left, mile 22.4, to High Rock Conservation Camp, which is situated on the hillside above the freeway. The Avenue then drops from the ridgetop, moving through a forest of mature redwoods. After passing several memorial groves, the route reaches an unmarked paved road, right, at mile 22.8. A turn here leads first to a small parking area, from which the northern end of the High Rock-Eel River Trail begins. Those who crane their necks skyward will be rewarded with a curious sight: attached part way up the side of a large redwood is a framework of aging timbers that juts out several feet from the tree's trunk. This seemingly inexplicable structure is, in fact, the last remnant of a pulley system that once hauled up gravel hoppers from the riverside for the Mercer-Fraser Company, a local construction firm. The side road continues east, dropping past several twinberry bushes to come out upon a long river bar; nearby are a pair of large, deep fishing holes: a right turn on the bar leads south 0.5 mile to the site at High Rock, while directly east from the road's end is Lower High Rock.

North of the side road, the Avenue moves across a tree-filled benchland; on the left at mile 22.9 is a marked trailhead that lacks a pullout [p. 185]. This starts the short Drexler Grove Trail, which rises to a knoll and forms a brief circuit; two spur trails descend northward to reach a roadside parking area at mile 23.0 of the Avenue, just past the sign for the grove.

The Avenue continues a short distance farther along the flat, the surrounding forest sprinkled with the stumps of trees that were cut for shingle bolts long ago. The bench-land then tapers off and the Avenue runs beneath a rocky cliff; to the right is a postcard perspective of the Eel as it heads north towards Larabee and Holmes.

Alder and bigleaf maple join the redwoods briefly, until the route begins climbing at 23.4 miles. Sheltered by heavy forest, fat false Solomon's seal sticks its stems out from the roadbank.

Across the Avenue from a colorful collection of cliffside clintonias is a turnout, right at mile 23.8, for the

Mercer-Fraser Tree

Geraldyne and McIntyre Faries Grove. A sign visible only to southbound traffic indicates the start of the Plaque Loop Trail, which drops down the bank from the turnout [p. 194]. The loop offers a short stroll through mixed forest, passing a plaque-embedded log bench along the way. As the Avenue continues uphill, a single large madrone juts jauntily from the surrounding forest to project out over the roadway.

The Daly Memorial Grove is marked to the right at 24.0 miles, just as the road reaches the top of the grade. On the left at mile 24.1 is an offramp for southbound freeway traffic.

It is here that two sections of the Avenue merge. The road segments were established several years apart, each with its own set of mileages, and the distances posted on their respective milepost markers were never brought into conformance. As a result, the markers now suddenly show an increase of 15 miles, so that the next milepost reads "39.17" instead of the expected "24.17." Travellers who use the markers to determine the distance from the Avenue's southern end should thus reduce the posted numbers accordingly for the remainder of the route. (Posted rather than the actual mileages will be used hereafter in describing the last part of the Avenue.)

Beyond the offramp the Avenue enters the environs of Englewood, which is centered around a large, nearly level clearing. The spot was first settled in the 1870s by a pair of brothers from England; they honored their homeland by naming the southern end of the wood-fringed valley Englevale and the northern part Englewood. Although the vale is more striking than the wood, it is the latter name which has stuck. In early days, travellers passing along the county wagon road would stay here at the George Ranch. The relative importance of the guests was reflected by the charges for accommodations: a barn stall for a horse cost fifty cents, while a room for its rider was only two bits. The Englewood Inn later replaced the George stopping place, serving the many motorists who drove the new highway.

While the local timber supply lasts, stacks of large logs line the roadway at mile 39.3, right, awaiting the sawblades of the Englewood branch of Eel River Sawmills. Ponderous Peterbilts and other log- and lumber-laden trucks may be encountered near the mill entrance.

Beyond the mill are the fields and orchard of the Childs Ranch, mile 39.5, right. Located on the property is the historic Englewood School-house, now more than a century old. In the early 1980s the building was disassembled, relocated, and rebuilt by Richard and Robert Childs, brothers who have lived on the ranch since their parents purchased it in 1914. The schoolhouse has been outfitted with period furniture and accessories, and a short distance away are a replica bell-tower and privy, built by the indefatigable Childses to complete the schoolyard setting. Also nearby is a small structure that houses the brothers' collection of early logging equipment and other implements of yesteryear; highlights of the mini-museum are several huge drag saws and an old bootlegger's still that was found near the 101 Freeway west of the ranch. (During the summertime, Park tours visit the Childs Ranch; contact the Visitors Center for details.)

The restored Englewood School

Opposite the ranch is a turnoff, left, that connects with the 101 Freeway 50 yards to the west. The Avenue then enters the hilltop town of Redcrest, population 50, elevation 382, which, because of its height above the Eel, was the only town along the northern Avenue to survive the 1955 and 1964 floods intact. The small business district includes a post office, store and gas station, motor court, cafe, laundromat, and gift shops. Midway through town, the Eternal Tree House, left, offers a free look at the inside of a large redwood stump. A room was hewn out of the stump's interior in the 1910s by Harry McLeod, an expert wood splitter who relied on ax and adze for the job; the walls still bear the marks of his work — mementos of an all-but-lost art.

Redcrest got its start in the days before World War I, when a tie camp was established on the hilltop to serve the railroad that was building its way upriver across the Eel. In summer the ties were hauled by wagons that forded the river near Shively, while in winter the cargo was moved by ferry boat. The tie camp owner, L. L. Chapman, also operated a general store; its present-day successor is housed in the original building. How the town received its name is a subject of some dispute. One version gives the credit to early-day store owner Ruby Rodenberger, who noted the community's location at the top of the hillcrest. By another account, the inspiration was Mabel "Red" McHenry, a motor

Original Redcrest store

court proprietor who sported a shock of brightly colored hair. In any case, the difference between Ruby and Red seems slight.

North of town, the Avenue descends into the canyon of Chadd Creek, passing a lone Redcrest redbud, mile 40.0, right; the route parallels the tree-filled stream gorge, left, until mile 41.1, where Holmes Flat Road exits right. This paved route leads to Holmes, a riverside agricultural area, and Larabee, a locality of ranches and Pacific Lumber Company timberland that lies across the Eel.

Side Trip to Holmes and Larabee

The county road leads northward onto Holmes Flat, soon turning right and crossing through a collection of farm buildings and small fields. This fertile benchland, which the Lolangkoks knew as Kahstes-be, was once covered with enormous redwoods; the Happy Camp shingle bolt company took out some of the trees before the turn of the century, and then, in the early 1900s, the Holmes-Eureka Lumber Company bridged the Eel with a railroad spur and soon levelled what timber remained on the flat. Unlike most logged-over land, the property here was subdivided and converted into small farms.

At 0.8 mile is the faded storefront of the one-time Holmes post office, left. In 1965, Holmes gained a bit of fame, albeit at a price, when *Life* magazine used a photo of the flood-wracked flat to illustrate a story about the region's rampaging rivers. The main road turns right at a junction, 1.4 miles; a left turn at 1.5 miles then leads to the Eel River, which can be crossed (at low water) on a narrow concrete bridge at mile 1.7. On the far bank is remote Larabee, mile 1.9. In the 1940s, the Pacific Lumber Company's ranch here ran a thousand head of cattle and 35 quarter horses on 20,000 acres of cutover land. High winter water on the Eel often isolated the residents of the area; the teacher at Larabee's Georgeson School often had to be rowed across the river to reach her classes.

The road turns right, mile 2.1, running next to the rail line, and at mile 2.5 crosses Larabee Creek—Slahn-ko to the Lolangkoks. To the left, a dark-timbered railroad trestle spans the creek. After passing several small fields and a few houses, the county road ends at the southern part of Larabee, 3.0 miles from the Avenue.

From the Holmes turnoff, the Avenue bends west, crossing Chadd Creek and then running through a series of small redwood groves. A parking area, right at mile 41.4, is for the privately owned Immortal Tree. According to a sign at its base, this often-scarred redwood is nearly a thousand years old, having survived the "logger's ax" in 1908, fire and flood in 1965, and an undated blast of lightning that removed the top 50 feet of its trunk.

The roadway then enters a striking stand of redwoods, reaching the Helen High Daniels Grove at 41.8 miles. Here the lush forest floor is covered with trail plant, redwood sorrel, inside-out flower, trillium, and smooth yellow violet; above them are sword fern, lady fern, five-finger fern, and thimbleberry.

Beyond the grove, bigleaf maples beautify the roadway; to the right is the channel of Chadd Creek, which meets the Eel just above a westward bend in the Avenue, mile 42.2. As the road passes beneath a steep riverside cliff, contortionists can twist their heads far to the right for a view back upriver of Holmes Flat.

Parts of the cliffside, left, are covered with cream bush and clumps of sticky monkey flower. Crumbling from the road cut is a type of sedimentary rock known as the Wildcat Group; this is the only place within the Park where the formation can be easily seen.

sticky monkey flower, orange bush monkey flower
(Mimulus aurantiacus)

One of the wildflowers often found on sunny roadcuts is the sticky monkey flower, which clings to the cliffs in tightly packed orange and green clusters. It blooms in early spring and lasts through most of summer, providing a reliable supply of nectar for hungry hummingbirds. Indians crushed the raw leaves and stems and used them to dress wounds; when young, the same parts of the plant can be eaten in salads. Left in place, this drought-tolerant flower will long greet the passing traveller. [blooms March-August]

Visible across the Eel at mile 42.5 are the tree-fringed fields of Shively Flat. From this vantage point, motorists can determine if the Shively summer bridge is in place; this structure provides the only convenient access to the riverside agricultural area on the far bank. The road to the river crossing is a short distance ahead.

A bridge takes the Avenue over Bear Creek, mile 43.0, while just to the left is the larger span for the 101 Freeway. In 1917, the benchland beyond the creek was the site of a heavily attended rally at which war bonds were sold to the locals by a war-bonnet-bedecked Indian chief.

Bear Creek bond rally, 1917

Beyond the creek, the Avenue runs through a narrow strip of red-woods; left at mile 43.4 is a two-lane paved road that leads westward a short distance to the freeway. A marked dirt road exits right at mile 43.5. It descends to the summer bridge connection with Shively, a fertile fruit and vegetable growing area that was once a wild watering hole for the work crews building the Northwestern Pacific Railroad.

Side Trip to Shively:

After crossing the Eel, the side road rises to the flats on the far bank, turning to one-lane pavement. It cuts its way around wide fields until reaching the old townsite at 1.9 miles. Here the long-closed Shively store slumbers next to the railroad tracks, the numbers on its lone, rusting gas pump frozen at thirty-five cents a gallon. Shively Road then rambles over the forested hillsides north of the Eel, passing the logging roads of Pacific Lumber; the company first cut the area more than 80 years ago. At mile 9.4 the road drops to the bottom of a narrow canyon, where a dirt side route exits left, leading to a railroad crossing that was once Elinor Junction. The train stop was linked to the south bank of the Eel by a ferry, which ran from the farming community of Elinor. Shively Road continues above the river until it meets the 101 Freeway at 12.2 miles, just north of the freeway bridge across the Eel.

On the Avenue beyond the Shively side road is a pullout, left at mile 43.6, for the Percy French Loop Trail. Here a short path winds its way through the fern-filled foliage of three memorial groves [p. 192]. The roadway then curves left, exiting the forest. Immediately there is a turnout, left, for the Drury-Chaney Loop Trail, mile 43.8, which provides access to the Newton B. Drury and Ralph W. Chaney groves; the stands honor two leaders of the Save-the-Redwoods League [p. 185].

The road now makes a wide bend left, turning west at mile 44.0 as it enters Pepperwood, population 50, elevation 200. Across the Eel is the Shively Tunnel, where one of the Northwestern Pacific's worst train wrecks occurred.

*   *   *

THE ONE-EIGHTY-FOUR
CLAIMED THREE TIMES THREE

On the night of August 6, 1937, Beatrice Keesey and her husband were asleep in their tent beside the Eel at Pepperwood; suddenly they were jolted awake by the sound of a terrific crash. The couple immediately rushed down to the river, heading in the direction of the noise. Looking across the water, they could see that a train had wrecked just north of the Shively tunnel. The Keeseys hurried back to Pepperwood and called Scotia, the first town up the line, where they alerted the local constable about the accident. A rescue party was soon on its way by handcar to the scene.

They arrived too late to be of much help. The train's engine, #184, had fallen through a burned trestle; the boiler had burst, engulfing the engine crew in scalding steam. Both engineer Ed Weatherbee and fireman Carl Bartlett were already dead; brakeman George Sill, badly burned, would later die at the Scotia hospital. The unfortunate Sill was supposed to have been riding in the train's caboose, but he had traded places with the regular front brakeman, Delbert Atwell, who had not been feeling well.

It was the second time that the 184 had claimed three members of her crew. Nine years earlier, the engine had been pulling a string of freight cars north through Mendocino County when the first calamity struck. Not far from Ukiah the freight plowed into a passenger train from Eureka. Thirty-two passengers were injured, and the three railway men in the cab of the 184 were killed.

The jinxed engine was repaired after both of its first two wrecks, and was still running in January 1953 when it hit a slide at the Scotia Bluffs and plunged 45 feet down the bank. For the third time in her sad history, the 184's engineer, fireman, and front brakeman all died.

It was to be the last chance the ill-fated locomotive had to harm anyone. The shattered engine that lay beside the river was now only a pile of twisted junk, soon to be scrapped; her mournful whistle would sound no more along the Eel. She had taken nine trainmen to their graves, but the 184's number was finally up.

The Jinx Engine

The flat at Pepperwood had been known as Ahn-sin Ken-tes-be to the Lolangkoks, but by 1873, white settlers were calling the area the "Laurel Bottoms," using another name for the "pepperwood" trees which grew in abundance throughout the area. Ten years later, the fertility of the riverside land had been discovered, and it was reported that

> . . . a number of settlers have claim here, and have made small clearings, on which they raise corn, peas, and potatoes and produce vegetables, bacon, butter, and eggs—the dainties back-woodsmen may be most lavish in enjoying.

Pepperwood served as a stop for the Overland stages that traversed the county wagon road in the early 1900s, with both the Lucas Hotel and Barkdull Ranch housing travellers. A mill was established to process the laurel/pepperwood trees; for a time it was owned and operated by John French, whose son, Percy, later became the first superintendent of the region's state parks. The trees' straight trunks made good masts for sailing ships, while the rest of the wood was used for furniture or to finish the interiors of vessels built during World War I. So many laurels were logged that by 1918 Pepperwood had few of its namesake trees left. There were still redwoods in the area, however, and they soon came to serve a strange purpose: sheltering the money taken in a Fortuna bank robbery.

* * *

FORTUNA BANK BOOTY: SALTED AWAY IN PEPPERWOOD?

When Lawrence "Chief" Mahach and Marion Rube robbed the bank in Fortuna, one May morning in 1922, they made off with a sizeable haul — more than $36,000 in coins and bills. The two Indians were soon speeding towards the Van Duzen River in a stolen getaway car, their faces still covered with the white powder they'd used as a disguise.

They were about to have some problems, though. Unbeknown to the robbers, they'd been seen while still in the bank. The alarm had sounded moments after they'd left, and at that moment, Fortunan Bobby Wise was in hot pursuit, gunning his Studebaker touring car up to the then-breakneck speed of 35 miles an hour. In addition, authorities had phoned the towns along the escape route, and in Carlotta, armed guards waited at the Yager Creek bridge.

The stolen car never reached the roadblock. On the approach to Carlotta the vehicle slowed to a stop by the roadside, its wheel bearings burned out. Mahach and Rube separated and continued on foot. After being seen and shot at by the bridge guards, Mahach was found hiding in the woods. It took longer to track down Rube, but the following week he surrendered to Deputy Sheriff Jack Long at Rube's home in Pepperwood.

Rube and Mahach were convicted of robbery and each sentenced to 25 years in the San Quentin penitentiary. Mahach was killed by a fellow inmate three years later; in 1928, Rube escaped from a prison road camp. He paid a brief visit to his wife Alice before going to hide out in his home country, the Hoopa Indian Reservation in northeastern Humboldt County. Not long afterwards, Rube shot and killed a man who he mistook for a deputy sheriff; a large manhunt ensued, but nothing came of the search. Once again, the elusive Rube seemed to have vanished. Then, on December 18, 1928, Rube and another man held up a bank in Coquille, Oregon. In the chase that followed, Rube was shot dead.

The tale of Marion Rube had ended, but not the story of the missing Fortuna bank money. Some $3,400 in gold and silver was found near where Mahach was captured, but over $32,000 in currency never turned up. A local historian, writing about the robbery in 1988, interviewed Alice Rube, who was then 92 years old. She stated that before *surrendering to Deputy Long, Rube told her that he'd concealed the money in three separate places on the mountain in back of Pepperwood. Alice Rube said she later looked for the loot in the locations her husband had indicated, but at each spot she found only an empty hole.*

Perhaps the money had already been taken; perhaps Alice Rube looked in the wrong places, and the booty was later carried off by a flood. Or perhaps some aging sacks yet lie hidden in the forest behind Pepperwood, still holding — if the rains and rats have been kind — the long-lost legacy of Marion Rube.

* * *

For a time, produce from Pepperwood and nearby Shively rode the rails far and wide. During the 1930s the two towns shipped "luscious Humboldt tomatoes" to Oakland, San Francisco, Los Angeles, and even to Reno, Nevada. The area continued to support dairying, poultry ranching, and farming in the years that followed, but the floods of 1955 and 1964 proved too much for most of the local residents. They had no flood insurance, and although some rebuilt in 1955, most gave up after the second flood. One Pepperwoodian who refused to quit was Angus Russell; after losing his home in 1964, he decided to reclaim some of the land the river had washed away and to build a flood-resistant house in the process. Russell trucked load after load of river silt back onto his property, forming it into a large mound. He built his new dwelling atop this born-again landform, and "the only hill in Pepperwood" has kept him dry ever since.

Holmes store, Pepperwood, 1949

Except for Russell's high-elevation home, present-day Pepperwood consists chiefly of a small collection of trailers, a few vegetable patches, and several summer produce stands. The southern entrance to the dwindling community is marked by a large but faded replica of an ear of corn — once perhaps impressive but now, like the little town, well past its prime.

The Avenue runs west through the fields of Pepperwood until it enters a stand of redwood at mile 44.7. The oft-flooded flatlands north of the road, mile 44.8, are now filled with young redwoods; the fledgling forest is part of a Park rehabilitation project. Across the Avenue is a deeply shaded Park road that winds south through several scenic redwood groves to reach the site of the historic Barkdull Ranch [p. 183].

A bower of bigleaf maples overhangs the Avenue as the route passes a pair of memorial groves, left. Here large stumps and decaying logs mingle with sword fern beneath a roof of mature redwoods. A few California laurel, a.k.a. pepperwood, pose as reminders of their long-lost local prominence. The Georgia Russ Williams Grove, mile 45.2, is fringed with more bigleaf maple, while wild cucumber and thimbleberry edge the roadside.

thimbleberry
(Rubus parviflorus)

Many a shadowy redwood grove is brightened by a thicket of thimbleberry, whose glowing green leaves vibrate in the gentlest breeze. The foliage which so dazzles the darkness once produced color of a different sort, for it was used as a rouge substitute by pioneer women. The soft, fine leaf hairs proved mildly irritating when rubbed against the skin, bringing a pleasing rosiness to the cheeks of the resourceful females. A paler glow comes from the thimbleberry's flower, whose yellow center is surrounded by five delicate, white petals. The centers ripen into rich red berries that are shaped somewhat like thimbles, but which also resemble tiny, mouse-size skullcaps. The tart berries are edible either cooked or raw, and a potent liqueur can also be made from them. The flowers, which measure one to two inches across, are among the largest of any berry plant, raising a question about why this plant was given the Latin name *parviflorus*, which, of all things, means "small flowered."
[blooms April-July]

At the Ethel Bancroff Richardson Grove, 45.7 miles, various sizes of redwoods shelter redwood sorrel, thin false Solomon's seal, Siberian candyflower, poison oak, and sword fern. The Greeenlaw Creek Bridge, mile 46.1, is followed by more bigleaf maples and additional redwoods. Left at mile 46.3 is an Avenue of the Giants Auto Tour pamphlet box for southbound motorists.

An unmarked paved road exits to the right at 46.4 miles. A little-used segment of the old highway, it soon passes the turnoff for Elinor Road, right, which leads to the elegiac benchlands of Elinor, a nearly forgotten farm village that failed to withstand the 1955 flood. The highway remnant continues to a turnaround at mile 0.2, whence the Old 101 Trail starts [p. 191].

ELINOR

When three-year-old Alice Barlow and her family arrived at Elinor in 1909, the little riverside ranching community was already a quiet place, and over the years, it grew more so. First the ferry stopped running, so there was no longer a way to reach the train station at Elinor Junction, across the Eel; later the school closed, which meant that the town's few children had to be bussed all the way to Scotia. By the 1950s, Elinor

Elinor School, 1949

was nothing more than a string of five ranches that reposed along a short, dead-end road. Ranch life meant "early to bed, early to rise," so it was highly unusual when, on the night of December 21, 1955, most of Elinor's residents huddled around their televisions and radios until far into the night.

The ranchfolk were listening to the news bulletins. There had been flooding earlier in the month, and now a huge new storm had moved in, dropping rain by the bucket full. About midnight the power went out; leaving the community with no way to learn that upriver as much as six inches of rain had fallen during the day. By now, though, people could step outside and get their own weather report: water from the rising Eel was beginning to cover Elinor Road.

At their ranch next to the old school, Alice Barlow Mortenson and her husband Jim took precautions. Jim tied a boat to the back porch in case they were forced to evacuate; for some reason, he also removed his carpentry tools from the barn and brought them into the house.

The river continued to rise, and the Mortensons finally decided it was time to leave. When they went to get their boat, however, they found that the floodwater had pinned the back door shut; there was no way for them to get out.

By this time, water was pouring into the house. The Mortensons began retreating to the attic, but Lucy Barlow, Alice's elderly mother, couldn't negotiate the steep stairs. Fortunately, Jim thought of his tools. He quickly sawed through the living room ceiling, and, after perching Mrs. Barlow on a dresser, the Mortensons lifted her into the attic. A few moments later, the swirling floodwaters swept the dresser away.

In the attic Mortenson again put his tools to work, cutting an opening that provided an escape hatch to the roof. Not long after daylight, two neighbors came by in a boat and took the family to safety.

When they returned after the flood, the Mortensons found that their ranch, as well as almost everything else in Elinor, had been wiped out. The family car was still there, only now it rested on top of a magnolia tree, supported by a tangle of irrigation pipe that had wedged beneath it. In other trees, ghastly apparitions greeted the returnees — drowned cattle were hanging far up in the limbs.

The destruction was too much for Elinor's other residents, who all moved elsewhere. The Mortensons, however, decided to stay. They rented the Dixon house, the only place left standing, and gradually rebuilt their ranching operation. A year and a half later they moved near Fortuna, but the couple continued to work the Elinor property, camping out there in the summers. The Mortensons kept the ranch until the late

1970s, when the Save-the-Redwoods League bought it for inclusion in Humboldt Redwoods State Park.

By then, Alice Mortenson had been in Elinor for nearly 70 years. It had proven to be a pleasantly uneventful experience, except for that one December evening — when she'd had a lifetime of excitement.

*   *   *

From its intersection with the old highway, the Avenue curves left, and at mile 46.5 (actually 31.5 miles from its southern starting point) it ends at an interchange with the 101 Freeway. Ahead lies the Pacific Lumber Company mill at Scotia, and beyond it, the small cities of Fortuna, Eureka, and Arcata. Farther north will be more groves of great redwoods, but none will surpass those just seen along the Avenue of the Giants . . . or in the rest of Humboldt Redwoods State Park.

Note to southbound motorists
regarding access to the Avenue:

Just south of Stafford, an offramp at freeway milepost 47.0 leads to a vista point and an Avenue of the Giants map. The overlook here provides views of the Eel and the Elinor area. An onramp then returns traffic to the freeway just west of the Jordan Creek bridge. Immediately past the bridge, at milepost 46.0, is an exit marked "Avenue of the Giants — Pepperwood"; a left turn at the bottom of this offramp begins the southbound Avenue.

TRAILS OF THE NORTHERN AVENUE

[for map showing trails, see p. 165]

BARKDULL RANCH ROAD

Summary: A redwood-shaded ramble to a historic ranch site, this charming course passes through magnificent forestland before entering a half-hidden woodland prairie.

Distance: 1.6 miles, round trip

Elevation change: negligible

Location: The road exits from the left side of the Avenue at mile 44.8, just west of Pepperwood; the route ends north of the 101 Freeway at the old Barkdull Ranch.

Description: Barkdull Ranch Road leads past a metal Park gate into a grove of old-growth redwood; in winter, bigleaf maples litter the way with their leaves. Redwood sorrel, thimbleberry, and log-lounging licorice ferns fill much of the lower forest. The route rises a few feet to an elevated benchland and then bends left, mile 0.1, passing a marker for the Helen Canfield and Marian Andrews Grove; the flat at Pepperwood is visible intermittently through the trees to the left.

The redwoods on the benchland are striking; massive trunks rise cleanly up to the forest canopy, their bark richly bright even among the shadows. Below, several small cascaras struggle for survival; although common on the coast, the tree is seldom found within Humboldt Redwoods.

Barkdull Ranch Road is the only dirt roadway in the Park's lowland redwood forests; narrow and leaf covered, its appearance recalls the early photos of rustic Humboldt routes, where dark, high-topped autos and their occupants pose ponderously between the thick trunks of huge trees.

The route passes a marker for the Newton B. Drury Grove, mile 0.4, followed by an intersection with the Drury-Chaney Loop Trail. At mile 0.5 of the road is a grove sign for the trail's other namesake, Ralph Works Chaney. Fairybells form a conspicuous roadside attraction.

A clearing suddenly opens at mile 0.6. The road straightens and runs south through the prairie beside a row of willows; the grassland forms a large, redwood-fringed rectangle, dotted with boggy patches and small trees. This is the site of the old Barkdull Ranch, first established by Joseph Barkdull a century ago when he fled the foggy Eel River delta for a healthier inland clime; for a decade the ranch maintained a way station called the Travellers Inn. Barkdull eventually relocated to Rio Dell, but the ranch remained in the family until it was sold to the Park. Even then, Madeleine Barkdull Holmes retained lifetime title to the property; when she died in 1991, Humboldt Redwoods assumed control, just a year shy of the ranch's hundredth anniversary.

Cascara sagrada
(Rhamnus purshiana)

First used by the Indians as both a rheumatism remedy and as a laxative, the bark of this large shrub was so valued as a medicine by the California mission padres that they named it *cascara sagrada* — "the sacred bark." In more recent times, it became the premier commercial cathartic and was heavily exported. Since the plant will die if it loses its bark, overharvesting nearly exterminated the cascara before a decline in the laxative market granted it a reprieve. Long ago, the shrub with the sacred bark was also blessed with several secular names: in Monterey County it was called "yellow boy" or "yellow root," while in Sonoma County it was known as "pigeon berry," because of that bird's consumption of its fruit. For a while cascara was also called "California coffee" — this during the brief time that its seeds were marketed as a coffee substitute. The scheme quickly failed when it was discovered that although the seeds indeed resembled coffee beans in appearance, they possessed no other coffeelike qualities, lacking even a similar smell when roasted.

The northern variety of cascara that grows in the Park, Rhamnus purshiana, is somewhat larger than its southern counterpart. In Oregon, the purshiana species has been given several colorful but sometimes mystifying nicknames, including "chittemwood," "bitter bark," "bear wood," "bee plant," and the wonderfully obscure "wahoo."

Nestled among the roadside willows are several large piles of debris and sticks — woodrat nests. One resourceful rodent has even strengthened his construction with a round of chicken wire, creating a sort of rat recycling project.

Farther south, the road bends right as blackberry vines rampage across the vacant ranch site; nearby a plot of recently planted redwood seedlings testifes to a Park rehabilitation effort. The road then approaches the 101 Freeway, ending at mile 0.8 next to several large stumps. A rutted track heads west a short distance to reach the freeway, but most hikers will now want to retrace their steps to the Avenue. In doing so, they'll encounter a stunning spectacle on their return along woodrat row: a wall of towering redwoods looms before them, visible from trunk bottom to tree top. Their foliage glows golden green in the afternoon sun, in perfect contrast to their rosy trunks . . . a resplendent reward for those who seek out this little-known but lovely route.

DREXLER GROVE TRAIL

Summary: This plant-packed path loops across a hilltop and crosses a lovely small stream.

Distance: 0.5 mile, one way

Elevation Change: 100-foot gain and loss

Location: The southern end meets the Avenue near mile 22.9; the northern end leaves a parking area on the west side of the Avenue, mile 23.0, near the Drexler Grove.

Description: A pair of trail spurs lead up the hillside from opposite ends of the paved parking area. Both pathlets soon crest a small knoll; here they connect with a loop trail that circles through a partially open stand of redwoods and tanoaks. Baneberry makes an infrequent Park appearance along the way. The loop branches meet at the southeast corner of the knoll, mile 0.3, and the trail then descends on switchbacks into a small, deeply shaded stream canyon; milkmaids, western bleeding heart, trillium, and vanilla leaf beautify the banks. The route crosses the placid, pool-filled creek on a downed redwood as a variety of ferns and some thimbleberry cluster about. After turning left, the path follows the canyon to the Avenue, ending at mile 0.5.

DRURY-CHANEY LOOP TRAIL

Summary: A shaded passage through redwood, lady fern, redwood sorrel, elderberry, and California laurel, the trail honors two leaders of the Save-the-Redwoods League.

Distance: 2.3 miles, round trip

Elevation Change: negligible

Location: The trailhead is on the west side of the Avenue at mile 43.8, near the eastern end of Pepperwood.

Description: Starting at a pullout beside the Avenue, the route crosses a lawnlike patch of grass before being engulfed by the grove. Large redwoods shelter a lush lower cover of vegetation; wild cucmber intertwines with big bushes of coast red elderberry, and together they overhang the path as it rises from a small gully.

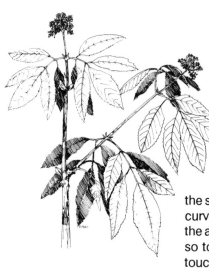

coast red elderberry
(Sambucus callicarpa)
[blooms March-June]

The trail then winds its way westward through masses of redwood sorrel and lady fern; a huge field of thin false Solomon's seal appears at mile 0.1. The forest understory now also displays the strange, arching forms of many California laurels – the "pepperwood" for which the nearby town was named. Suppressed by the surrounding redwoods, the laurels curve gracefully but weakly through the air, their spindly trunks sometimes so top heavy that they bend back to touch the ground. The route comes to a spur trail, left at mile 0.3, that leads a few feet to a log which has a seat carved out of it. A plaque set into the back of the seat announces:

RALPH WORKS CHANEY MEMORIAL GROVE
PRESIDENT, SAVE-THE-REDWOODS LEAGUE 1961-1971
FOUND METASEQUOIA DAWN REDWOOD IN CHINA 1948

. . . and thereby hangs a tale.

*   *   *

THE DAWNING OF THE DAWN REDWOOD

One day in 1944, near the remote Chinese village of Mo-Tao-Chi, forester T. Wang noticed a curious tree growing on top of a small temple. The tree was unlike any Wang had seen before; he therefore collected some samples and took them to the university in Nanking for identification. The resident expert shook his head in bafflement, so Dr. H. H. Hu of the Fan Memorial Institute in Beijing was consulted.

Since the tree appeared to have no living counterparts, Dr. Hu decided to compare Wang's samples with fossil impressions from ancient species. In time, Hu found an exact match – with a tree thought to have last been alive 20 million years ago! It was a type of sequoia, and it soon came to be called the "dawn redwood."

Word of the amazing find spread, and in 1948, Dr. Ralph Chaney, a paleontologist at the University of California at Berkeley, flew to China to investigate. He was accompanied by Milton Silverman, science

Temple dawn redwood, Mo-Tao-Chi

editor for the <u>San Francisco Chronicle</u>; their trek to the site of the dawn redwood proved to be nearly as exciting as the tree's discovery.

The pair landed in Chongquing, boated down the Yangtze River, and then continued on foot over three mountain ranges. Picking up an escort of armed soldiers to protect them from roving bandits, Chaney and Silverman finally reached Mo-tao-chi. After Chaney examined Wang's tree, the party continued on to the even more remote Valley of the Tiger. Here they found dozens of dawn redwoods, along with ancient species of oak, sassafras, birch, sweet gum, laurel, and katsura. "We have come a hundred miles by trail," Chaney declared, "and a hundred million years in history."

The return trip was charted to avoid the local bandits' stronghold. The route "began as a muddy, rocky path," reported Silverman. "[It] then followed an old streambed, and finally disintegrated completely into a slimy smear that wound around the hills." Despite the detour, the bandits appeared the next day, but the escort quickly drove them off; one robber was killed and two others wounded. The journey then continued peacefully until Silverman and Chaney arrived in Hawaii and tried to clear customs. Chaney had brought some dawn redwood seedlings back with him, and the confused officials were unable to find any regulations governing such items; it seemed the cargo would be confiscated. The day was saved when it was decided that the seedlings were not plants but antiques.

Chaney cultivated his "antiques" on the Berkeley campus, and soon seedlings were being sent far and wide; a dawn redwood was proudly displayed outside the Dyerville headquarters of Humboldt Redwoods State Park. Other transplanted trees survived the winters of Alaska and British Columbia, while one—perhaps the hardiest of the lot—was photographed flourishing in Cleveland, Ohio. The dawn redwood had indeed come a long way from the Valley of the Tiger.

*   ⋆   ⋆   ⋆*

The route crosses Barkdull Ranch Road at 0.6 mile; this bucolic byway connects the Avenue with an old ranch site. The trail continues west, and shortly beyond mile 0.7 it comes to the branches of a loop; a sign directs hikers to the left. The path in this direction encounters a patch of false lily-of-the-valley and then crosses a pair of small bridges as it zigzags west and north.

At 1.2 miles the route bends right and begins its return, soon coming to a short spur, left, that ends at another plaque-adorned log, this one for the Helen Stanford Canfield and Marian Farr Andrews Groves. After passing a big, barkless snag, the path completes its loop at mile 1.7; the remainder of the route retraces the first portion of the trail, arriving back at the Avenue at mile 2.3.

THE FIVE ALLENS TRAIL

Summary: Short but exerting, this climb leads to a haunting grove of hillside redwoods.

Distance: 2.6 miles, round trip

Elevation Change: 1,000-foot gain and loss

Location: The trailhead is on the west side of the Avenue, mile 21.1, at a pullout for the Maria McKeen Allen Grove.

Description: Leaving the Avenue, the trail ascends steeply through mixed forest before crossing the 101 Freeway through an underpass; the route then resumes rising, passing many milkmaids, until it reaches a bridge that spans a small, sparkling waterfall, 0.2 mile. Clustered on the nearby banks are thimbleberry, five-finger fern, lady fern, seep-spring monkey flower, vanilla leaf, and bedstraw.

The trail then alternates between level traverses and steep, zigzagging climbs, the way frequently brightened by trillium and clintonia. At mile 1.0 the route winds between a pair of large downed redwoods; hundreds of licorice ferns cover the top of the second log. A piece of plank spans a small, clear stream, 1.1 miles, where both deer fern and lady fern border the banks. Beyond the brook, the trail forks at a striking, sword-fern-covered glade.

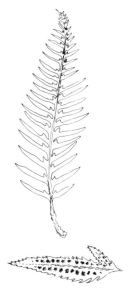

western sword fern
(Polystichum munitum)

This sturdy fern derives its name from the small perpendicular projection on each of its frond segments that resembles a sword hilt; the segments, or pinnae, are appropriately hard, sharp, and bladelike. Northwest Indians ate the fern's rhizomes and also boiled them to make a pain-relieving tea. One tribe tied the fronds together with maple bark to serve as mattresses. Florists frequently use the fronds in funeral sprays.

From the junction, the route to the right travels 50 yards to a marker that opaquely commemorates "The Five Allens." Left leads around the hillside past the eerily blotched leaves of numerous fetid adder's tongues; the trail subsequently ends at a redwood stump, mile 1.3. A plaque here states: "In memory of Elisabeth Achelis 1880-1973." Surrounding the marker, a grove of stately redwoods raise their reddish brown trunks from the steep hillslope, living pillars in a temple of green.

HIGH ROCK-EEL RIVER TRAIL

Summary: The only Park trail that offers access to the main Eel River, this rambling route passes large collections of both fat and thin false Solomon's seal on its way south to a scenic overlook atop High Rock.

Distance: 1.5 miles, one way, including the spur to High Rock

Elevation Change: 100-foot gain and loss

Location: To reach the trail's north end, turn right at mile 22.8 of the Avenue onto an unmarked, paved side road; proceed a hundred yards to a small parking area, from where the route departs south. Two paths start from the southern end: an undesignated path on the right side of the Avenue at mile 21.7, and a marked entrance at the Arbor Day Grove, mile 21.9. There is also a connection with the middle of the trail at mile 22.3 of the Avenue, just at the crest of the High Rock grade.

Description: The northern trailhead is in a stand of large redwoods that comprise the Andy Bowman Grove. The route immediately passes a variety of forest-floor flora dominated by thin false Solomon's seal.

thin false Solomon's seal
(Smilacina stellata var. sessifolia)
[blooms March-May]

At mile 0.1 the trail divides, passing around several wide-spreading patches of cestrum, an exotic shrub from the tropics that inexplicably has found a home here; the route reconnects at mile 0.2, having encircled the Madison Lewis/Elizabeth Lewis Grove. Just ahead, large patches of western bleeding heart and vanilla leaf embellish the adjacent Fanny Haas and Starr groves.

The route winds downhill to cross a small creek; a pathside bench then marks the Wentworth Grove. Near a viewpoint of the Eel River, mile 0.3, are a pair of striking spring wildflowers: trillium and calypso orchid. The trail then climbs the hillslope to arrive at a junction, mile 0.4. Left is a spur that soon reaches a beach to the north of High Rock; the main route turns right and climbs steeply, passing a side trail, right, that leads to a parking area at the Avenue. The main path turns left to ascend the side of High Rock.

Atop the ridge saddle just west of High Rock is a junction, mile 0.5. A left turn climbs past fat false Solomon's seal to the top of the High Rock ridge, whence the path continues east to a stunning view of the Eel. On the cliff below the overlook are toyon, canyon live oak, sticky monkey flower, soap plant, and Indian warrior; milkwort grows on the ridgetop beside the trail.

A right turn at the junction goes but a few feet to another fork; from here the way right immediately exits onto the Avenue, while the main trail bears left and drops down the south side of the ridge. Near the bottom of the slope, a poor side trail departs right and climbs steeply to the Avenue; the main route turns left and arrives at another fork, mile 0.7. Left here leads to a small beach beneath the southern base of High Rock. The through trail goes right, soon crossing fern-lined Matthews Creek on a redwood slab bridge, and then passing over an unnamed stream, mile 0.8, on a construction of old logs. The trail climbs out of the creek gorge to regain the benchland, encountering some pathside Siberian candyflower; at mile 0.9 it crosses through a covering of western bleeding heart and vanilla leaf. Overhead are full-size redwoods.

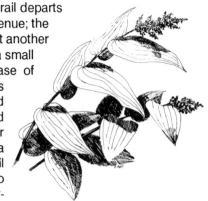

fat false Solomon's seal
*(Smilacina racemosa
var. amplexicaulis)*
[blooms March-May]

Soon the main trail turns left; a spur then branches right, mile 1.1, and heads toward the parking area at the Arbor Day Grove. Along the main route, a thicket of thin false Solomon's seal recalls a similar setting at the trail's start. At 1.3 miles the pathway crosses through a large redwood log and meets the Avenue.

OLD 101 TRAIL

Summary: This redwood-lined passage follows a ghostly stretch of abandoned highway at the northern end of the Avenue.

Distance: 0.5 mile, round trip

Elevation Change: negligible

Location: At mile 46.4 of the Avenue, an unmarked, paved road branches right; the trailhead is at a turnaround 0.2 mile along this route.

Summary: A path leads around a large redwood log that blocks further vehicle travel along the roadway. After following the old roadbed for 50 yards, the trail jogs past another fallen tree and then returns to the aged pavement of the erstwhile Redwood Highway; occasionally a fragment of faded white line appears through the cover of forest litter. At the roadside, well-kept signs for the memorial groves add an eerie contemporaneity to the decaying surroundings.

The road crosses Jordan Creek on the Robert H. Madsen Memorial Bridge, mile 0.2; the moss-covered concrete bears the date "1938" on its railings. Workers, including college student Madsen, were paid sixty cents an hour while building the bridge, seventy-seven cents when pouring concrete. The wages were apparently too high; although the contractors charged $21,000 for the job, they made only a $35 profit.

Red alder and bigleaf maple line the rocky creekbed. At the far end of the bridge a trail exits left, passing a log bench and then looping a short distance through redwoods before regaining the road at the Roberta Oliver Greenlee Grove. The roadbed ends in another 50 yards; a path continues to the base of a hillside, mile 0.3; the 101 Freeway passes along the slope above. The return trip provides panoramic views of the tall roadside redwoods as thimbleberry and other eager plants encroach on the remains of the nearly forgotten highway.

PERCY FRENCH LOOP TRAIL

Summary: Offering three groves in one swoop, this brief double loop wanders through lush corridors of lady fern, also passing the memorable Girdled Tree and encountering a Park rarity—leather fern.

Distance: 0.7 mile, round trip

Elevation Change: negligible

Location: The loop starts from the west side of the Avenue, mile 43.6.

Description: A sign by the roadside pullout proclaims:

ACCESS TRAIL TO THOMAS A. GREIG
ENOCH PERCY FRENCH   WINIFRED BROWN BELL.

Two markers helpfully point the way across an open space to the start of the trail, which departs southwest into a near jungle of forest foliage;

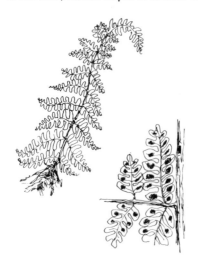

poison oak, unless recently trimmed, predominates. The route moves across a gently rolling benchland, soon passing through thick masses of lady ferns.

lady fern
*(Athyrium filix-femina
var. sitchense)*

The lady fern has large, light green fronds with deeply fringed, lacy pinnae. Like most ferns, it favors very moist areas, but unlike many of its kin, the lady fern dies back annually; each year it sends out tightly curled new fronds that unroll gradually. Medieval herbalists used lady fern roots and leaves to treat a diverse quintet of ailments: jaundice, gallstones, sores, hiccups, and worms.

Girdled Tree

At the Enoch Percy French Grove, mile 0.1, the pathside scenery seems to have sprung from a storybook – a Lilliputian landscape of tiny hills and dales, its cover a forest of redwood sorrel. Of a different scale is the huge Girdled Tree, 0.2 mile, a wide-trunked redwood that is missing much of its lower bark. An interpretive sign explains that the tree was partially peeled in 1901 by J. H. French and his sons, one of whom – Percy – later became the Park District's first superintendent. The tree was on the property of the Pacific Lumber Company, which sent the bark to San Francisco to be part of a convention display.

leather fern
(Polypodium scouleri)

A memorial bench just beyond the tree bears a dedication to Percy and Viola French; the trail forks at the French Bench, with the left branch leading past more lady fern to a pair of picnic tables and the short Winifred Brown Bell Grove loop at mile 0.4. The route skirts the southern edge of the grove, beyond which a gloomy thicket of second-growth redwood shows the result of clear-cut logging. From the Bell Grove loop, the trail retraces its route to the French Grove; a left turn at the benchside junction, 0.5 mile, continues the initial loop.

The trail winds past redwood sorrel and red elderberry, cuts through more lady fern, and encounters some dangerously proximate stinging nettle. At mile 0.6 the path passes through an opening in a large log; the fallen redwood sports a pair of leather ferns — pretty but infrequent inhabitants of the Park. Just ahead is the junction with the loop's start; the way left returns to the Avenue, mile 0.7.

PLAQUE LOOP TRAIL

Summary: Hairy honeysuckle highlights this hillside forest circuit.

Distance: 0.2 mile, round trip

Elevation Change: negligible

Location: The trail leaves the right side of the Avenue at mile 23.8.

Description: After dropping over the roadbank, the route soon levels as it moves through open mixed forest. Yerba buena mingles with more commonly seen flowers; salal provides a thick groundcover. In 100 yards the trail forks, forming a short loop that winds past several large stumps. At

hairy honeysuckle
(Lonicera hispidula)
[blooms May-June]

the loop's apex is a large log into which is set a plaque for the Geraldyn and McIntyre Faries Grove; a charming cascade of hairy honeysuckle falls from the top of the log to picturesquely frame the plaque.

THE BULL CREEK BACKCOUNTRY: A CANYON FOR THE CURIOUS

Over half the acreage of Humboldt Redwoods State Park lies within the Bull Creek watershed, a collection of remote ridges and rocky ravines that curves in a wide, 10-mile-long arc around the western and northern sides of Grasshopper Peak, the highest point in the Park. A region once ravaged by logging, fires, and floods, it also contains one of the most magnificent forests found anywhere on Earth.

Motorists enter this large and varied landscape by a single route, Mattole Road, which starts from the site of old Dyerville at mile 20.8 of the Avenue. The road runs briefly above the South Fork Eel and then enters the canyon of Bull Creek, dodging the redwoods of the Rockefeller Forest as a single-lane route before widening to two lanes. After passing though the old Bull Creek townsite, Mattole Road leaves the valley floor and climbs, via a series of hairpin curves (called "elbows" by the old-timers), to the Park's western boundary at Panther Gap; from there the route descends to the Mattole River at Honeydew.

An elaborate network of trails and dirt roads covers the Bull Creek drainage, linking together an array of camping areas, scenic attractions, and historic sites. More than a score of hiking, biking, and horseback riding routes are reached from Mattole Road; they can be grouped conveniently into four units within the watershed.

1. Lower Bull Creek Canyon:

Beginning at the Rockefeller Forest and continuing to the Bull Creek cemetery, a half dozen low-elevation routes run through the lower canyon; they usually parallel the creek and are often within sight or sound of it. The short Rockefeller Loop provides a stunning introduction to the sights of the region, while the Bull Creek Flats and Big Trees-Albee Creek loops offer extended jaunts among giant redwoods in the depths of the forest; the Horse Trail runs a wider-ranging course that includes Rockefeller tall trees, mill sites, and ranch orchards. Finally, a pair of dirt roads lead to the Park's two walk-in environmental camps, which are both situated in small stands of redwoods. The routes of lower Bull Creek are readily accessible, generally easy to hike, and filled with some of the Park's most spectacular scenery — they provide a perfect prelude to the canyon's more remote, upper countryside.

2. The Northwest Ridges:

North and west of the lower canyon, Peavine Ridge and the Big Hill-Fox Camp ridgeline offer elevated destinations that can be reached by a quintet of dirt routes. Varied vegetation, steeply sloping prairies, and challenging climbs mark the courses; an easier approach to the area begins at the southern end of Fox Camp Road. History seekers can survey sites along the Indian Orchard Trail, the Addie Johnson Grave Trail, Look Prairie Road, and Fox Camp Road. Big Hill, on Fox Camp Road, provides one of the best panoramas in the Park, while remote Peavine Road reveals a rare ridgetop old-growth forest. Pole Line and Thornton roads climb through vast, sunny prairies; after their own climbs, mountain bikers will love the death-defying descents from Peavine. The ridge region is hard to reach, but well worth the effort.

3. Grasshopper Peak/Squaw Creek:

The center of the Bull Creek backcountry is the elevated area around Grasshopper Peak and Squaw Creek Ridge. The peak rises more than 3,000 feet above the valley floor and features an extensive, exhilarating view from its summit. On the mountain's deeply shaded and steeply inclined north face, the Johnson Camp Trail reaches an old tie-cutting operation that now serves as a backpackers' camp, while Grasshopper Road rises up a heroically hard climb to the lookout atop the peak. Grieg Road traverses the easier and sunnier southern approach, running along the top of the Canoe Creek drainage before arriving at Grasshopper Trail Camp. To the west, Squaw Creek Ridge Road travels through secluded forestland, meeting the steep Baxter-Squaw Creek Cutoff Trail before arriving at wooded Whiskey Flat Trail Camp; farther south, the route meets Hanson Ridge Road, which leads to the Hanson Ridge trail and group camps. Connecting the Squaw Creek Ridge-Hanson Ridge region with the Grasshopper-Grieg area is Preacher Gulch Road, which passes three beautiful prairies on its ascent from upper Bull Creek. Backpackers and bikers will find plenty to accommodate their interests in this heart of the Humboldt Redwoods hinterlands.

4. Upper Bull Creek Canyon:

A landscape of rugged stream canyons, once nearly ruined by logging but now recovering, the upper Bull Creek drainage offers open country, relics from an old ranch site, and some of the most remote roadways in Humboldt Redwoods. Bull Creek Road follows its namesake to the upper end of the canyon, passing the Bull Creek Trail Camp, ceanothus-scented hillslopes, and young stands of mixed forest. Kemp Road and Tanbark Road both start at crossings of Bull Creek and then rise rapidly to meet Perimeter Road, a lengthy but nearly level route that runs around the southern rim of the drainage. In the middle of the upper canyon, Gould Road and South Prairie Road climb the grassy hillsides of the old Hazelton-Bull Creek Ranch; a pair of weathered barns repine for the ranch's long-vanished livestock. This little-visited part of the Park offers enough history and hill climbing to attract the adventuresome.

The four quarters of the Bull Creek backcountry beckon, luring the leisurely away from the Avenue. Both highway and high country are vital parts of the Park, and no experience of Humboldt Redwoods is complete without sampling both of them.

Upper Gould Barn,
Hazelton-Bull Creek Ranch

MATTOLE ROAD:
THE ONLY WAY TO GO

Mattole Road has long been the major thoroughfare between the mouth of the South Fork Eel and the Mattole River country, far distant to the west. Seventy years ago, the region's ranchers used the road to drive their hogs, sheep, and cattle to the train station at South Fork; tanbark was packed out along the same route. Log trucks later lurched down the roadway in great clouds of dust, bound for mills beyond the locality. Today, the road still serves area residents, but many of its travellers are now Park visitors, lured by Bull Creek's steep-sloped, sunny uplands or the towering spires of the Rockefeller Forest.

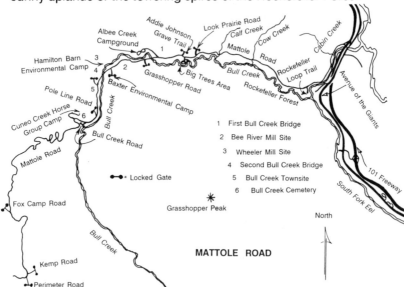

1 First Bull Creek Bridge
2 Bee River Mill Site
3 Wheeler Mill Site
4 Second Bull Creek Bridge
5 Bull Creek Townsite
6 Bull Creek Cemetery

●—● = Locked Gate

✳ Grasshopper Peak

North

MATTOLE ROAD

One-lane, paved Mattole Road exits, left, from mile 20.8 of the Avenue at a junction just north of the South Fork Eel bridge. After crossing under the 101 Freeway, the route runs above the river as it hugs the mostly open cliffside, passing Indian warrior at 0.2 mile. The road enters upon a redwood-covered terrace, mile 0.3, and then crosses the fern-filled gorge of Cabin Creek, mile 0.7. Open hillslopes return at mile 1.2; on the bank, right, is a changing display of brightly colored flowers: springtime Indian pink followed in summer by redwood penstemon.

redwood penstemon
(Penstemon corymbosus)

Look for redwood penstemon on rocky outcroppings and open cliffs, where its dark green leaves and tomato-red flowers contrast brightly with the typical gray-brown bankside background. The flower's bright coloring and tubular shape make this penstemon especially attractive to hummingbirds; in addition, its late bloom offers the busy birds a final local nectar source before they migrate elsewhere in search of food. [blooms July-October]

Presently the route enters the magnificent Rockefeller Forest, mile 1.4, a collection of gigantic redwoods that inhabit the fabled Bull Creek Flats. At the entrance to the forest, a steep but paved side road, left, leads downhill 0.1 mile to a parking area for the Rockefeller Loop Trail [p. 223]; directly east is the Federation Grove, reached by a summer bridge across the South Fork Eel.

Mattole Road then leaves the river valley and turns up the canyon of Bull Creek; enormous redwoods cover the flats, left. The creek appears downhill to the left at mile 1.7, marked by a striking redbud at the road edge; this spindly but sturdy specimen rises some 25 feet skyward, its top annually crowned with a regal bloom more purple than it is red.

western redbud
(Cercis occidentalis)

Many a springtime passer-by will pause before the purple-pink blossoms of a roadside redbud; the dazzling flowers glow in perfect counterpoint to the new-green foliage of the surrounding plants. The shrub's next phase is more subdued, as it produces a covering of round, notched, softly colored leaves. The fruit, which matures in late summer, consists of dense clusters of rhubarb-colored, pealike pods. Various Indian tribes, including the Hupa and Yuki, used redbud as a material for making baskets. Indians also utilized the redbud's astringent bark in a tonic to treat diarrhea and dysentery, while its wood was made into bows.

The redbud is sometimes called "Judas tree," a reference to an allied species from Palestine; when Judas Iscariot hanged himself from one of the trees, its white blossoms reputedly blushed pink from shame. Perhaps because of this stigma, medieval Europeans thought that witches would rendezvous next to redbuds; the shrubs were thus considered dangerous to approach at night. [blooms March-April]

Black huckleberry, thimbleberry, vanilla leaf, and California hazel beautify the route as it continues west through the forest. The lichen-choked limbs of several Pacific yews droop near the roadside just before the crossing at Cow Creek, mile 2.8. This year-round stream was once called Corduroy Creek, perhaps in reference to the local roadbeds that were "corduroyed" with timbers to make them passable in wet weather.

A tusklike root projects from the roadbank at mile 3.2; the protuberance is decorated by a drooping tendril of honeysuckle. Calf Creek is soon announced by a thick patch of roadside vanilla leaf, mile 3.5. This stream was earlier called Coon Creek, but as ranching spread through the valley, calves became more common than coons, and the name of the creek has been changed accordingly.

Cow Creek, upstream
from Mattole Road

The grassy, slumping hummocks of Luke Prairie run down to the road, mile 4.0, while Bull Creek rushes by on the left. Look Prairie Road [p. 238] and the Horse Trail [p. 219] exit right, mile 4.2, at a small parking area. Mattole Road then immediately crosses Harper Creek, known in bygone days as Jenny Johnson Creek after Roxanne "Jenny" Johnson, the second wife of Bull Creek pioneer Tosaldo Johnson. Roxanne-Jenny, also called "Huckleberry Jane," was somewhat of a local legend, being known to walk the hillsides with a revolver strapped to her leg, so she probably deserved having three names.

Creek-less coon

* * *

WHEN GNOMES ROAMED THE ROCKEFELLER FOREST

Long before the Ewoks were rollicking around the redwoods in Return of the Jedi, *the lives of other forest-dwelling creatures were being depicted in films. Harry Pritchard, a California Division of Forestry supervisor, discovered this one day while on his way to a fire in upper Bull Creek.*

In the middle of the Rockefeller Forest, a group of distraught men blocked the narrow roadway, waving frantically for Pritchard to stop. Believing himself to be in the midst of another emergency, Pritchard halted his vehicle and asked for an explanation. One of the clamoring contingent breathlessly explained that they were part of a movie crew from Disney Studios and were filming a fun-filled frolic called The Gnome-Mobile; *a sequence was in progress just ahead. If Pritchard would only wait until they were finished with this particular scene . . .*

The entreaty was drowned out by the sound of Pritchard's truck, siren blaring and lights flashing, as it roared away up the road. Nothing, it seems, can stop a CDF fire engine for long — not even gnome-mobiles.

* * *

Left at mile 4.4 is the turnoff to the Big Trees Area. A paved side road leads 0.1 mile to a parking lot, a pair of creekside picnic tables, and portable restrooms. The Bull Creek Flats Loop Trail [p. 212] and the Big Trees-Albee Creek Loop Trail [p. 208] meet here; the spot is also the closest access point to the Johnson Camp Trail [p. 257]. Three world-class redwoods reside in the neighborhood: the Giant Tree, which has replaced the downed Dyerville Giant as the Champion Redwood, stands to the south across a bridge over Bull Creek, as does the strikingly shaped Flatiron Tree; the misnamed but nonetheless very large Tallest Tree is situated a short distance west of the parking area.

Unmarked Johnson Prairie Road exits right at mile 4.5. This dirt route travels 200 feet to a junction with the Horse Trail, where an informal parking area marks the start of the Addie Johnson Grave Trail [p. 225].

After passing through a sublime stand of large, beautifully proportioned redwoods, Mattole Road comes to the Albee Creek Campground turnoff, right at mile 5.0. This one-lane, paved route leads 0.3 mile to the canyon's main camping facility, which occupies a lovely, open setting: to the east, Albee Creek runs along the edge of the Rockefeller Forest, while Bull Creek rushes by to the south, just below a small prairie; most of the campsites nestle northward, next to the base of a forested hillside. An old fruit orchard covers part of the prairie; it once belonged to John Albee, who for a time carried the mail into the valley. The campground is only open in summer; its 34 sites will each hold trailers up to 21 feet long and motorhomes no longer than 33 feet. The facilities include piped drinking water and restrooms with showers, but there are no laundry tubs; a solar shower is situated on the prairie. The Horse Trail runs through the campground [p. 219], while the Big Trees-Albee

Drinking fountain,
Albee Creek Campground

Creek Loop Trail [p.208] also connects here and Thornton Road departs northward on its way to Peavine Ridge [p. 247].

Bobcat – Bull Creek canyon inhabitant

The Big Trees-Albee Creek Loop Trail intersects Mattole Road at mile 5.2. Another part of the loop follows the road when it crosses the first Bull Creek bridge just ahead; the trail then branches left off the roadway. The original road up the canyon sometimes went through the streambed itself, and early travellers often found their way impeded by the creek's heavy salmon runs.

Beyond the bridge, the roadway widens to two lanes; it then leaves the western edge of the Rockefeller Forest, mile 5.3. Grasshopper Road exits left here [p. 250]. A parking area lies 50 yards south along this dirt route. Mattole Road now enters the eastern end of what was once the community of Bull Creek, an isolated logging and ranching town that survived the devastating 1955 flood only to succumb to the Park's acquisition program during the following decades.

Although Bull Creek in its early days was a three-day ride from Scotia, the nearest town of any size, a dozen hardy families were living in the canyon by 1895. Homesteaders ranched hillside prairies or openings on the canyon bottom, raising hogs, sheep, and cattle while also tending orchards of pears, apples, nuts, and plums; surplus produce was hauled to Dyerville and then sent downriver by boat to market. Some locals would leave the valley for summer work, returning in the fall to supplement their larders by hunting and fishing. Prohibition brought a new source of income, as the basin's numerous narrow side canyons often served as sites for small stills, some of which were conveniently located inside goosepen trees. Tanbarking and tie hacking were done on many of the canyon slopes, and several lumber mills at one time or another operated on the valley floor. During the Douglas fir boom in the late forties and early fifties, the upper Bull Creek basin was heavily logged, an activity that was held responsible for the disastrous effects of the 1955 flood. To prevent further damage to the basin, the Save-the-Redwoods League began purchasing Bull Creek properties in the 1960s, subsequently transferring them to the Park. Today, few signs of the community remain; besides the cemetery and a few bits of concrete, there are just three old barns, two homes, and a weathered outhouse. Only in spring, when the aging apple trees brighten the flats with their sweet, white blossoms, does the little valley recall the time when it was home to over 300 residents.

Continuing west, Mattole Road passes a large open space, right, mile 5.7, where the Bee River Mill once stood. A light fixture, still hanging from a lone tree, waits for another chance to illuminate the long-vacant mill yard.

The dirt road to Baxter Environmental Camp [p. 208] exits left at mile 6.2. Grace Johnson Baxter, the daughter of Tosaldo and Roxanne Johnson, once had a home here. The town's first store was near the creek opposite the camp turnoff.

Bull Creek School

At mile 6.3 the road crosses the second Bull Creek bridge. On the right at mile 6.5 is the dirt road entrance to the Hamilton Barn Environmental Camp [p. 216]; opposite this turnoff is the site of the second Bull Creek store. The school was on the right a short distance ahead, as was the town's first church. The local congregation apparently felt uncertain about the future of religion in the area, for the church was built on ski-like runners and had a canvas roof. It was in fact later skidded a short way south and made over into a home, but by then, another house of worship had taken its place.

"Maple Rest" once stood on the creekside flat to the left. This large, tree-sheltered structure was an early dance hall, but the building later lapsed into middle-aged propriety after it was converted into a set of apartments.

A large field that once served as the Bull Creek rodeo grounds then appears on the right. Beyond it is one of the canyon's two remaining houses, now a Park employee's residence.

Next the route comes to dirt Pole Line Road [p. 245], which departs, right at mile 7.3, on its way over the Bear River divide and into Happy Valley. Mattole Road then crosses the gray, gravel-filled bed of Cuneo Creek, a three-stemmed stream that courses through the heavily eroded canyons to the northwest. After passing another Park employee's house, the road begins climbing out of the valley. On the flat to the left was the original Bull Creek cemetery, which was washed out by the 1955 flood. The trees of Noah Lewis's fruit orchard can be seen a short way up the creek.

The dirt Bull Creek Road [p. 266] branches left, mile 7.6; opposite it is the southern end of the Horse Trail [p. 219]. Ahead on the right is the second Bull Creek cemetery, the well-maintained resting place of many valley pioneers. The property was donated by long-time resident Bruce Lewis, who died shortly after his bestowal and came to occupy the first plot in the new graveyard.

Above the cemetery is the gravel entrance road to the Cuneo Creek Horse Group Camp, right at mile 7.9; the one-lane route winds through a small, gently sloping prairie that formerly belonged to the Lewis family. On the right at 0.2 mile is the pale concrete pad of what was once the Bull Creek dance pavilion. In early summer, the surrounding meadow is colorfully covered by a field of blue-hued miniature lupine.

miniature lupine
(Lupinus bicolor ssp. umbellatus)

This small lupine is a common resident of the Park's numerous prairies. Several blue and white flowers grow on the top portion of each erect stalk, often allying themselves in hued harmony with the large golden petals of near-by California poppies.

Other, non-native varieties of lupine also grow in Humboldt Redwoods. The genus is a true survivor, as witnessed by the discovery, in 1967, of lupine seeds found frozen in a lemming burrow; although estimated to be 10,000 years old, they germinated within 48 hours of being planted. [blooms March-June]

The camp access road then meets the Horse Trail, which enters from the right just as the road turns and begins to drop steeply downhill. A mound of grape vines, right, marks the entrance to where a tiny house once sheltered Frank Howe, a grandfatherly man who in old age wore a long, white beard more commonly seen in an earlier era.

At mile 0.5 the access road levels next to a patch of cut-leaf black-berry, left, and enters the Cuneo Creek Horse Group Camp. The road makes a small loop around the camp area, circling a pair of Spanish chestnut trees; the home of Bruce and Ida Lewis once stood nearby, but it burned many years ago in dramatic fashion.

*   *   *

THE MOON THAT CAME TOO SOON

Bruce Lewis awoke one night bothered by a strange, uneasy feeling. He looked out the bedroom window; the ranch yard below basked in the bright moonlight.

The elderly Lewis reflected a moment and then sprang from the bed. He awoke his invalid wife, Ida, before rushing out into the yard. A moment later Lewis was struggling with a large wheelbarrow, trying to get it into the house.

The wheelbarrow scraped its way inside; Lewis picked up his wife and placed her in it. He was panting too hard to answer Ida's rapid questions; besides, there was no time to lose.

Gathering his strength, Lewis raised the wheelbarrow and began pushing it across the room. Soon he had burst out the front door and was rolling Ida across the yard. Behind him, flames danced on the roof of the ranch house.

The building was beyond saving, but at least Ida was all right. Now there was time for Bruce to tell her how he'd known about the fire. "It was too bright out for this time of month," Lewis explained. His wife understood what he meant; farmers always know the phases of the moon.

*   *   *

The Horse Group Camp occupies the gently sloping ground above the rocky channel of Cuneo Creek; it will accommodate 50 people and their horses. There are tables, barbecues, solar showers, and primitive toilets for the humans, while their steeds get troughs, corrals, and hitching posts; the only shade is provided by the trees in the campground's central circle. The Indian Orchard Trail exits from the north end of the campground [p. 234].

After passing the Horse Camp access road, Mattole Road begins climbing the hillside on a series of sharp switchbacks, rising past a view of the badly eroded Cuneo Creek watershed, mile 10.1. A side road branches left at mile 10.3, leading to an old but still-used quarry. Another view of the Cuneo devastation opens to the right at mile 10.7, followed by a prospect of upper Bull Creek, left at mile 11.1. Soon the road begins to straighten and level as it heads southwest, crossing the cascading headwaters of Burns Creek, mile 11.4, where hound's tongue, giant chain fern, western coltsfoot, flowering currant, giant horsetail, and other water-loving plants cover the banks. At mile 12.6 the route passes a turnout, right, where dirt Fox Camp Road exits to the extreme right [p. 229].

Mattole Road continues south, running beside a bank of farewell-to-spring, mile 13.5, before arriving at Panther Gap, mile 14.4; here Kemp Road [p. 273] and Perimeter Road [p. 274], both dirt, depart to the left. At this point Mattole Road passes out of the Park and begins its descent to the Mattole River and Honeydew.

Mountain lion, a.k.a. panther

ROUTES OF LOWER BULL CREEK

BAXTER ENVIRONMENTAL CAMP ROAD

Summary: Several tree species line this entrance to a pair of pleasant campsites.

Distance: 0.6 mile, round trip

Elevation Change: negligible

Location: The route turns left off Mattole Road, 6.2 miles west of the 101 Freeway.

Description: After passing a locked gate, the road runs beside a leafy profusion of Oregon ash, red alder, California laurel, and bigleaf maple. The base of Squaw Creek Ridge rises to the left, while on the right is a broad benchland that runs west to Bull Creek. At mile 0.2 the route comes to a second locked gate. A continuation of the road, open only to Park vehicles, crosses a log bridge just beyond the gate; the first campsite is here to the left in a grove of medium-small redwoods. The road ends at a grassy clearing, mile 0.3, near a water tap and pit toilet. Two paths depart the area: the track left is the Baxter-Squaw Creek Cutoff Trail; the way right runs south to cross a small bridge and then enters a secluded stand of redwoods wherein lies the second campsite.

BIG TREES-ALBEE CREEK LOOP TRAIL

Summary: This curving course circles through the western end of the Rockefeller Forest as it connects the Big Trees Area with the Albee Creek Campground.

Distance: 2.5 miles, round trip

Elevation Change: 100-foot gain and loss

Location: The trail's eastern end is at the Big Trees Area parking lot, located off Mattole Road, left, 4.4 miles west of the 101 Freeway; the western end is at the Albee Creek Campground.

Warning: *This route requires crossing Mattole Road and also briefly walking along the road on the bridge over Bull Creek; be alert for traffic when on the roadway.*

Description: The trail begins by following the short pathway to the Tallest Tree, which exits the Big Trees access road at a marker between

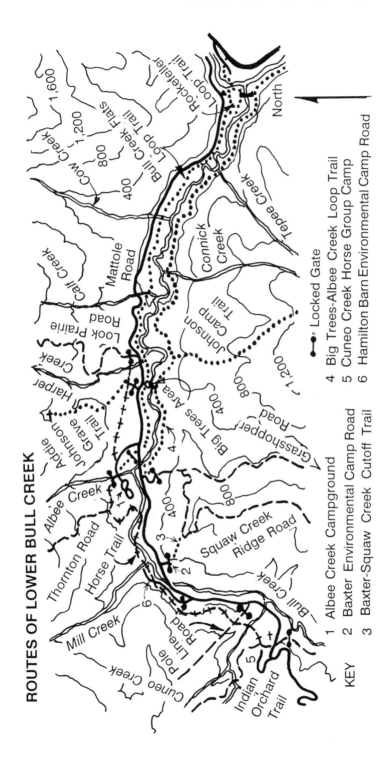

ROUTES OF LOWER BULL CREEK

KEY

1 Albee Creek Campground
2 Baxter Environmental Camp Road
3 Baxter-Squaw Creek Cutoff Trail
4 Big Trees-Albee Creek Loop Trail
5 Cuneo Creek Horse Group Camp
6 Hamilton Barn Environmental Camp Road

•••• Locked Gate

the first and second set of parking spaces. To the right is a large hollow log which, during the wet season, displays dozens of licorice ferns.

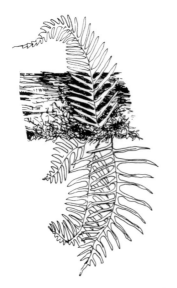

licorice fern
(Polypodium glycyrrhiza)

The licorice-flavored root rhizomes of this small fern have long been chewed raw; for a time they were even used as a sweetener for plug tobacco. The roots' distinctive taste is due to a componet called glycyrrhizin, which is also present in fennel and anise. Recent experiments have revealed an important new use for the substance — shrinking tumors. Appropriately, the fern's rhizomes have a history of other medicinal applications, most notably as an ingredient in cough drops. Licorice ferns grow on mossy rocks, logs, and tree trunks, often in large groups. Their fronds depend on the moisture contained in the moss, and when this dampness dries out, the ferns die back until after the next rain.

Thirty yards from the parking area, a little loop to the erroneously titled "Tallest" Tree commences to the right; this trail leads to a 360-foot redwood whose stature is somewhat less than its name implies; it is thus sometimes referred to as the Rockefeller Tree. Although surpassed in height by a trio of Redwood National Park behemoths, it does vie with the nearby Giant Tree for being the tallest tree in any state park.

The Big Trees-Albee route continues left from the junction; in 50 feet it leaves the Tallest Tree loop by crossing a low wooden railing, left, and striking out on its own along the benchland beside Bull Creek. Large, solemn redwoods shelter shade-loving ground covers such as thin false Solomon's seal, sugar scoop, and sweet-scented bedstraw as the trail wanders westward. After passing a Pacific yew, mile 0.4, and a patch of yerba de selva, mile 0.6, the course crosses Mattole Road at mile 0.8. The route then follows a wide dirt track that soon passes a small stream-gaging station, left. Now narrowing again to a path, the passage runs northwest above the tree-lined bank of Bull Creek; a border of black cottonwood, red alder, and bigleaf maple are sweetened by a comely cluster of hairy honeysuckle. The trail reaches the mouth of Albee Creek at mile 0.9. It follows this stream to the campground entrance at the Albee Creek bridge, 1.0 mile. Here the route meets the Horse Trail, which briefly follows the campground access road on its way west.

The return from Albee Creek Campground backtracks down along the streams to Mattole Road, mile 1.3. Here the route now turns right, following the road west across Bull Creek. At a marker 100 feet beyond the bridge, the trail leaves the south side of the road, plunging into thick forest. The route winds past ferns and a Pacific yew, meeting a side trail on the right, mile 1.6, that originates at Grasshopper Road, 0.2 mile to the west.

Continuing left from the junction, the main trail soon ascends a low ridge spur, reaching a viewpoint at mile 1.7; the towering trunks of numerous redwoods are visible on the far side of Bull Creek. The path then drops off the ridge, offering, as it does so, an elevated view of the flat below. At the bottom of the descent, a fresh green ground cover of redwood sorrel is embellished by milkmaids, fetid adder's tongue, wild ginger, windflower, and sweet-scented bedstraw.

Another ridge spur forces the trail up to a second overlook; an outstanding view stretches north across Bull Creek to another group of giant trees. The route then returns to the lowlands, and at mile 2.1 passes a stretch of benchland thick with trillium.

A wonderful, gargoyle-like burl perches on the side of a redwood trunk at mile 2.3; near it is a stunning, blackened snag that rises a hundred feet in half-burned grandeur and still bears living limbs near its lightning-blasted top. Other redwoods lay shattered upon the forest floor, crisscrossing each other like giant pick-up sticks; they all form a prelude for the startling Flatiron Tree, mile 2.4, a leaning leviathan that has sent out a huge buttress at its base to help keep it upright. The result is a strangely flattened lower trunk that narrows to a wedge-shaped point on one side; a cross section of its base thus resembles the sole plate of an old-fashioned flatiron. The tree enhances its eye-

trillium, western wake robin
(Trillium ovatum)
[blooms February-April]

catching appearance with a ropy, high-ridged bark that bends its way up the trunk like a covering of great, gray jungle vines. In a forest where size is everything, the tipsy, tilted Flatiron Tree is a magnificent misfit, living proof that it's what shape you're in that counts.

FLATIRON TREE

7.5FT ←17.5FT→

TYPICAL CROSS SECTION

Flat but flamboyant

Two trails leave the opposite side of the Flatiron Tree. The one right leads east to the Giant Tree, while the way left continues the main route, which joins the Bull Creek Flats Loop Trail just before crossing the creek on a wooden bridge. On the far bank is the path's end, mile 2.5, at the parking lot for the Big Trees Area.

BULL CREEK FLATS LOOP TRAIL

Summary: This nearly level loop winds along both sides of lower Bull Creek, passing through the heart of the Rockefeller Forest.

Distance: 8.2 miles, round trip

Elevation Change: negligible

Location: The route can be commenced from either of two starting points. The first departs from the Rockefeller Loop Trail; to reach it, proceed west on Mattole Road 1.4 miles to a narrow paved road that drops abruptly downhill to the left; this leads to a parking area for the Rockefeller Loop. Take the right fork of this path 0.2 mile to another junction. A right turn here leads a few feet to the Bull Creek Flats Loop Trail; turn right to start the loop. The second starting point is at the Big Trees Area, 4.4 miles west of the 101 Freeway, off of Mattole Road.

Warning: *In winter, the seasonal bridge near the mouth of Bull Creek is removed; fording the stream there at high water may be unpleasant and/or unsafe.*

Description: After leaving the Rockefeller Loop, the route heads upstream along the northern side of Bull Creek. Giant horsetail and scouring rush stipple the surroundings; small creekside alders to the left contrast sharply with tall redwoods on the right. There are rough patches of pathway at mile 0.5 as it passes more giant horsetail and scouring rush. The trail crosses a clearing at 1.1 miles next to a stretch of Bull Creek riffles.

California spikenard, bigleaf maple, iris, and blueblossom enjoy the southern exposure at mile 1.4, just before a bridge crosses a side creek. The route then winds northward into the forest, emerging at 1.9 miles to a view of the large redwoods that line the opposite side of Bull Creek. Soon the trail enters its own stand of trees, passing over Cow Creek at mile 2.0; then a grassy flat, 2.3 miles, provides access to several summer wading spots in Bull Creek. A return to the forest brings another stream crossing, followed by an opening at mile 2.6; a log bench here provides a rest spot.

Now the trail turns north, opposite an eroded bluff on the far side of Bull Creek, and enters a grove of good-sized redwoods at 2.9 miles. The trailbed is lined with the lacy tendrils of sweet-scented bedstraw.

sweet-scented bedstraw
(Galium triflorum)

What bedstraw lacks in appearance it makes up for in usefulness. Its tiny, whitish green flowers and whorls of small, narrow leaves make it an easy plant to overlook, but it was prized for its practicality by pioneers and Indians alike. As its name implies, bedstraw was often harvested for stuffing mattresses; it also perfumed packed belongings. It was used, along with rennet, in the preparation of cheese, and some varieties of the plant have served as a coffee substitute; a cold infusion of bedstraw provided a treatment for fevers. Bedstraw also functions as a powerful diuretic, useful for inducing weight loss and treating edema. Boiled, its roots produce a beautiful red or purple dye, especially valued by some Indians for its use on wool, quills, and horsehair. The Cowlitz tribe believed that if a woman first performed certain rituals and then rubbed bedstraw on her body while bathing, she would then have a successful romance. Bedstraw grows close to the ground as a spreading vine and favors moist, shaded areas. [blooms April-July]

Calf Creek spreads a wash of alluvium across the trail at mile 3.0. The route then rises to run next to Mattole Road; after briefly dropping back to the flats, it regains the roadside, mile 3.5, just east of Luke Prairie. A spur route joins the trail, right, near a large parking area south of the prairie. Another side path exits right at 3.8 miles; it leads to Mattole Road just opposite Look Prairie Road. The main route then crosses Harper Creek on a wooden bridge and soon returns to the side of Bull Creek. After passing over another bridge, the trail arrives at the Big Trees parking lot, mile 4.4.

Leaving the parking area, the route heads south, immediately cross-ing Bull Creek on a sturdy log footbridge. Just beyond the bridge a side route branches right; this is part of the Big Trees-Albee Creek Loop, which leads in 50 yards to the Flatiron Tree. The Bull Creek Loop turns left and presently reaches its own large redwood, the fence-enclosed Giant Tree.

This stout-trunked specimen has succeeded the now-fallen Dyerville Giant as the "champion" coast redwood, a designation based on its combined height, circumference, and crown size, which now surpasses that of any other sempervirens. Although the Giant Tree is some 357 to 363 feet tall, its towering top is invisible, hidden by a tangle of limbs high above; what is most striking is the enormous girth of the tree's lower trunk, which crowds its surroundings, dwarfing the fence railings at its base as if they were toothpicks. The Giant's heavy bark is covered with dark, pocklike marks and a mottling of thick moss – everything about the tree bespeaks strength born of struggle, for it has stood here since the age of Charlemagne, a still-growing monument to survival.

Departing the Giant, the trail bears right, winding past widowmakers that jut from the ground like huge pins in a cushion. At mile 4.7, five varieties of ferns – sword, giant chain, lady, five-fingered, and bracken – nestle in the hole of an uprooted redwood; shortly thereafter, the babbling waters of Squaw Creek are spanned by a rustic, single-log bridge. The stream's unfortunate name refers to a massacre of Lolangkok Indians that reportedly occurred on the flat here.

The Johnson Camp Trail forks right, mile 4.8, amid a stand of large redwoods. The main route wanders across the fertile flat, encountering an especially pleasing collection of ferns and flowers at mile 5.0.

After passing a pair of yews and a hollow, "walk-through" log, the trail crosses little Miller Creek on a fallen, railed redwood, mile 5.5; Bull Creek has now turned south, forcing the trail against the hillside. At mile 5.7 a former meander of the creek has carved a pocket out of the higher ground to the south; a semicircle of bluffs rims the pocket, while a prairie-ringed stand of redwoods rises from its center. The path crosses the neck of the meander; in spring, a speckling of western blue flax floats

GIANT TREE
BY CIRCUMFERANCE 53 feet

The champion redwood

over the grassy trailside like stars above a green sea. Snowbrush and blueblossom bask in the light of the opening.

Leaving Bull Creek, the trail climbs to an elevated benchland. A switchback soon takes the path down into the surprisingly deep gorge of tiny Connick Creek, mile 5.9, a repository of mossy rocks and many ferns. The route then runs beneath spectacular redwoods, and at mile 6.3 passes beneath the unique Giant Braid, a trio of redwood trunks that twist together high overhead. Soon afterward, the trail encounters a stately stand of sword ferns.

At mile 6.4 the trail passes a pair of small openings in the forest canopy that are filled with clusters of sunlight-loving bracken ferns. The route runs over lightly rolling ground, twisting among giant logs that dwarf a delicate trailside speckling of milkmaids.

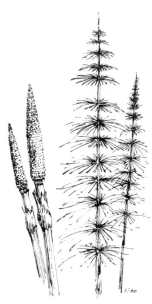

Bull Creek is heard but not seen at mile 7.1, its proximity indicated by a ribbon of red alder and scouring rush. Giant horsetails rise like a pale green fog beside the bases of several huge redwoods.

giant horsetail
(Equisetum telmateia)

The redwood of the equisetum genus, this large species of horsetail can grow up to 10 feet tall. A simple-looking but complexly constructed plant, it has sheaths of fused leaf whorls that grow at regular intervals from nodes on the stem; below the sheaths are additional whorls of thin, dark green branches that form a bottlebrush shape and are the horsetail's most distinctive feature. Indians of the Pacific Northwest delighted in eating both the new shoots and heads of the plant. The Swinomish Indians used the plant for scouring and for polishing arrow shafts. With shoots strong enough to burst through pavement, this horsetail's hardiness won it fame as the first plant to regenerate amid the destruction of Mount St. Helens.

After crossing Tepee Creek at mile 7.5, the trail drops slightly to run a narrow course between Bull Creek and the steep cliffside. The route comes out onto a streamside gravel bar, 7.7 miles, but soon climbs back onto the flat. It then crosses a protruding hill shoulder on a set of switchbacks and drops into a stand of awesomely large redwoods. The Burlington-Bull Creek Flats Trail enters from the right at mile 8.1; here the main route turns left, dropping from the flat past clustering California spikenard and then crossing Bull Creek on a seasonal bridge. Following a short climb up the bank, the loop concludes, mile 8.2, at the connecting spur for the Rockefeller Loop Trail.

HAMILTON BARN ENVIRONMENTAL CAMP ROAD

Summary: This pleasantly winding roadway passes a beautiful old apple orchard, a pair of interesting willows, and leads to the sites of both a sawmill and a ranch.

Distance: 1.4 miles, round trip, including the trail through Hamilton Barn camp

Elevation Change: 50-foot loss and gain

Location: The route exits from mile 6.5 of Mattole Road.

Description: Turning a sharp right from Mattole Road, the route immediately heads uphill to a locked gate. A hundred feet past the gate, a side road branches left; it leads to a series of open, grassy areas and a Park employee's residence. The main route continues straight ahead briefly before bending left to cross a small, tree-lined streambed. A large walnut tree, right, precedes the crossing, while a group of Oregon ashes gather just beyond the gully, left.

At mile 0.1 the road enters a large, redwood-edged apple orchard; in springtime the trees' white blossoms billow above the new grass like a sun-brightened cloud. The property once belonged to Amos Cummings, whose King apples won a gold medal at the 1914 San Francisco Apple Show. The road dips briefly after leaving the north end of the orchard, mile 0.2, where two dramatically different willows rise from a small creekbed on the right.

Pacific willow, yellow willow
(Salix lasiandra)

More than a hundred species of willow are native to North America, most of them growing as shrubs. The Pacific and Scouler willows are among those that attain tree size, sometimes growing 50 feet tall; they are also among the more easily identified members of the Salix family.

The Pacific willow produces narrow, sharply pointed, dark yellow-green leaves that have a distinctive wart at their junction with the stem. Sometimes also called the black willow, its wood was once used for the saddletrees of Spanish Californians.

The leaves of the Scouler willow are paddle shaped and rounded at their upper end; the leaf tops are colored dark green while the undersides often bear a reddish gold hairiness. A type of pussy willow, it derives one of its names from its proclivity for occupying burned areas; its other moniker honors John Scouler, a friend of botanist David Douglas.

Scouler willow, fire willow
(Salix scouleriana)

coyote brush

(Baccharis pilularis

ssp. consanguinea)

[blooms August-December]

The route now moves through open forest; a side road, left, soon joins the Horse Trail. A short downhill pitch leads to a clearing at mile 0.3; here another side road, left, crosses the Horse Trail and then climbs northwest beside Mill Creek before ending on the hillside. Blueblossom and coyote brush fill much of the open flatland.

A small parking area at mile 0.5 marks the end of the main road. The trail to the environmental camp leaves the parking area, dropping to cross Mill Creek on a wooden bridge.

The path then enters a thick stand of second-growth redwood, passing three of the campsites. At mile 0.6 the route comes out onto a small prairie; a fourth campsite is in the woods to the left. The trail now cuts across the grassland, going by several graying timbers that were once part of the Hamilton Barn. At mile 0.7 the route ends at campsite #5, a pleasantly isolated spot sheltered by a string of fruit trees. Bull Creek noisily splashes by some 50 feet to the northeast.

*   *   *

A TREE-MENDOUS WEDDING

On a late spring day in 1910, Bull Creek resident Hugh Hamilton married Ruby Butler, who hailed from Burlington. The couple had planned to hold the wedding indoors, but they had invited so many guests that none of the available buildings could contain the group. After pondering the problem, Hugh and Ruby found a solution available only in redwood country — they would be married inside a tree!

A large, hollow redwood was selected, which was then lined with ferns, roses, and redwood lilies. During the ceremony, the minister, bride, groom, bridesmaid, and best man all squeezed inside the trunk, while the wedding guests stood in front of the improvised chapel.

The newlyweds took up residence on the Hamilton Ranch, which stood on a bluff above Bull Creek. Hugh ranched there until his death, and Ruby stayed on after him. Finally, 54 years after she came to the canyon as a bride, Ruby sold out to the Park and left the valley that had become her home. All the ranch buildings were eventually removed; now only a few pieces of bleached barn wood remain to mark the site.

There is even less left of the Hamilton's marriage tree; it stood in the path of the Redwood Highway and was cut down just a few years after housing the ceremony. The sylvan sounds of the wedding march have been followed by decades of humming, honking traffic. At the abandonded ranch up in Bull Creek, only the stream breaks the silence.

* * *

HORSE TRAIL

Summary: This broad but bridgeless pathway follows the northwest side of the Bull Creek canyon, connecting with eight other routes, the Cuneo Creek Horse Group Camp, and the Albee Creek Campground.

Distance: 4.6 miles, one way

Elevation Change: 710-foot gain and 440-foot loss, northeast to southwest

Location: The trail's northeastern end is at the junction of Mattole Road and Look Prairie Road, 4.2 miles from the 101 Freeway; its southwestern end is at mile 7.6 of Mattole Road, opposite the start of Bull Creek Road.

Warning: *All four major stream crossings lack bridges—this is primarily a horse route and hikers will have to wade or rock hop at the fords. Bicycle use is prohibited.*

Description: The Horse Trail heads through mixed forest that is thick with black huckleberry. Soon the route fords Harper Creek at the bottom of a rocky gully; giant horsetail, western coltsfoot, and lady fern repose beneath an awning of California hazels. Late summer will find a large patch of California harebell blooming to the right of the trail at mile 0.2.

Continuing west, the path crosses the roadlike start of the Addie Johnson Grave Trail, mile 0.4; Mattole Road is only 200 feet to the left. The route then runs along the base of the hillside, passing a host of low-growing plants: sugar scoop, redwood sorrel, thin false Solomon's seal, redwood violet, smooth yellow violet, milkmaids, and vanilla leaf. An occasional lichen-draped Pacific yew poses like an escapee from some southern bayou.

Now the trail climbs a short distance onto the slope above the flats. In summer the graceful,

California harebell
(Asyneuma prenanthoides)
[blooms June-September]

California hazel

(Corylus cornuta var. californica)

[blooms January-March]

green-leaved limbs of several California hazels reach over the route.

After descending to cross a small bridge, mile 1.0, the trail proceeds through fetid adder's tongue, calypso orchid, and redwood inside-out flower. A small mill, right, is used by the Park to cut salvaged redwoods.

The path presently crosses the entrance road to Albee Creek Campground; 50 yards farther the trail again meets the road, this time following it across the Albee Creek bridge and into the campground, mile 1.2. The Horse Trail turns right immediately past the bridge, following a gravel campground road along the side of Albee Creek. The route soon reaches a locked metal gate, which marks the start of Thornton Road; the Horse Trail follows the road up the hillslope to mile 1.6, where it branches left onto its own trailbed.

The liberated pathway runs briefly across the hillside before reaching a junction with an abandoned section of the trail. The new route branches left and descends, at times very steeply, through mixed forest until it reaches the western edge of a large grassland; the Albee Creek Campground lies just to the east. Remnants of the Albee family's orchard still dot the area, and in winter, fountainesque cascades of red rosehips cover the meadow's many bushes. The Horse Trail cuts part way through the prairie, turning right at mile 1.9 to reach the first Bull Creek ford. On the south bank, the route curves right and picks up an old roadbed, bending around a log barrier at mile 2.0; to the left is a residue of scrap wood from the long-departed Bee River Mill. The path skirts the edge of the old mill yard, turns left to approach Mattole Road, and then descends, right, mile 2.3, into the rocky bed of Bull Creek.

Alder and white sweet clover cover much of the appoach to the wandering, sometimes-divided stream. The trail twists across the rocky creekbed, finds one or more places to ford, and then ascends the west bank into a sheltering cluster of bigleaf maples. After cutting through a large log, mile 2.5, the route makes an abrupt left turn; here an abandoned section of the Horse Trail forks to the right.

The way then follows an old roadbed, which soon enters thick forest; below on the left is the Hamilton Barn Environmental Camp. After dropping briefly, the trail fords Mill Creek, mile 2.7, and then climbs to a small flat where a most unusual lumbering operation once stood.

*   *   *

FROM MISSISSIPPI TO MILL CREEK: HERSHELL WHEELER AND HIS MOVEABLE MILL

In 1953, Hershell D. Wheeler returned to his home in Mississippi after a long trip. He had just been to Northern California, where he purchased some property in the little community of Bull Creek.

When it came time to move west, Wheeler took more than a few family belongings. He packed up the machinery from the mill he'd been operating, loaded it onto trucks, and had a half-dozen of his top mill hands drive it all out. He would use the equipment—and the workers— to upgrade the old Littlepage Mill that sat next to the Hamilton property at the mouth of Mill Creek.

The Littlepage Mill had also travelled a bit. First known as the Taylor Mill, had been situated on the divide between Bear River and Bull Creek, where it was used to cut fir logs in the twenties and thirties. Following the war, the mill was moved down the mountainside and operated by three different owners before Wheeler purchased it.

Wheeler increased the mill's capacity, mainly cutting logs trucked in from the Mattole River basin. After the 1955 flood, his crew dug the mud out of the mill and resumed operations, only to have new flooding the following year again cause a halt. Some 28 millhands were temporarily put out of work.

Undaunted, Wheeler once again started up the mill. This time it ran until 1962, when it burnt.

A fire and two floods might not have been enough to keep Wheeler down, but the Park acquisition program was. He sold out to the state after the blaze, just nine years and three disasters after he—and his moveable mill—had migrated from Mississippi.

*   *   *

Coyote brush crowds the trailside as the course rises from the flat; at mile 2.8 the route crosses an abandoned dead-end road that climbs the hillside next to Mill Creek. The path then passes through mixed forest, reaching a road spur, left at mile 3.0, that connects with the road to Hamilton Barn Camp a short distance below. Ahead on the left is a set of cement steps that once led to the door of a Bull Creeker's house but which now rises to nothingness, like a plinth without its statue.

After crossing a shallow gully, the trail runs along the western edge of the old and lovely Cummings apple orchard, 3.1 miles, before dropping into another small streambed. Four Oregon ashes assemble to the left; they are among the largest found in the Park.

Oregon ash
(Fraxinus latifolia)

The Oregon ash has an eye-catching compound leaf, usually composed of five to seven light green leaflets that are attached in opposite pairs on the stem, with the final leaflet positioned at the stem tip. The tree prefers moist soils near streambeds, often sharing spots with black cottonwood, red alder, and willow; when growing in drier areas, its usually straight trunk often manifests the stress by becoming crooked. Its wood is used for furniture, flooring, paneling, and boxes, but in earlier days, the tree served another purpose — according to a botanist of the time: "An opinion prevails in Oregon among the hunters and Indians that poisonous serpents are unknown in the same tract of country where this ash grows, and stories are related of a stick of the black ash causing a rattlesnake to retire with every mark of trepidation and fear . . . ."

Past the valley of the ashes is a grassy flat that features a few fruit trees, a Park employee's trailer, and a dirt road; the latter originates 50 yards east at the Hamilton Barn Road and continues west, ascending to its terminus on a terraced prairie. After crossing the flat, the Horse Trail plunges into another diminutive defile. It then rises to pass a patch of grassland and arrives, mile 3.4, beneath a small stand of Douglas fir.

Continuing south, the route runs through another stretch of prairie, climbs a small rise, and then cuts across a much larger meadow.

At mile 3.7 the path enters a hillside grove of small oaks and madrones, twisting its way uphill until it reaches yet another

Northern flicker —
Horse Trail habitué

prairie. In summer, the slopes here display both farewell-to-spring and woolly blue curls.

woolly blue curls, vinegar weed
(Trichostema lanceolatum)

This plant is noticeable both for its small, hair-covered leaves and its far-reaching, "vinegary" smell. As its name implies, the pale blue flower curls upon the end of its floral tube, which itself curves grace-fully back to connect with the stalk. Indians had several uses for the plant's leaves: crushed, they were thrown into streams to stun fish, which could then be caught more easily; packed around teeth, they relieved inflammation; combined with the plant's flowers, they served as a cold remedy. [blooms June-August]

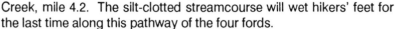

Pole Line Road cuts across the trail at 3.9 miles; the route then drops down the tree-dotted prairie to reach the crossing at Cuneo Creek, mile 4.2. The silt-clotted streamcourse will wet hikers' feet for the last time along this pathway of the four fords.

On the benchland west of the crossing is the Cuneo Creek Horse Group Camp. The route passes a solar shower and reaches the camp access road; 50 feet to the right is the start of the Indian Orchard Trail. The Horse Trail turns left to follow the access road, soon climbing steeply uphill. At 4.4 miles the trail exits the road, branching left and skirting the eastern edge of a grassland. After passing the Bull Creek cemetery, the trail ends at Mattole Road, mile 4.6, just opposite the start of Bull Creek Road.

ROCKEFELLER LOOP TRAIL

Summary: This charming path circles beneath some of Humboldt Redwoods' biggest trees and beside a wealth of smaller plant life.

Distance: 0.6 mile, round trip

Elevation Change: negligible

Location: The trail starts at the end of a short paved access road that exits left from Mattole Road at mile 1.4.

Description: The path leaves the southwestern edge of a small parking area, reaching a fork in 50 feet; sugar scoop, smooth yellow violet, milkmaids, and redwood sorrel blanket the rolling forest floor, while huge, stately redwoods rise into the foliage-filled air high above. The way right twists through the trees, arriving at a spur route, right at mile 0.2, that promptly connects with the Bull Creek Flats Loop Trail.

A left turn at the junction continues the Rockefeller Loop, which soon bends left again to run above the northern bank of Bull Creek. A pair of big redwoods at 0.3 mile feature picturesque burls; the second tree sports a snoutlike excrescence at the base of its trunk. As the route nears Bull Creek at mile 0.4, the vegetation is diversified by bigleaf maple, California laurel, fairybell, wood rose, and thin false Solomon's seal. Ahead on the left is a marker for the forest; the petro-profits of the Rockefeller family were here happily converted into a perpetually preserved resource.

Siberian candyflower, western spring beauty
(Montia siberica)
[blooms April-September]

Past the commemorative plaque, the trail arrives at a large log that has had a section of its underside removed, thus allowing hikers to pass beneath it. A short spur route branches right to reach the confluence of Bull Creek and the South Fork Eel. The loop trail crosses under the crenelated log and then bends around the stump end of a large fallen redwood; the base of the tree's trunk is surmounted with a crown of Siberian candyflower.

The trail soon passes another spur, right, which descends through a mass of encroaching vegetation to the South Fork Eel. Hikers who want to reach the nearby summer bridge to the Federation Grove would do better to take the well-maintained pathway that descends from the eastern edge of the Rockefeller Loop's parking lot. The main trail finishes at the lot, mile 0.6.

ROUTES OF THE NORTHWEST RIDGES

[see map, p. 228]

ADDIE JOHNSON GRAVE TRAIL

Summary: This hike to a secluded grave site climbs a rolling hillside prairie and encounters an abundance of oaks.

Distance: 1.6 miles, round trip

Elevation Change: 600-foot gain and loss

Location: The trail starts along what was once Johnson Prairie Road, which exits Mattole Road 4.5 miles west of the 101 Freeway.

Warning: *Unless recently maintained, the middle part of the trail is likely to be covered with broom; this yellow-flowered bush grows in thick clusters that are sometimes all but impenetrable. Check with Park headquarters for the route's current status.*

Description: Unmarked Johnson Prairie Road branches right from Mattole Road a short distance beyond the Big Trees Area turnoff. The route runs north 50 yards to the base of the hillside; at an intersection with the Horse Trail is a small place for parking. The road slants uphill through mixed forest and soon passes a locked metal gate. At 0.2 mile it enters the bottom of Johnson Prairie; the grassland rises northwest along a ridge spur. A string of oaks—both California black and Oregon white—rises in accompaniment along the roadside.

Heavy patches of broom, an invasive exotic, often impinge on the roadway at mile 0.3. The route now narrows to become a trail, although it continues to follow the old roadbed. Back to the southeast is a view of Grasshopper Peak, whose steep northern slope rises high above the Bull Creek Flats.

broom
Cytisus sp.; Spartium sp.
[blooms March-June]

California laurel, madrone, Douglas fir, and oak border the prairie as the road continues climbing; at mile 0.6 it arrives at a junction. To the left is the abandoned continuation of Johnson Prairie Road; it immediately crosses the gully of Gopher Creek and then follows the grassland west, finally entering the forested canyon of Albee Creek. The road becomes badly overgrown only 0.1 mile ahead, just past a trio of rusting farm implements that stand beside the roadway as monuments to the vanished Johnson homestead.

The Addie Johnson Grave Trail branches right from the junction. The route climbs north, cutting through a ribbon of trees; Oregon white oak and California black oak grow side by side, their fallen leaves mingling on the grass.

The trail then crosses the prairie, turning left at a wall of trees and running uphill along the edge of the grassland. The route picks up an old roadbed and follows it briefly before making a concluding climb onto a shaded knoll, mile 0.8. Here is Addie Johnson's grave, surrounded by a low picket fence; a pair of cypresses stand beside a weathered wooden grave marker.

California black oak

California black oak
(Quercus kelloggii)

Oregon white oak
(Quercus garryana)

The Park's many hillside woodlands are often graced by a gathering of California black and/or Oregon white oaks. Although somewhat similar in appearance, the two trees can be distinguished by their leaf lobes, which are rounded on the white oak and pointed on the black — if you can jab your finger with the leaf end, it's a black oak. The trees'

names indicate a second difference: their bark. Black oak bark is usually dark brown, while that of the white oak is light grey or whitish. The black oak is difficult to overlook in springtime, for its young, uncurling leaves are covered with fine hairs and are tinted an eye-catching purplish pink. In autumn, the white oak often creates its own display by reddening some of its leaves, while those of the black oak turn a more subdued yellow or brown.

Indians once used the black oak's slow-burning bark for parching seeds, while ranchers cut its wood for fencing. The more resilient white oak also provided fence posts — and was sometimes called the "post" oak as a result; more recently it has been used for shipbuilding, agricultural tools, interior finish, cabinetwork, furniture, and other types of construction. Uncut, both trees array themselves on the prairies above Bull Creek in a summertime blanket of shimmering green.

Oregon white oak

ADDIE JOHNSON FINDS HER RESTING PLACE

In the 1860s a rancher named Tosaldo Johnson travelled from California to Texas to buy some cattle; while there, he married Addie Stewart. The couple came west, and in 1872 they homesteaded 160 acres on a sunny prairie above Bull Creek.

One day several years later, Addie Johnson hiked up the prairie in search of a lost lamb; she eventually came to a lovely promontory that looked down on the family's homestead. Enchanted by the spot, Addie told her husband it was there she would someday like to be buried. Sadly, Tosaldo Johnson had to honor her request just a few months later when she died in childbirth.

Tosaldo Johnson married Roxanne Hanlon three years after Addie's death. The second Mrs. Johnson planted four cypress trees by the grave of her predecessor, two of which survive to this day.

Late in life, Tosaldo and Roxanne Johnson moved north to Rio Dell, but they both chose to be buried at the cemetery in Bull Creek. They had realized, like Addie, that the beautiful valley was meant to be their final home.

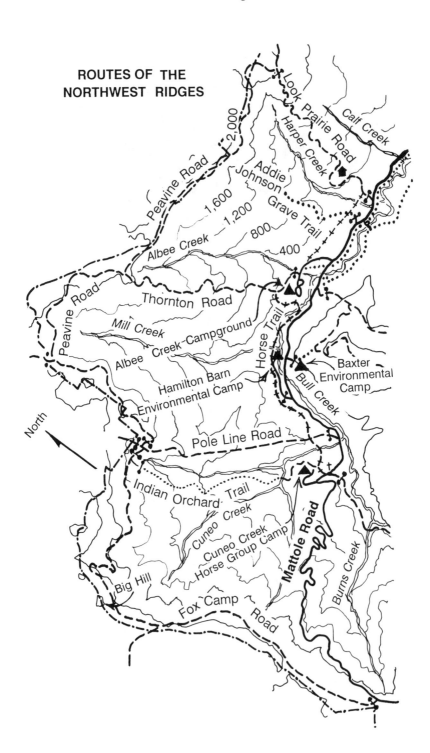

ROUTES OF THE
NORTHWEST RIDGES

FOX CAMP ROAD

Summary: A historic high road, it passes the site of Fox Camp Ranch, skirts the edge of panorama-topped Big Hill, and meanders through lovely madrone thickets on its way around the northwestern rim of Bull Creek.

Distance: 6.7 miles, one way

Elevation change: 500-foot gain and 1100-foot loss, south to north

Location: The route's unmarked southern end is at a large roadside pullout on Mattole Road, 12.6 miles west of the 101 Freeway; the northern end forms a junction with the Indian Orchard Trail and Pole Line Road.

Description: Starting at a metal gate, the route immediately climbs northward through thick woods. The road forks and then reconnects twice in quick succession, passing a prairie, left at 0.2 mile, before topping a hill crest at 0.4 mile. On the right is the debris from a demolished cabin, once used to house a Pacific Lumber guard who kept hunters off company land.

The route then crosses over lightly wooded, rolling hills until another prairie, left, opens out along the ridge at 1.4 miles. A thicket of Douglas fir engulfs the road at mile 1.8, but the grasslands soon re-emerge; a dirt track along the ridgetop sometimes leaves the Park to enter private property. The yard of the Fox Camp Ranch appears below the road, mile 2.1, nestled in a forest-framed clearing.

* * *

FROM FOX CAMP TO ONRAMP:
MAX CRISMON'S MANY RIDES

In 1922, when Max Crismon was in the fifth grade, he had to get up very early to go to school. Once he was dressed and fed, there was the horse to saddle up, and then, even using the cutoff trail, the ride down to the Bull Creek School took an hour and a half. There wasn't much of the day left when Max rode back onto the Fox Camp Ranch after class let out.

The ranch had been in the family as far back as the 1880s, but the Crismons had sold it in 1910; now Max and his parents, Arch and Coral, rented the property while they raised cattle, hogs, and turkeys. The ranch ran to more than 700 acres, leaving the Crismons all alone on their stretch of the ridge. A few years later, the family moved down to Bull Creek and the days of Max's long rides came to an end.

One summer a few years later, Max finally had a chance to get back in the saddle. A bad fire broke out in the high country, up by Rainbow Ridge and Fox Camp, and the 16-year-old Crismon went in with Irv Kelly to get Irv's stock out. It was a tall order; Kelly had 25 head of bucking horses up there that he kept for the Fortuna Rodeo, and it was a long way to safe pasture. There were just three wranglers to do the job: Max, Irv, and the herding dog.

The route they took was better suited for a mountain goat than a stock drive. First they headed north around the side of Big Hill, where a misplaced hoof could send a horse—and its rider—crashing a thousand feet down the cliffside towards Cuneo Creek. After crossing the Bear River divide and dropping into Happy Valley, they climbed all the way up massive Monument Ridge; the final run took them down the mountainside to Rio Dell and west, around the bluffs, to a grazing ground above the Eel River. It was a gruelling trip, done all in a day—but worth the price, since, as Max put it, the fire up by Fox Camp "burned the country to a frazzle."

By then Max may have seen enough excitement around Bull Creek, for he took a job repairing bridges for the Northwestern Pacific Railroad. He moved all over the southern county during the next few years, working at different sidings on the rail line.

Later Max settled in Fortuna and took up logging. His job, as it turned out, was with Louisiana-Pacific at Big Lagoon, halfway up the county to the north. For years, he made a daily round trip of 148 miles to work and back. Even after the freeway went in, it took about an hour and a half each way, but spending all that time driving didn't bother Max much—after all, he already knew a thing or two about long rides.

*　　*　　*

A concrete foundation juts up from the clearing, marking the remains of the old ranch house. Twice during its ill-fated history the structure burned to the ground; for good measure, ranch owner Lorenzo Roman's barn, which sat a few hundred yards to the south, on its own occasion also burnt. Now gooseberry, creambush, and poison oak rise from the high grass of the ranch yard, while several decaying apple trees struggle to send out a few blossoms. In the middle of the dying orchard, a small stream still seeps from the hillside—Fox Camp Spring, which flows into the main fork of Cuneo Creek.

Fox Camp first appeared in the news on October 19, 1869, when it was reported as the scene of a "homicide." According to the laconic account, William S. Jones, originally of Illinois, was standing in his yard when Thomas J. Moore approached. Jones then "came to his death by blows inflicted with a gun."

creambush, ocean spray
(Holodiscus discolor)

Flower fanciers can choose what they call this shrubby plant: if the clusters of small flowers are noticed for their color, it is creambush; if the wavelike arrangement of the blossoms is more striking, then it is ocean spray. Its straight branches were made into arrows by Indians, leading to a pair of more practical names, ironwood and arrowwood. The Lummi Indians of Washington used the plant's leaves to heal sore lips and feet.

One of the early residents expansively reported "thousands of foxes" in the vicinity of the aptly-named camp.   An epidemic later killed them off, along with most of the gray squirrels. Elk also roamed the region for a time; hunted extensively, they were gone by the 1920s.

The route continues through prairie until mile 2.6, where it enters a dense stand of Douglas fir. Just ahead, the road again divides temporarily, the right fork offering the longer but gentler grade. Along this route, an enormous madrone languishes downslope among the dark firs. At 3.0 miles the road switchbacks sharply left, soon reaching another stretch of prairie. To the right are the remains of a small corral, its frail fencing now no more able to enclose cattle than it can hold back the wind. The two road forks converge just beyond the corral; the route

Gray fox

immediately turns right, climbing sharply along the narrow spine of the ridge. To the left is a view of the Rattlesnake Creek drainage as it descends to the Upper North Fork Mattole River, a waterflow long in name but short in distance.

At the top of a small rise directly ahead, the route forks; the better roadway branches left towards the ranches of Rainbow Ridge, while a fainter track to the right is the continuation of Fox Camp Road. A blue Park boundary sign sticks up from the prairie, right, conveniently marking the junction.

Following the Park road, right, the route crosses a rocky grassland to the base of Big Hill, 3.5 miles, a landmark which rises to the north like a giant haystack. A track branches left, leading up to a saddle below the hill; a short, steep climb then reaches the 3,042-foot summit.

From the hilltop there stretches a wide view of the southern Humboldt landscape: west is the forested mass of Rainbow Ridge, with South Rainbow Peak rising up only two miles away; southwest is the notched ridgeline of the King Range, the slopes on its far side plunging straight to the sea; southeast are the jagged Bear Buttes, and closer at hand, Grasshopper Peak, with the Bull Creek drainage falling away in front of it; east are the distant Yolla Bollys and also the conical Lassics; northwest, looming through a fringe of trees, is the apparatus-crowned top of Monument Peak, where the presence of several relay stations maintain the mountain's long history of usefulness, which began with its service as a survey meridian in the previous century.

Fox Camp Road bends around the base of Big Hill and plunges into a thicket of Douglas fir, where the little-used route clings to the hill's steep eastern cliff. Bigleaf maples cover the rocky roadbed with a litter of crackly leaves, but their sound is soon replaced by the sweet scent of California laurel, a grove of which clusters about the road.

At mile 4.1 the forest opens briefly to offer a vista of Pole Line Road; the route then descends gradually to a 180-degree right turn at the base of Thomas Hill, mile 4.4. Now the road drops quickly, reaching another switchback at a rushing rivulet, mile 4.8, that forms part of Cuneo Creek.

The road levels and at mile 5.1 comes to a second small branch of Cuneo Creek. Here exists a sort of oasis within the forest, the overstory of tanoak, Douglas fir, and madrone now supplemented by sword fern, redwood sorrel, giant horsetail, and gooseberry. The route then turns east, running gently downhill through a mixed forest made notable at mile 5.2 by several groups of lovely large madrones.

As the road continues to drop, it passes through several sunny patches of grassland, finally reaching a locked gate at 6.7 miles. The route ends just ahead at a junction with the Indian Orchard Trail and Pole Line Road.

Pacific madrone
(Arbutus menziesii)

Few trees offer more contrast to their surroundings than the Pacific madrone. Perhaps most often, it will be found arching gracefully over some thickly forested hillslope, growing in delicate defiance of the surrounding straight-trunked Douglas firs and tanoaks. When seen by the roadside, it colors the darkest woodland with the pink and green hues of its underbark, which it often exposes by exfoliating its thicker, brownish red outer covering.

By the edge of a springtime prairie, the trees gleam in the gloaming, their foliage framing the pale light of hundreds of creamy white flowers. The madrone stands out wherever it is found; in a region ruled by redwoods, it has claimed its own province.

Madrone berries were eaten, either raw, boiled, or dried, by various Indian tribes, who also brewed the tree's roots and leaves into tea. Whites had a less peaceful use for the madrone, using charcoal from its burned wood to make gunpowder of commercial quality. [blooms March-May].

The estimable tree even prompted the following explosion of poetic high eloquence by Bret Harte, a one-time resident of Humboldt County:

Captain of the Western wood,
Thou that apest Robin Hood!
Green above thy scarlet hose
How thy velvet mantle shows:
Never tree like thee arrayed.
O thou gallant of the glade!
. . . .
Where, oh where shall we begin
Who would paint thee, Harlequin?
With thy waxen, burnished leaf,
With thy branches' red relief,
With thy polu-tinted fruit,
In thy spring or autumn suit, —
Where begin, and oh, where end, —
Thou whose charms all art transcend?

INDIAN ORCHARD TRAIL

Summary: This winding path ascends the wooded canyon slopes above Cuneo Creek; along the way it passes a haunting, half-hidden apple orchard.

Distance: 2.8 miles, one way

Elevation Loss/Gain: 1,100-foot gain, south to north

Location: The southern trailhead is at the Cuneo Creek Horse Group Camp; the northern end is at the Fox Camp Road/Pole Line Road junction.

Description: The trail begins between a pair of fence rows at the northern end of the campground loop; it runs north as a faint road and soon drops over the edge of the camp area onto the benchland beside Cuneo Creek. At 0.2 mile the trail swings left; a Park sign marks the route's descent, right, to a ford on the main fork of Cuneo Creek; the track left ends after briefly running along Cuneo's south fork.

The main trail crosses the creek amid a confusion of boulders, small alders, and silt. Far upstream to the left, the hillside is scarred by a huge, grayish gash, the site of a major mudslide that generates much of the creek-clogging material.

North of the crossing, mile 0.3, the path switchbacks up the bank to run along another benchland on an old, gently rising roadbed. To the right is the north fork of Cuneo Creek, while the end of Cuneo Ridge ascends steeply on the left. Atop the ridge stood an orchard belonging to John Cuneo, an early farmer famed for his chestnuts.

Blueblossom and creambush cluster near the pathway at mile 0.9 as the route continues its gradual ascent. At 1.2 miles a wooden sign proclaims "Cuneo Road," although there is no noticeable change in the trail, which continues to follow the old roadbed. The path then drops to cross a side branch of the Cuneo North Fork, passing giant chain fern and seep-spring monkey flower that lurk in the bankside shadows.

Past the crossing are views of Grasshopper Peak, Squaw Creek Ridge, and, east across Cuneo Creek, the oak-dappled ridge on which Pole Line Road runs. Bigleaf maple and Pacific starflower enhance the closer, pathside scenery.

The trail begins a series of zigzags, mile 1.5, that climb the steepening side of the Cuneo Creek drainage. The route then straightens northward and at 2.0 miles reaches the vegetation-choked entrance to Indian Orchard, left. A hundred feet along this access path, the foliage parts to reveal a small, boggy glade filled with a dozen long-neglected apple trees.

THE LAST LOLANGKOK OF BULL CREEK

Once the spot now called Indian Orchard was known only as "the Indian's." It was named for the man who had settled there — "Indian George" — a Lolangkok whose original name was Ah-da-dil-wah, but who the whites called George Burt. He had been born in the middle of the previous century on the flats beside Bull Creek, where his people had a village they called Kahs-cho-chi-net-tah. Within a few years of his birth, Burt's tribe had been virtually destroyed; the whites who had taken over the valley renamed the site of his village, calling it "School-house Flat."

A victim of the so-called "Indian wars," Burt was taken from his homeland while still a child, spending time at both the Smith River Reservation in Del Norte County and at the reservation in Hoopa. He survived these ordeals and returned to live along the South Fork Eel; for a while he was at Sa-bug-gah-nah, a Lolangkok community above Myers Flat. He may also have lived for a time along lower Bull Creek, dwelling in a goosepen redwood on the flats between Luke Prairie and the Big Trees area. Eventually Burt and his wife Tu-ha-ka, or Sadie, a member of the Lassik tribe, acquired a homestead above the north fork of Cuneo Creek. They built a house there, framing it not with lumber but with peeled logs. Burt also began growing apple trees, which he started from seed; the county directory for 1905-06 listed his occupation as "farmer." Five of the Burt children, three boys and two girls, would troop down to the site of their father's old village to attend school.

The Burts moved to Fortuna in their later years, but for a time they returned to their homestead in the summers. Bruce Lewis, who lived at the bottom of the canyon, would haul up supplies to the Burts' place on a horse-drawn sledge. The youngest Lewis child, Albert, once painted three lines on his chin when the Burts came through; it was to imitate Sadie Burt's "one-eleven" tatoo that was traditional among the local Indian women.

In 1922 the linguist C. Hart Merriam interviewed Burt, who was then one of but a few remaining Lolangkoks; the aging Indian provided Merriam with an extensive list of tribal place names, along with a few folk tales and bits of other information. Back on Cuneo Creek, the orchard homestead now lay vacant, the little cabin gradually falling apart. A neighbor who visited the abandoned house found a scattering of love letters that had been written to one of the Burts' daughters. Little else, except for the apple trees, was left.

The Burts sold the property in 1928. Two of the new owners, George Wrigley and his son Irving, were themselves apple growers, although they had purchased the place not for its orchard but to use as a vacation *spot and hunting camp. Irving Wrigley did take an interest in the apple trees, however, especially one that grew near the house and produced apples with a purplish pink flesh. He tried to propagate the species back at his home, but came up with a different variety instead.*

Wrigley had been charmed by the little canyon orchard and by the man who had started it. He kept the new tree, and named the apple it produced "George Burt." It was a fitting tribute to a fellow apple grower—and to the last Lolangkok of Bull Creek.

*   *   *

The orchard reposes in a sort of wistful half-light, shaded by the surrounding forest and overgrown with grasses and poison oak. It is rent down the middle by a deep gully, which a weathered wooden bridge still struggles to span. The access trail turns left to cross the bridge and then leaves the orchard to ascend a low, fir-covered rise. A water faucet and a privy mark the site of a now-abandoned trail camp. The privy works; the faucet doesn't.

Two paths depart the spot. The one left passes the privy and then drops south to a lovely little stream that gurgles over a mass of mossy rocks. The route continues downhill a short distance to meet the Indian Orchard Trail about 0.1 mile below the main entrance to the orchard.

The path to the right heads toward the base of a small ridge, passing a carpet of several dozen calypso orchids along the way. This gathering of entrancing flowers will likely bloom several weeks later than those found elsewhere in the Park.

calypso orchid
(Calypso bulbosa)

One of the few places where this delicate flower grows in abundance is Humboldt Redwoods State Park. Sending up a slender stem from a basal leaf, the plant produces a stunning flower noted for its protruding pink and white lower petal, which droops like a pouting lip. In early spring numerous calypso orchids dot the duff of shaded forest areas, their intriguing appearance inspiring many a lingering look. The flower's name refers not to some syncopated song of the Caribbean, but to the Greek goddess Calypso, an Aegean beauty who lived in island solitude unless prompted to snatch a sailor from the sea for temporary amusement; like its namesake, this orchid is something of a recluse. It is also called "fairy slipper"—by those who see its puffy bottom petal as a shoelike shape. [blooms March-June]

Be it ever so humble. . .

Beyond the orchids is another, older outhouse that was built by a relative of the Wrigleys. Now the privy is home to a later orchard resident, an ambitious woodrat that has built a four-foot-tall nest of sticks in the middle of the tiny building.

Leaving Indian Orchard, the main route resumes its gradual northward climb along what has become a wide roadway, soon offering a vista of Grasshopper Peak to the right. A roadside creeklet supports a string of red alders, which in turn shades a blanket of Siberian candyflower.

The Cuneo Creek North Fork flows under the trail via a culvert at 2.6 miles; several clumps of California spikenard cling to the damp streambanks. The route then makes its final, gradual ascent; it passes a rusting, locked metal gate at 2.8 miles and then meets the eastern end of Fox Camp Road. A few feet to the right is a junction with Pole Line Road.

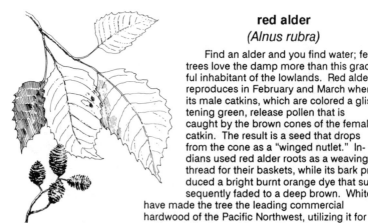

red alder
(Alnus rubra)

Find an alder and you find water; few trees love the damp more than this graceful inhabitant of the lowlands. Red alder reproduces in February and March when its male catkins, which are colored a glistening green, release pollen that is caught by the brown cones of the female catkin. The result is a seed that drops from the cone as a "winged nutlet." Indians used red alder roots as a weaving thread for their baskets, while its bark produced a bright burnt orange dye that subsequently faded to a deep brown. Whites have made the tree the leading commercial hardwood of the Pacific Northwest, utilizing it for pulp and also for making tool handles, furniture, and cabinets. When burned, alder wood produces an aromatic smoke that is excellent for curing salmon. Alder roots contain nitrogen-fixing bacteria, which enable them to serve as a natural soil enhancer.

LOOK PRAIRIE ROAD

Summary: One of the most scenic routes in the Park, this road winds its way up to Peavine Ridge through varied woodlands, past exquisite flowers, and across a charming prairie complete with rustic barn.

Length: 3.4 miles, one-way

Elevation Change: 2,000-foot gain, south to north

Location: The southern end of the route is at Mattole Road, 4.2 miles west of the 101 Freeway and just before Harper Creek; the northern end joins Peavine Road.

Description: Look Prairie Road promptly passes a locked metal gate as it begins to climb out of the Rockefeller Forest. After a sharp switchback, the route winds through grassy woodlands that in spring are dotted with two-eyed violets.

Soon the road crosses the western edge of Luke Prairie, mile 0.2, at a point called "Blue Slide." Here masses of blue-gray earth slump downhill in rolling, grass-covered heaps. This slow-moving "earthflow" contrasts sharply with the spectacular "mudflows" of Cuneo Creek, where huge sections of the mountainside have slid into the streambed far below.

Leaving Luke Prairie, the route climbs gradually as it passes near the wide-spreading limbs of several Oregon white oaks. Just ahead, the center of the roadbed fills with a springtime profusion of long-beaked storksbill geraniums.

long-beaked storksbill,
broadleaf filaree
(Erodium botrys)

This immigrant from Europe, a member of the geranium family, is notable for its eye-catching seed pods — the thin and sharply pointed containers from which the plant derives its most commonly used name. Emphasizing another facet of the pods' shape, some people call the plant *alfilaria* ("little pin" in Spanish), filaree, or pin clover. At the base of the flower's "bill" are several small cups that are connected to the top of the bill by tiny, springy bands. These bands contract as the seeds ripen, finally breaking the cups and curling up. The force of this action flings the seeds away from the cups, sometimes to a distance of several feet. The curled bands are left delicately twisted into striking shapes. In earlier times, children would stick the flowers on their clothes and then watch them unwind, causing the multi-named plant to also be called "clocks." [blooms March-May]

*   *   *

LOOKING FOR LUKE AND LOOK

Look Prairie Road crosses through two grasslands on its way to Peavine Ridge. Most commonly the lower area is called Luke Prairie and the upper one Look Prairie, but the similarity of the two names often leads to confusion.

Late in the last century, the upper meadow was called Darby Prairie; it became the home of a former stagecoach driver, Allan Look, his wife Sara, and six sons. Allan raised cattle and hogs, leaving in the summers to work as a wagon painter in the Eel River valley; the still extant ranch barn was built by Allan and his sons. In 1905, the family sold the property to Bull Creek pioneer Tosaldo Johnson, who had homesteaded the next prairie west; Johnson subsequently renamed the prairie for the Looks. In more recent times, Tony Look, a grandson of Allan and Sara, founded the Sempervirens Fund, an organization which has done much to enhance another state park, Big Basin Redwoods.

Bill Luke was born in Phillipsville and later lived at several other locations in southern Humboldt County. For a time he drove a six-horse team between Briceland and Shelter Cove, hauling tanbark for shipment to the tanneries farther south. Luke then helped build the Redwood Highway, while his wife Mary cooked for the road crew. In the early 1940s, the Lukes rented the Look Prairie ranch and used it to raise sheep; during their stay the ranch house burned and had to be rebuilt.

Bill Luke later went back to driving, this time piloting the mail truck between South Fork and Piercy. He must have liked the job, for he kept at it until he was 85.

Allan Look and Bill Luke both gained fame as early-day drivers in southern Humboldt; it seems fitting that their names should each be attached to a pretty patch of local landscape. Others might disagree, but it all depends on how you "look" at it.

* * *

Appropriately close to the storksbill is a flock of birdsfoot buttercups. California black oaks line the route as it approaches the shaded confines of Harper Creek, mile 0.5. The road now straightens and cuts through a patch of sloping prairie, passing a struggling, solitary apple tree before entering a dark stand of redwood and Douglas fir. At mile 0.8 the route emerges from the forest onto a flat grassland. Directly ahead, framed by a wide-branching oak, is the Look Prairie Barn.

A barn worth many a look

THE LOOK PRAIRIE BARN

The aging building seems almost engulfed by the ground, its low-pitched roof flattened against the prairie. It appears that the barn might disappear into the grass at any moment, yet there is a feeling that it has been waiting, with utmost patience, for yet another traveller's visit. Did its builder stand at this spot when he first formed the barn's image in his mind's eye? It seems so, for the structure fits the setting as if it were part of a painting.

A latticework of poison oak climbs beside the barn door. Inside, the ground floor is nearly empty; the stalls to either side still have a sense of snugness. Some bottles, bleary with age, have been placed on the stall sills, and a few rusty implements have been hung overhead. A pile of ancient hay reposes in a corner. At the rear, a ladder ascends to the loft, its rungs well worn but still able to hold weight. The loft floor is made of huge redwood planks, three inches thick, that even now bear the marks of their hewing. Spikes the size of dinner knives anchor the planks to the beams underneath. Here in the loft there is a quietness, a feeling of farmer's peace, that fills the space beneath the broken shingles. All around is the smell of old, dry wood.

The loft door opens out to a view of the ranch yard. In spring, the ground below is filled with the progression of the season: daffodils nearly past flowering, periwinkle in purple bloom, iris yet to be. One fruit tree colors the air above the yard, the trunk of a second now only a shattered silhouette. Down the hillside from them sounds the thin trickle of a creek. Over all spreads the darkened limbs of the old oak. Above, a gray sky; below, the still prairie.

*   *   *

The road passes between the barn and the ranch yard, drops to cross a creeklet, and then winds uphill along the western edge of an old orchard. Rising amid the decaying apple trees is the larger form of a single Spanish chestnut. The route turns right at the base of a steep hillside and climbs eastward past a large, rounded bigleaf maple; just ahead, patches of popcorn flower rise from the road. At mile 1.1 the route enters a stretch of burned forest and bends left to follow the canyonside above a branch of Calf Creek. The forest duff here is home to numerous two-eyed violets and calypso orchids; the small and delicate flowers are nearly obscured by the litter of redwood needles.

two-eyed violet, heart's-ease
(Viola ocellata)
[blooms March-June]

On the bank to the left at 1.5 miles is an opening to the upper end of Look Prairie. A short climb off the road leads to the madrone-fringed prairie summit—an ideal picnic spot. From here, the grassy hillside descends gently southward to a knobby knoll that offers good views of Grasshopper Peak and the Bull Creek canyon. The prairie itself is also worth a look, for this is the best spot in the Park to find the native bunch grasses that once covered such open areas; other Park prairielands saw greater encroachment of domestic grass species as the result of ranching, but this spot was somehow spared. Beyond the knoll, the prairie drops down a ski-run-like slope that ends just above the orchard and barn. The madrones that rim this section of prairie have strangely clipped lower foliage—browsing deer have eaten everything they could reach.

From its meeting with upper Look Prairie, the road rises through mixed forest, twisting up gentle, shaded switchbacks. A small spring drips from the bank at mile 2.2, watering a group of giant chain ferns. The route passes through a lovely grove of medium-size madrones and then encounters a wandering branch of Calf Creek, mile 2.8. Salal and black huckleberry flourish in the vicinity.

Near another, larger tributary of Calf Creek, a number of burned and broken snags mark the course of an earlier fire. The road then passes a locked metal gate; beyond it is a junction with Peavine Road, mile 3.4.

PEAVINE ROAD

Summary: This long, remote and often scenic roadway traverses the northern rim of the Bull Creek drainage; the highlight is a stunning stand of mature mixed forest midway along the route.

Distance: 7.1 miles from its junction with Look Prairie Road to its meeting with Pole Line Road (Note: The eastern section of Peavine Road, which runs through a small section of the Park before entering private timberlands, is not included.)

Elevation Change: 1,000-foot gain and 1,600-foot loss, east to west

Location: Peavine Road connects with the tops of three valley-to-ridgetop routes: Look Prairie Road to the east, Thornton Road in the middle, and Pole Line Road to the west.

Description: From its junction with Look Prairie Road, the route turns left and soon begins twisting uphill through mixed forest. At 0.5 mile the road reaches a hilltop and then drops sharply towards a ridge saddle. The course crosses the bottom of the saddle, mile 1.0, amid a young second-growth forest; the road along here could well be called "Wall Street," for the canyon of *Bear* Creek descends to the right and that of *Bull* Creek to the left.

As it rises from the saddle, the road passes a patch of stinging nettle before gaining the top of a knobby ridge crest, mile 1.2. Here taller trees shade redwood sorrel, redwood violet, and smooth yellow violet.

stinging nettle
(Urtica dioica)

When touched, stinging nettle indeed stings, but the unpleasant prickly sensation is short lived. For those who can't wait for the discomfort to diminish, the crushed leaves of elderberry, plantain, bracken fern, horsetail, thimbleberry, or curled dock can be applied to provide relief.

This nettlesome plant does have its positive side, however: it has served as a fodder crop in Sweden and Russia, a hair tonic, a scalp conditioner, a growth stimulant, and as a tea for colds. Indians wove stinging nettle fibers into cords for both nets and fishing lines; nettles have been prepared in soups and salads, and have also been made into beer. Three varieties of discriminating caterpillars eat the plant's leaves. A Japanese novel even bears the title *Some Prefer Nettles*.

Perhaps the nettle's most interesting use occurred during World War I, when cotton-starved Germans revived the medieval practice of processing the plant to produce fabric. Since it took 90 pounds of raw nettles to make a shirt, supplies of the wild plant were quickly exhausted, and a new crop had to be cultivated. The experiment was soon discontinued, however, with the resultant loss of nettle shirts apparently little lamented. [blooms June-September]

The route crosses another once-logged saddle, mile 1.6, and climbs past a view of Grasshopper Peak, left. At mile 1.9, large beds of pale Douglas iris grow in the midst of old logs and stumps—an inviting rest stop.

Douglas iris
(Iris douglasiana)

Douglas iris features the drooping, delicately-shaped petals common to the iris family; it grows in a range of colors — from cream white through pale yellow to blue violet. The side ribs of the leaves provided a fiber which Indians converted into a strong, rope-like string that was used for hunting and for fish nets; the string-making process was slow: according to one Indian, it took "nearly six weeks to make a rope 12 feet long." Some northern tribes wrapped their babies in the leaves. The Douglas iris is never eaten more than once, since all parts of it are poisonous. [blooms March-May]

An older Douglas fir/redwood forest begins to enclose the road at mile 2.1. The trees grow in stature as the route moves west; such large redwoods are seldom seen at this high an elevation – 2,200 feet. Even more impressive are the mature, thick-trunked tanoaks, mile 2.4; those found in the Park are usually small, spindly second-growth, but here an entire stand escaped the tanbark crews, and they are magnificent.

Mixed old growth continues until mile 3.0, where large stumps mark a logging site beside a branch of Albee Creek, left. The remains of an old cabin lie hidden in the woods to the right, just before a junction with Thornton Road, left, at mile 3.1. From here, Peavine turns right and rises up a hillslope. At mile 3.7 the road levels and then begins a long, gradual descent west. Between miles 4.3 and 4.6 the route crosses three tributaries of Mill Creek; soon the slopes of Snow Prairie appear above on the right. More meadow rises next to a junction with an old logging road, right at mile 4.9. Peavine Road then bends left around the top of Mill Creek; at mile 5.1 the route rises slightly as it traverses the top of the ridgeslope, moving through medium-small Douglas fir and tanoak.

The route winds south and west; at mile 5.5 it heads downhill into a small saddle, reaching some madrones at 5.8 miles and then climbing slightly. The land here is the only part of the Bull Creek watershed not owned by the Park. Until recently it was in private possession, but the property was confiscated by the Federal Government after a marijuana plantation was discovered on it.

Having levelled at mile 6.1, the road begins dropping abruptly down the southwestern end of Peavine Ridge through mixed forest. Several switchbacks later, mile 6.9, the route turns left; the small stream that flows through the shaded canyon, right, is the beginning of Bear River. Beyond a locked gate the way turns right, crossing the top of a small, cattail-fringed pond that forms Bear River's source. Peavine Road then meets Pole Line Road at mile 7.1.

common cattail
(Typha latifolia)

Cattails usually cluster together in groups, often wagging the tops of their tall stalks when caught by the wind. Northwestern Indians wove the stalks into mats that were then used as baskets, rain capes, kneeling pads in canoes, and for other diverse purposes. The spike contains a soft down that has been used as a pillow stuffing and a dressing for burns and wounds. As the summer progresses, the spikes often break open, allowing wisps of the down to float away on the wind – a wistful reminder that fall will soon follow. [blooms June-July]

POLE LINE ROAD

Route Summary: A stiff but short hillside climb, this route crosses two large prairies, passes glorious groves of oaks, and leads to the headwaters of Bear River.

Distance: 2.6 miles, one way

Elevation Change: 1,200-foot gain, south to north

Location: The south end of Pole Line Road is at Mattole Road, 7.3 miles west of the 101 Freeway; the north end is at the Park boundary, 0.3 mile beyond the Bear River divide.

Description: The first power lines into the community of Bull Creek came down Pole Line Road after passing over Monument Ridge to the north; they were strung by Charlie East in the days before PG&E consolidated the region's utilities. Today, the roadside is still stippled with poles, but their importance diminished when the town disappeared.

The route branches right from Mattole Road, reaching a locked metal gate in a hundred feet; it then climbs up the end of a broad ridge, moving through bigleaf maple, madrone, willow, Douglas fir, and blueblossom. Much of the area is covered by enormous thickets of poison oak.

At a small, grass-covered saddle, 0.2 mile, the road crosses the Horse Trail and then resumes climbing, soon curving around the hillside to enter a large ridgetop prairie. A forest of young oaks rises up the hillslope on the right; to the left are views of erosion-wracked Cuneo Creek and of the Horse Camp near the creek's mouth. In summertime, blue-eyed grass, California poppy, and buttercup speckle the grass-land, which the road then leaves at mile 0.7.

California blue-eyed grass
(Sisyrinchium bellum)

A pretty plant, but one misleadingly named, its "blue eyes" are narrow-veined purple flowers with yellow centers, and, rather than being a grass, the plant is actually a type of iris. The Latin name seems to make even less sense, for it means "handsome pig snout." This apparent insult is actually a garbled reference to the interest swine show in the plant's roots. Look for blue-eyed grass in meadow areas and oak woodlands. [blooms March-May]

After meandering among small firs and madrones, Pole Line Road comes out onto a second lengthy prairie at 0.9 mile. The remains of an apple orchard, left, mark part of John Cuneo's homestead site; a road once dropped from here to the creek which bears his name. On the right are views northeast of Thornton, Johnson, and Look prairies. In the distance are ridges near the main Eel River, and beyond them, far to the east, the pointed peaks of the Lassics.

This second prairie rises more gently than the first, providing a pleasant place to picnic. Near its upper end, a stately California black oak spreads its dark limbs above a bright patch of buttercups. The view back down the prairie includes the whalelike hump of Grasshopper Peak, along with Squaw Creek Ridge, Hanson Ridge, and the upper Bull Creek watershed.

At 1.2 miles the road leaves the prairie, passing into a woodland of Douglas fir, California laurel, and oak. On the right side of the road is scarlet pimpernel, a small, alien flower whose name is more famous as the title of a book and several movies.

The route continues climbing northward and at 1.5 miles passes a group of Oregon white oak and California black oak; blue-eyed grass looks up from the roadside. Then, at 1.8 miles, Pole Line Road bends around a high point of the ridge. In summer, the grassy hillside above the roadbank offers a colorful collection of flowers, including farewell-to-spring, blue dicks, miniature lupine, California poppy, buttercup, and popcorn flower. Farther afield, a wide panorama spreads to the west: Bear River divide, Thomas Hill, Big Hill, and the area near Fox Camp.

Below this ridgeline is the North Fork of Cuneo Creek—the Indian Orchard Trail can be seen running along the benchland above the streambed.

At 2.1 miles, two road remnants branch right; the main route bends left and begins its final ascent to the ridge saddle. The bank above the road at 2.2 miles is decorated with bright yellow clusters of seep-spring monkey flower, which, like the neighboring giant chain ferns, seeks out seeps. Across the road are shaded clumps of another moisture lover, California spikenard. A short distance ahead, the prolific upper roadbank displays creambush, California hazel, inside-out flower, and the petite goldenback fern.

**seep-spring
monkey flower**
(Mimulus guttatus)
[blooms April-June]

Soon the route arrives at a junction, left, with Fox Camp Road and the Indian Orchard Trail. The route continues uphill to meet Peavine Road at mile 2.3; it then runs north on its way out of the Park, passing a marshy pond, right, that forms the headwaters of Bear River. At mile 2.6 it comes to a locked metal gate that marks the start of private property.

goldenback fern
(Pityrogramma triangularis)

This tiny, triangular-shaped fern clings to damp, dark hillsides, sometimes barely seen in its shaded surroundings. The plant's underside is coated with a waxy powder, colored either gold or silver, which rubs off easily. The fern's black stems were woven into basket patterns by California Indians.

THORNTON ROAD

Summary: The steepest north slope road, Thornton offers a challenging climb through grasslands, madrone thickets, and mixed forest.

Length: 2.5 miles, one way

Elevation Change: 2,000-foot gain, south to north

Location: The southern end of Thornton Road starts in the Albee Creek Campground; after crossing the Albee Creek Bridge at the entrance to the camp, immediately turn right and proceed to site #39—the route begins at a locked gate just ahead. At its north end, Thornton Road meets the middle of Peavine Road.

Note: A section of the Horse Trail follows the southern part of Thornton Road, exiting onto its own trailbed 0.4 mile from road's start.

Description: The road is named for a family that once owned the property where the campground is now located. Hugh Thornton led local opposition to the Park's upper Bull Creek acquisition program.

Beyond the gate, the road begins climbing abruptly. Downhill to the left is mixed forest; a rising prairie covers the hillside on the right.

At 0.4 mile the Horse Trail branches left; Thornton Road proceeds sharply uphill, passing through Douglas fir, California laurel, and California black oak. Near the road edge are several small, moundlike growths of California laurel that owe their shrunken size to browsing deer. A few Oregon white oak now appear at the roadside; then, left at 0.6 mile, several California buckeyes cluster downslope.

California buckeye
(Aesculus californica)

The appearance of the California buckeye's large, cream-white flower spikes is a sure sign that spring has come to the North Coast. The cylinder-shaped clusters extend erectly from the plant's bushy mass of dark green leaves, giving the buckeye a bristly, hedgehog-like appearance. Growing as either a large shrub or small tree, the buckeye has shed its leaves by fall, exposing large, nutty capsules bigger than golf balls; this fruit is poisonous to people unless leached in boiling water. Unlike humans, both chipmunks and squirrels can eat the raw capsules, but bees are killed by both the nectar and the pollen. Indians would throw the ground capsules into fishing holes, stupefying the fish and thus rendering them more catchable. Cabinet makers often use the buckeye's wood, which, when kiln dried for several weeks, takes on a mottled green coloration resembling that of onyx. The California buckeye can grow to 25 feet in height, often spreading grandiosely as if it were a miniature oak; it is the only variety of its genus native to the west, far removed from Ohio — "the buckeye state." [blooms April-June]

Prairie alternates with woodland as the rough, rutted road continues climbing to the northwest; it crosses a tributary of Mill Creek, mile 0.9, before finally levelling out amid many small madrones. A scattering of scrub oak lines the roadway.

A large meadow opens on the hillside to the left, mile 1.6, offering views of Big Hill and the Mill Creek drainage. Farther along the opening are vistas to the south of Bull Creek and Cuneo Creek. The gently sloping grassland offers a good resting spot.

Beyond the prairie, Thornton Road enters a large grove of medium-small madrone. With their thin, twisted trunks and partially flayed, skinlike bark, the young trees seem strangely vulnerable, as if suffering some lingering torment of the forest. Only at mile 2.0 does the grove's intensity lessen, as Douglas fir and tanoak gradually supplant the suppliant madrones.

At 2.4 miles, the road passes a derelict wooden gate and soon rises to cross a small prairie. At the north end of the prairie, 2.5 miles from its start, Thornton Road ends at a junction with Peavine Road.

ROUTES OF GRASSHOPPER PEAK
AND SQUAW CREEK RIDGE

[see map, p. 251]

BAXTER-SQUAW CREEK CUTOFF TRAIL

Summary: This hillside shortcut connects Baxter Environmental Camp with the middle section of Squaw Creek Ridge Road.

Distance: 0.7 mile, one way

Elevation Change: 750-foot gain, west to east

Location: The route's western end begins in the middle of Baxter Environmental Camp; the eastern end is at mile 1.8 of Squaw Creek Ridge Road.

Warning: *The trail's lower section is very steep and in poor condition; it can be dangerous on descents, especially for backpackers.*

Description: A sign near the environmental camp's restroom indicates the start of the trail, which branches left to cross a small grassy area; in a hundred feet the route meets the base of a steep bank. The trail now climbs very abruptly on a poor, slippery track, turning left and levelling after another hundred feet to cut across the hillside beneath a covering of tanoak and madrone.

The route turns right at mile 0.1 and follows the spine of a ridge spur uphill. After bending left, mile 0.2, the incline increases; the trail then picks up an old roadbed, passing some California black oaks before reaching a patch of blackberries at mile 0.4.

California blackberry
(Rubus vitifolius)

This prolific plant is as pesky as its berries are tasty. It can form impenetrable thickets that no hiker would hazard, and in more subtle guise can dangle a few thorny vines by the trailside, waiting to catch and scratch the unwary. From a distance, however, blackberry bushes can be stunningly scenic as they encroach upon a decaying barn or form islands of rough-textured color in an otherwise drab field. The closely related *Rubus ursinus*, which, along with the California blackberry, is sometimes called "dewberry," has been hybridized to develop such food store favorites as youngberry, boysenberry, and olallieberry. The California blackberry has three leaves per stem and relatively small stem prickles; also found in the Park are the Himalaya berry, with wide leaves on a thick stem, and the cut-leaf blackberry, with sharply slashed leaves; both have five leaves per stem. [blooms April-August]

The path continues its steep climb; the appearance of a group of large, ruddy redwoods signals the forthcoming ridgetop. At mile 0.7 the trail meets the Squaw Creek Ridge Road.

GRASSHOPPER ROAD

Summary: Steep but shaded, this northern approach to the Park's highest peak is a favorite of cyclists and an important connecting route for backpacking trips.

Distance: 6.9 miles, one way

Elevation Change: 3,200-foot gain, 120-foot loss, north to south

Location: The route's northern end is at Mattole Road, 5.3 miles west of the 101 Freeway; the southern end is at the top of Grasshopper Peak.

**Andrews' clintonia,
red clintonia**
(Clintonia andrewsiana)
[blooms April-July]

Description: After leaving Mattole Road, the route passes a shaded parking area and then rises briskly on steep switchbacks, soon arriving at a locked gate in the midst of heavy mixed forest. The climb continues to a junction with Squaw Creek Ridge Road, right, mile 0.7, at which point Grasshopper Road finally levels. The course then runs high along the mountainside, dipping and rising only slightly; in the canyon far below are the rushing waters of Squaw Creek. At mile 1.7 a collection of clintonias cluster on the upper roadbank opposite two large stumps.

After crossing Squaw Creek at mile 2.6, the road turns east and begins to rapidly ascend the north side of Grasshopper Peak. Giant chain fern fills a small stream

ROUTES OF GRASSHOPPER PEAK/SQUAW CREEK RIDGE

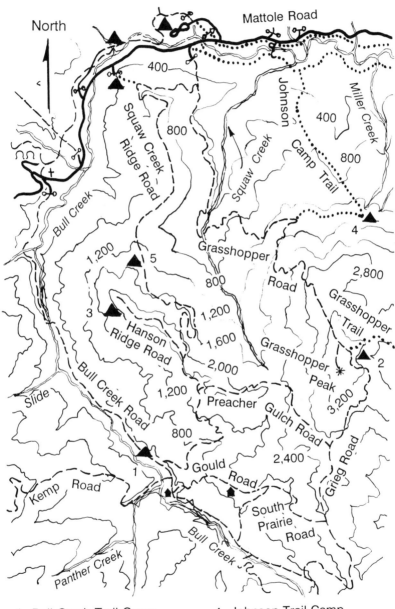

1 Bull Creek Trail Camp
2 Grasshopper Trail Camp
3 Hanson Ridge Trail Camp
4 Johnson Trail Camp
5 Whiskey Flat Trail Camp
Barn   Camp

canyon, right at mile 3.7, as mixed forest continues to cover the hillslope. At a small opening, mile 4.2, Grasshopper Road makes a wide turn and meets the Johnson Camp Trail, which joins from the left. A pair of cabins once fronted the junction, but now all that remains is a piece of old furniture, hidden in the woods.

* * *

GRASSHOPPER'S GRUELLING GRADE

In the summer of 1950, Marie Moore set up housekeeping in a small cabin near Johnson Tie Camp while her husband, Edgar, worked in the nearby woods. It wasn't easy for Marie; she had two young children, there was no electricity or running water, and worst of all, she had to travel down the mountain to the Bull Creek store when she needed food. Marie was fresh from the flatlands of Amarillo, Texas and was just learning to drive — Grasshopper Peak must have seemed like the Matterhorn as she coaxed her car back up the steep grade. Frequently the engine would overheat, and Marie would finish the trip on foot, a sack of groceries in one arm and her baby son in the other.

Thirty years earlier, motorists had a tougher time driving down Grasshopper Road than up it. When the little Overland car from a hillside tanbark camp made its first trip down to the flats, the vehicle quickly went out of control and nearly crashed. A small tree was then tied to the back of the auto on its downgrade runs, and this kept the Overland from going over the cliff.

Tom Hill, the Miranda store owner who supplied the camp with food, also grappled with the grade. His sturdy, high-bodied delivery truck usually made the trip without difficulty, but during one trip down the mountain, Hill failed to shift properly and the truck rolled along out of gear, rapidly gaining speed. Tom jumped from the cab and grabbed a fence picket he kept close at hand. He quickly thrust the piece of wood between the truck's wagon-type wheel spokes; the picket held, and once he found the right gear, grocer Hill finished descending Grasshopper's hill.

Today the redoubtable road is open only to authorized vehicles. The general public can no longer drive the hair-raising route, as Marie Moore and Tom Hill once did, but for some reason, there haven't been many complaints.

* * *

Leaving the junction, the route moves south through second-growth forest, climbing abruptly at mile 4.7; along the roadside are three dwellers of the darkness: phantom orchid, leafless wintergreen, and white-veined wintergreen. The route twists and then levels briefly, resuming a sharp incline at mile 5.4. After several brief pauses in the shadowed ascent, a very steep pitch at mile 6.0 brings the road out onto the northern arm of Grasshopper Peak. The grade now lessens and the thick forest recedes. A vista opens to the right at mile 6.1 amid a framing of snowbrush, canyon live oak, and hairy manzanita; Squaw Creek Ridge is visible in the middle ground, with the Fox Camp/Panther Gap ridgeline rising in the distance behind it.

hairy manzanita,
Columbia manzanita
(Arctostaphylos columbiana)

With its twisted, often peeling, red-brown bark and thick, leathery leaves, manzanita often appears to be a sort of junior madrone that hasn't quite grown up. This common shrub likes dry sites and is a major cover plant on Southern California hillsides. Near the turn of the century, a huge specimen was reported at St. Helena in the Napa Valley; it measured 35 feet tall, with a trunk eleven-and-a-half feet in circumference. A woodsman who was apparently unimpressed with its size nearly cut the massive manzanita down, but a plant-loving passerby paid him two dollars to lower his ax.

There are more than 40 kinds of manzanita, but only the Columbia, or hairy, variety is common in the Park. While other manzanitas also have hairy branchlets, the hairs of this one alone are bristly. In Spanish, *manzanita* means "little apple," a reference to the sweet taste of its small berries; the early Hispanic settlers gathered the fruit green, making it into both a type of soft drink and a jelly. The California Indians used ripe berries for cider, wine, baked cakes, and a pinole-like meal. Manzanita leaves and wood also were used for a variety of purposes, giving the little apple a big reputation as one of the region's most versatile plants. [blooms March-May]

In a sunny opening at mile 6.4 are popcorn flower and baby blue eyes. The road returns to heavier forest at mile 6.5, where it meets Grieg Road, left, a route that soon leads to the Grasshopper Trail Camp. The route then climbs to the right, passing hound's tongue and scarlet larkspur.

The open hillside displays snowbrush, blueblossom, canyon live oak, and a beautiful blue-colored penstemon. The latter plant is also found at the road's end, mile 6.9, next to the Grasshopper lookout tower. The peaktop panorama here ranges far and wide: from the mountains of Trinity County in the east, across the sprawling Eel River watershed to the south, and westward to the ragged ridgeline of the King Range, close beside the ocean.

**scarlet larkspur,
canyon delphinium
Christmas horns,**
(Delphinium nudicaule)

To the practical-minded California Indians, this lovely flower was called "sleep root" for its narcotic properties; tea made from the roots was used to stupefy gambling opponents. Above ground, the plant's bright scarlet flowers branch off from the tops of long, thin, leafless stalks; the petals have a crinkly texture, as if made from rolled-up paper mache. As with other delphiniums, each flower has a long spur — quite like a lark's hind claw — that tapers back from where the petals attach to the stem. Taken together, the petals and spur look like a trumpet, explaining why the flower is also called "Christmas horns." [blooms April-June]

GRIEG ROAD

Summary: A southerly, gradual approach to Grasshopper Peak, the trail's middle section straddles the ridge between the Bull Creek and Canoe Creek watersheds.

Distance: 4.1 miles, one way

Elevation Change: 1,960-foot gain and 200-foot loss, south to north

Location: The route's southern end is at mile 5.6 of Bull Creek Road; its northern end meets Grasshopper Road, 0.4 mile below the fire lookout.

Description: Grieg Road departs northward from Bull Creek Road, rising steeply through blueblossom and snowbrush. It bends right and gradually levels at mile 0.4, climbing again at 0.6 mile. After a sharp switchback left, mile 0.7, the route reaches the ridgetop and proceeds north along the Bull Creek-Canoe Creek divide; a thick mixed forest encloses the roadway. The course crosses a saddle at mile 0.9 and another at 1.2 miles, arriving at a junction with South Prairie Road, mile 1.5. Grieg Road bears right, moving uphill through a grassy opening that in early summer is enlivened by firecracker flower and winecup clarkia. After a short but steep rise, the route re-enters the forest; Oregon white oak and California black oak shelter both tarweed and a large, downslope patch of hound's tongue, mile 1.6.

After passing a prairie that drops leftward off the ridge, the route crosses another saddle. A dark section of forest at mile 2.0 contains good-size madrones and also several Douglas firs that have strangely large lower limbs. The road dips through a final saddle before climbing sharply past more madrones to an opening where it meets Preacher Gulch Road, left, at 2.3 miles.

western hound's tongue
(Cynoglossum grande)

This sedately beautiful, large-leaved plant is notable for two things. First, its flowers, which are colored an eye-pleasing combination of periwinkle and cream. Second, it is named not for its blossom, like most flowers, but rather for its large and floppy leaves, which indeed seem to loll like floppy tongues. An inhabitant of damp, forested areas, hound's tongue produces barbed nutlets that attach themseles to passing animals, thereby assuring dispersion of the plant's seeds. Its root was prepared by Indians to soothe burns and stomach aches; in a bygone era it was believed that dogs would refrain from barking at anyone who put the flower under their feet. [blooms March-June]

Grieg Road proceeds to the right, passing along the southeastern side of Grasshopper Peak. A pleasant prairie at mile 2.4 contains western blue flax and rigid hedge nettle, while canyon live oak, scrub oak, Douglas fir, and manzanita mingle around its border. The road rises through small patches of woodland and prairie, climbs past some large outcroppings of rock, and then reaches a badly eroded stream gully, mile 2.9, where bigleaf maple and California laurel thrive on the creekbank moisture. After another steep grade, the route levels, winding around the mountainside through an alternation of shade and sunlight; canyon live oak, woolly sunflower, and creambush embellish the road edge. At mile 3.3, a broad vista to the east reveals such landmarks as Tuttle Butte and the Yolla Bollys. Closer at hand are a trio of hardy bushes — snowbrush, blueblossom, and hairy manzanita. In a stand of mature Douglas fir, mile 3.6, a side road exits right; it drops a short distance into a canyon containing the headwaters of Canoe Creek's North Fork — a possible water source for users of the Grasshopper Trail Camp.

Beyond the creek canyon, a patch of prairie descends to the rising roadway; bankside lupine, poppy, and cream cups then mark a further stretch of fir forest. The route soon enters more meadow, reaching a ridgeline intersection at mile 3.8. Here the Grasshopper Trail rises past the trail camp, right, crossing the roadway on its way uphill to the fire lookout. Grieg Road bends left to move laterally across the steep north face of Grasshopper Peak; it runs through a dark, second-growth forest of Douglas fir, madrone, and tanoak before ending, mile 4.1, at a junction with Grasshopper Road.

HANSON RIDGE ROAD

Summary: This brief byway leads across a flower-filled prairie to a pair of trail camps and two huge madrones.

Distance: 2.0 miles, round trip

Elevation Change: 560-foot gain and loss

Location: The route begins at Squaw Creek Ridge Road, 0.3 mile north of Preacher Gulch Road; it comes to a dead end on the northern end of Hanson Ridge.

Description: The road heads northwest along the side of Hanson Ridge, dropping slightly as it crosses the top of a splendidly flower-sprinkled prairie. In summer, the grass is intermixed with Douglas iris, blue dicks, popcorn flower, miniature lupine, and California poppy.

California poppy
(Eschscholzia californica)

A versatile plant, the California poppy serves as both the state flower and a potent narcotic. Its large petals form a deep, richly golden bowl that rests precariously atop a slender stem; the top-heavy flowers waggle wildly when buffeted by afternoon breezes. A lover of sunlight, the poppy petulantly closes its petals at night and on cloudy days. In earlier times, its crushed leaves were used as a pain killer for sore teeth. [blooms February-September]

As the road passes through the prairie, a view opens across the canyon to the western slopes of the Bull Creek watershed; the route crosses onto the forested top of Hanson Ridge at 0.2 mile. After running along the ridgeline to mile 0.4, the road reaches a spur trail, left, that enters a thicket of wood rose and then comes out onto the prairie. The trail follows the cascading grassland down a steep hillside for 150 yards; there it arrives at fir-fringed Hanson Ridge Trail Camp. Some 50 yards to the west, just past a patch of gooseberries, the track ends at the Hanson Ridge Group Camp, a somewhat vague vicinity apparently situated under several sheltering trees. A sometimes faint but well-marked path runs south and west from the camps' outhouse to reach a small, shaded canyon; here a tank holds the untreated drinking water supply. Along the way, bracken ferns bring seasonal color to the prairie — bright green in summer, golden brown in fall.

A few yards past the camp access trail, Hanson Ridge Road curves right, climbing around a humpy hummock. The route then twists along the ridgetop and at mile 0.6 passes two enormous madrones that stand in twisted, bark-clad grandeur like a pair of massive monuments. The road continues northwest, rolling along the ridgeline; at 0.8 mile the ridge narrows and is covered by somber, medium-size Douglas fir. The forest then changes to a mix of small second-growth as the route first rises and then makes a final drop, ending at 1.0 mile in a tree-encircled turnaround.

bracken fern
(Pteridium aquilinum)

JOHNSON CAMP TRAIL

Summary: Rising through mixed forest, this route passes the remains of an old camp where railroad ties were once cut; the spot now shelters overnight backpackers.

Distance: 2.3 miles, one way

Elevation Change: 1,350-foot gain, north to south

Location: The trail's northern end leaves the Bull Creek Flats Loop Trail 0.4 mile east of the Big Trees Area parking lot; the southern end is at a junction with the middle part of Grasshopper Road.

Warning: *Damp, shaded Johnson Camp is notorious for its many mosquitoes; campers can hope that the site's screened-window shacks will provide some protection.*

Description: After branching right from the Bull Creek Flats Trail, the route heads south across a small section of redwood-covered benchland. In a hundred yards the path begins climbing the northern slope of Grasshopper Peak, soon moving into a zone of open mixed forest; the hard-packed trailbed is noticeably rutted. The shaded hillside provides springtime habitat for several non-green plants — members of the orchid and heath families which grow without chlorophyll and instead derive their nutrients from living fungi. One such entity, spotted coral root, sticks up from the trailside at 0.4 mile.

The grade lessens as the path reaches the end of a ridge spur, which it then follows south. At mile 0.9 the route passes two more non-green plants: phantom orchid and leafless wintergreen. Several bog wintergreens, a green-leafed variety, grow by the trailside at mile 1.2.

For a time, the path undulates gradually upward, going by more bog wintergreen and then passing a few calypso orchids. At 1.7 miles there is pipsissewa, a.k.a. prince's pine, and lots of redwood inside-out flowers; the predominant ground cover is black huckleberry. Soon Pacific starflower and spotted coral root also make appearances.

At mile 1.9 the route crests a small rise and levels out; the trail then meets an abandoned road that runs

**bog wintergreen
(Pyrola asarifolia)**
[blooms May-August]

along the hillside; the route turns right to follow the roadbed. Just ahead, a side path turns left and enters the grounds of Johnson Trail Camp.

The site occupies a narrow, forested gulch and part of the neighboring hillside. Four reconstructed but well-weathered shanties repose under a canopy of redwoods, imparting the flavor of the original camp. Next to a small central clearing are an outhouse and a watering trough; the latter is the last remnant of the days when Enoch Johnson ran a split-stuff layout here, his crews cutting railroad ties and other hand-hewn redwood products. The camp operated until the 1950s, providing work for the woodsmen of southern Humboldt.

From the camp entrance, the trail continues southwest, crossing a small branch of Squaw Creek at 2.0 miles. A short distance ahead is the only vista point along the route; it offers a view of Bull Creek canyon's distant north slope. After several more bends along the hillside, the trail meets Grasshopper Road at 2.3 miles.

phantom orchid
*(Cephalanthera
austinae)*
[blooms May-July]

DAVE CHADBOURNE SURVIVES
WORKING IN THE WOODS

One of the early-day employees at Johnson Tie Camp was Dave Chadbourne, who, like many of the locals, took work in the woods whenever it was offered. The jobs all had one thing in common — they were dangerous.

In the summer of 1922, Chadbourne and Jesse Ridley were falling tanoaks at DeYoung's bark camp in Bull Creek when one of the trees smashed into a madrone on its way groundward. Then, according to a breathless newspaper account, the men soon

> *. . . heard some queer noises and concluded it must be the same tree. While trimming another limb from their tree Jesse glanced up at this huge big tree it was coming towards them. Calling Dave's attention immediately, they both scampered for a get away. As it was heading toward them. Dave had very little chance of escaping the terrible death that awaited him. But his first, last, and only chance was just one and he dashed into the gulch below and under an embankment, just in time to hear the crash and report of the enemy which fell directly where the boys were working.*

Johnson Camp shack

A month later, perhaps hopeful of avoiding other "enemy" trees, Dave had switched to the seemingly safer job of tanbark packing, but the change offered little improvement:

David Chadbourne had his leg crushed quite badly one day recently while packing bark, one of the mules became frightened and on turning around caught one of his legs between the load of bark and a tree, he is getting along nicely.

On another occasion, a skittish mule prompted Dave to halt his tanbark loading; an investigation revealed a rattlesnake hidden within the bark packet. Dave quickly dispatched the hitchhiking reptile and continued with his work.

Life outside of working hours had its hazards, too. Twice Dave had a wheel fall off his Dodge car as he motored the roads of Bull Creek; shortly thereafter he was in an auto wreck but escaped injury. On horseback, things were no better; in February of 1923 he cut his hand "quite badly" on an ax blade he was carrying on his saddle. At a baseball game, Dave was injured when struck in the head by a pitch. It seemed that he had a poor chance of surviving to old age.

But survive he did, and in his nineties Dave could still smile as he recalled his death-defying earlier years. When asked about his stint with the Bull Creek baseball team, he replied, "The only place I ever played was behind the plate." It figures that Dave would have been a catcher—after all, it's a good position for someone who's used to getting hurt.

* * *

PREACHER GULCH ROAD

Summary: This wide-ranging route climbs to the divide between Bull Creek and Squaw Creek and then runs east onto a shoulder of Grasshopper Peak. A magnificent meadow lies near midpoint.

Distance: 3.7 miles, one way

Elevation Change: 2,200-foot gain and 450-foot loss, west to east

Location: The western end of Preacher Gulch Road is at mile 3.5 of Bull Creek Road; the eastern end is at Grieg Road, south of Grasshopper Peak.

Description: At the base of a large prairie, Preacher Gulch Road forks east from Bull Creek Road and soon begins ascending the hillside. Bracken fern borders the route like a band of green lace, while western blue flax rashly resides directly in the roadbed.

The road climbs quickly through mixed woodland and prairie, with the gulch itself lying hidden far downslope to the right. Manzanita, oak, and bigleaf maple enliven the usual forest mix at mile 0.5. After crossing two small streams, the route rises steeply; at mile 1.4 it enters the upper end of the long, hillside grassland that was first encountered at the trailhead. Above the roadbank, summer splashes of winecup clarkia, elegant brodiaea, and California poppy color the prairie red, blue, and gold.

western blue flax, wild blue flax
(Linum perenne)

These slender-stemmed flowers are often found by the side of little-used roadways, like stranded commuters waiting for a ride; their pastel blue petals appear faded from the sunlight, blending with the dry, tan earth below them. Several Indian tribes made cordage from the plant, which is a cousin of the utilitarian common flax that produces both linen and linseed oil. [blooms March-September]

After meeting Squaw Creek Ridge Road, left, mile 1.8, the route climbs with renewed vigor, soon gaining the western end of a long ridge. The road finally crests at mile 2.0 and passes a mat of yerba de selva, left, that covers the base of a dead fir tree.

yerba de selva
(Whipplea modesta)
[blooms April-June]

Immediately ahead is a dazzling ridgetop prairie that falls away southward towards Bull Creek. During summer, masses of true baby stars twinkle pinkly in the grass.

The road then runs gently downhill along the northern edge of the prairie. The view east could

true baby stars
(Linanthus bicolor)
[blooms April-June]

come from a painting: clusters of a silver-leaved lupine brighten the roadside, while a canyon live oak extends its dark form overhead; in the distance, framed by a fringe of trees, the grassland arches across the ridgetop like the back of some sleek-furred beast.

After passing through part of the prairie, the route bends left, mile 2.2, and drops over the ridge into the Squaw Creek drainage. The road descends through second-growth mixed forest, briefly bottoming out by the headwaters of Squaw Creek, mile 2.6, and then rising briskly. At mile 2.9 a sunny knoll offers a glimpse of the Grasshopper Peak lookout high above. A creek at mile 3.0 runs through the wooded confines of upper Preacher Gulch, which here has shrunk to the size of a mere gully.

*   *   *

HOW THE "PREACHER" GOT INTO (AND OUT OF) THE GULCH

Chauncey Gould was a businessman, and when business wasn't going well, he was not pleased. As he looked down into the wooded ravine north of the Bull Creek Ranch, his brow first furrowed in annoyance and then contorted into a scowl of rage. The new timber faller he'd hired had been making a hash of the forest, dropping the valuable redwoods so carelessly that they shattered into worthless splinters.

Gould was a large man, weighing some 265 pounds, and he now carefully made his way down into the gulch, mindful of his bulk. The timber faller, a part-time preacher from Oklahoma, looked up from his work.

"If you can't fall trees any better than that," bellowed Gould, "get the hell out!"

The livid Gould loomed large above the faller, but the Oklahoman held his ground.

"You can't talk to me like that," he answered, "I'm a man of the cloth."

"Reverend," Gould quietly replied, his voice rising gradually to a roar, "if you can't preach any better than you can fall trees, you can damn well get the hell out!"

The faller may in fact have sermonized better than he sawed, but he quickly left without arguing the point. He was not soon forgotten, however, for although miles from any pulpit, the scene of his hasty departure was henceforth known as Preacher Gulch.

*   *   *

Leaving the gulch, the route continues upgrade; a darkened fir forest is relieved by the bright leaves of Oregon white oak at 3.2 miles. After briefly lapsing back into fir, the road crosses through a large prairie, mile 3.4, that rises up the southern shoulder of Grasshopper Peak. Midway through the meadow, a pair of canyon live oaks bracket an Oregon white oak at a wide-angled overlook. The route then tops the shoulder, mile 3.7, and ends at Grieg Road.

SQUAW CREEK RIDGE ROAD

Summary: A slow-paced passage that meanders through thick forest on a generally gentle grade; along the way is Whiskey Flat Trail Camp.

Distance: 5.7 miles, one way

Elevation Change: 1,490-foot gain and 150-foot loss, north to south

Location: The northern end begins at a junction with Grasshopper Road, 0.7 mile south of Mattole Road; the southern end meets Preacher Gulch Road midway along its course.

Warning: *Whiskey Flat Trail Camp is now better known for its mosquitoes than its moonshine.*

Description: Squaw Creek Ridge Road forks right from Grasshopper Road, rising gently through mixed forest. After a switchback past a pair of large, leaning redwoods, the route levels and heads west at 0.5 mile; black huckleberry is the main ground cover. Just beyond a mossy roadbank, left at mile 0.8, is a nice patch of redwood violets.

redwood violet
(Viola sempervirens)
[blooms February-April]

The road switchbacks at 1.3 miles and again at mile 1.6 as it climbs onto the northern end of Squaw Creek Ridge. The route now follows the nearly level ridgetop south. The Baxter-Squaw Creek Cutoff Trail drops steeply downhill to the right, mile 1.8.

Following a long run along the broad, forested ridgeline, the road reaches a view of Hanson Ridge at 3.0 miles. The route soon begins climbing the ridge's shoulder, levelling somewhat as it enters a lush stretch of forest, mile 3.7, where trillium, milkmaids, redwood sorrel, Pacific starflower, sweet-scented bedstraw, yerba de selva, and various ferns congregate. At mile 3.8 the course crosses a small stream and drops to the Whiskey Flat Trail Camp, a verdant but insect-infested site, bordered by a substantial covering of salal.

Salal

(Gaultheria shallon)

[blooms April-July]

The camp derives its name from a Prohibition-era still that was located here inside a hollow redwood. The Bull Creeker who made the moonshine sold it for the then-astronomical price of $7.50 a fifth; he stayed in business as long as he paid off the revenue agents.

Immediately after passing the trail camp, the road crosses a second branch of the creek. The streambed upslope is filled with giant chain ferns.

Leaving the flat, the route bends uphill, turning south at mile 4.0 to make a long, rising run across the hillside. Grasshopper Peak and the upper Squaw Creek drainage are visible through the trees on the left. At mile 4.5 the road levels, but it soon makes a switchback and resumes scaling the eastern side of Hanson Ridge. After passing through the remains of a large landslide, the route reaches a second switchback, where it turns back towards the south.

giant chain fern, western chain fern

(Woodwardia fimbriata)

This large, eye-catching fern often perches on streambanks, spreading its sharply cut fronds over the water below. Its name refers to the chainlike arrangement of the spores on the underside of its fronds, recalling the phrase, "when it chains, it spores." The root fibers of the giant chain fern were colored with a red dye made from the bark of white alder and then used to create designs on Indian baskets.

As the road recrosses the slide area, the landscape opens to provide a view, left, that ranges from Johnson Prairie to Grasshopper Peak. The route begins to level, soon reaching the ridgecrest, mile 5.4. Here Hanson Ridge Road branches right, heading into a large prairie that spreads across the slope to the west; small California black oak and bigleaf maple border the eastern side of the junction. Keen-eyed observers may spot a turkey vulture or two as the soaring scavengers study the nearby grassland.

The road drops from the ridgetop into the upper Bull Creek drainage, passing sweet cicely, California poppy, miniature lupine, popcorn flower, tarweed, and western blue flax. At mile 5.7 Squaw Creek Ridge Road ends at a junction with Preacher Gulch Road.

Turkey vulture — a prairieland peruser

ROUTES OF UPPER BULL CREEK

BULL CREEK ROAD

Summary: An exciting and essential link in the upper Bull Creek road network, this route runs to the top of the drainage; it encounters a deep stream gorge, an old barn, and many memorable plants along the way.

Distance: 7.4 miles, one way

Elevation Change: 1,780-foot gain, north to south

Location: The route's north end is at Mattole Road, 7.6 miles east of the 101 Freeway; the south end meets Perimeter Road.

Description: Cut high onto the canyonside above its namesake, Bull Creek Road passes a locked gate and moves south on a nearly level grade; the bank to the right displays firecracker flowers in summer. Both creambush and snowbrush line the early stages of the route, which, after dropping downhill, offers two views to the left: upward to the snag-stippled side of Hanson Ridge, and downward to the canyon bottom of Bull Creek, where Noah Lewis's old apple orchard still blossoms brightly in spring. A side road, left at mile 0.6, leads to a shooting range for Park rangers.

After turning away from Bull Creek, the route comes to a stout wooden bridge, mile 0.8, that crosses Burns Creek. Years ago, the higher reaches of this stream canyon were a favorite site for moonshiners' stills, but the only liquid to be found now is bubbling brook water.

The road turns left at the bridge and runs east until it regains the bank above Bull Creek; canyon live oaks enliven a mix of smallish redwood, tanoak, and madrone. A seeping spring creates a cool, damp stretch of shade at 1.4 miles, as bigleaf maples overhang the roadway and California spikenard and western coltsfoot crowd the muddy ditch.

western coltsfoot
(Petasites palmatus)
[blooms March-May]

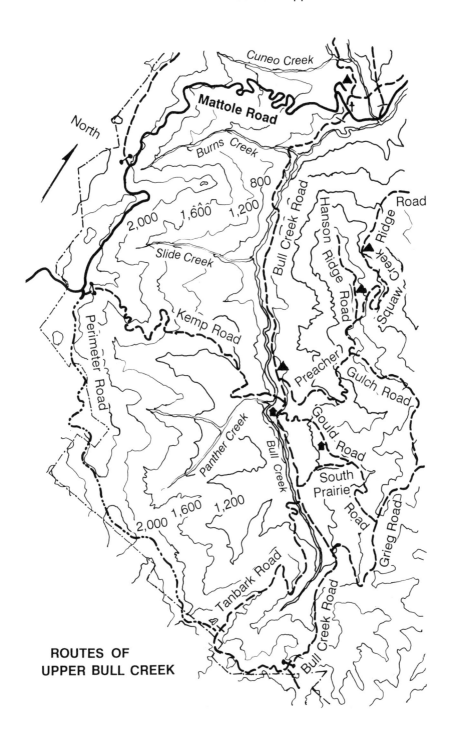

**ROUTES OF
UPPER BULL CREEK**

**blueblossom, blue myrtle,
California wild lilac,**
(Ceanothus thyrsiflorus)
[blooms March-June]

Just ahead, the steep bank on the right displays pearly everlasting, creambush, California hazel, tarweed, and alum root. The exhibit ends at the edge of Bull Creek, which the road crosses at mile 1.6. Below the bridge, alders rise from the depths of the boulder-clotted streambed as the creek's compressed waters swirl past. This section of the canyon is appropriately called "The Narrows"—the canyon walls rise almost perpendicularly from the creek bottom, forming a deep gorge. Masses of blueblossom enliven the eastern hillside here in spring; the plant is one of the two ceanothus species that range far up the watershed.

This pair of sweet-smelling shrubs ranks among nature's best healers, eagerly covering burned or cutover areas while helping to replenish nitrogen in the damaged soil. As beautiful as they are nurturing, both bushes bring clouds of color to the upland hillslopes, while the fragrance of their lilac-like blossoms perfumes entire canyons when warmed by the morning sun.

Blueblossom, which can reach 20 feet in height, blooms first, sending out clusters of rich blue petals in early spring. The white flower cones of the snowbrush arrive later in the season; this smaller ceanothus seldom grows taller than six feet. Indians made a tea from the flowers and leaves of the blueblossom, concocted a red dye from its roots, turned its stems into foundations for their baskets, and mixed the blossoms with water to produce a soap. On occasion, an Indian bride and groom would shampoo each other's hair with the aromatic suds as part of their wedding ceremony.

snowbrush, tobacco brush
(Ceanothus velutinus)
[blooms April-June]

East of the bridge, the roadway turns south, passing some ditchbound seep-spring monkey flowers and then rising sharply; a large slide scars the west side of the canyon, testifying to the instability of the steep slopes. Bigleaf maples dot the upgrade at mile 1.9. After topping a rise, the road comes to an overlook, mile 2.3, that provides a view of the creek far below. The road levels, and then undulates past pretty patches of Pacific starflower, mile 2.6, and yerba de selva, mile 3.1, before arriving at shaded Bull Creek Trail Camp, mile 3.4. A trail exits, right, to the compact campsite, which occupies a small flat east of the creek.

On the left beyond the trail camp is a rising, snowbrush-covered prairie; the opening continues to the junction with Preacher Gulch Road, left, mile 3.5. Bull Creek Road then curves along the edge of the canyon, coming to a bankside mass of Bolander's phacelia at mile 3.7.

The canyon broadens as the route arrives at Kemp Road, which exits right at mile 3.8, close beside Bull Creek. Beyond the junction, Panther Creek debouches from the west; a section of heavily-silted streambed shows the effects of continued erosion in the upper drainage.

Another sturdy wooden bridge appears at mile 4.0; this one crosses Preacher Gulch, an alder-choked streamcourse that descends from the left. Just to the south, Gould Road branches uphill, left; to the right an unnamed track runs 200 feet to the lower Gould Barn, a saltbox-like struc-

Bolander's phacelia
(Phacelia bolanderi)
[blooms May-July]

ture that was used mainly to store machinery for the Bull Creek Ranch. The barn's grainy timbers provide an intriguing interplay of light and shadow—a must for camera buffs who are keen on chiaroscuro.

Bull Creek Road now runs an almost flat course, the stream often close at hand, until a slight rise precedes the obscure junction with South Prairie Road, left at 4.7 miles. The beginning of this side route has been nearly covered by straw and plantings of grass, but a vague track is still visible.

Gooseberry, Pacific willow, and snowbrush fill gaps in the open woodland as the road crosses an unnamed creek. Tanbark Road departs downhill to the right, mile 5.0, and Bull Creek Road then rises with increasing intensity through second-growth mixed forest. There is a respite from the climb at 5.6 miles, where Grieg Road branches left, but after crossing a small stream and curving right, the route again ascends in earnest at mile 5.9.

Lower Gould Barn

Another creek crossing, mile 6.1, causes a lull in the grade, but the route then steepens increasingly as it moves through redwood, tanoak, and Douglas fir of various sizes. The road levels again — briefly — at 6.6 miles to bend across a small stream canyon. The uppermost section of Bull Creek runs through the forested ravine to the right; in times past, a plentitude of silver salmon was found near the headwaters.

Now Bull Creek Road begins its last, great climb, rising very steeply through open, mixed forest. At mile 7.2 is a view, right, of the Grasshopper Peak Lookout far across the valley to the north. The route at last levels slightly and meets Perimeter Road, mile 7.4.

GOULD ROAD

Summary: A rousing route, it switchbacks up a steep hillside to the Upper Gould Barn and the site of the Hazelton-Bull Creek Ranch; a pair of pleasant prairies lies along the way.

Distance: 1.2 miles, one way

Elevation Change: 720-foot gain, west to east

Location: The route's western end begins at Bull Creek Road, 4.0 miles south of Mattole Road; its eastern end meets South Prairie Road.

Description: East of the intersection at Bull Creek Road, little-used Gould Road rises gently along the shaded slope of Preacher Gulch; soon the way steepens and turns south, leaving the canyon. The hillside is covered by snowbrush and a mixed forest of young trees. The route bends left at mile 0.3 and runs along the upper edge of a steep prairie; in summer, a bankside group of firecracker flowers at mile 0.4 bursts colorfully above the roadway.

The track then turns left, leaving the prairie and moving through a roadcut where a pile of weathered fence posts reposes on the bank. On the left is a sylvan meeting of the states: California black oak and Oregon white oak fraternize within a few feet of each other.

After zigzagging through more oaks and a dotting of madrones, the road leaves the woodland at 0.7 mile and enters a large, gently rising prairie. The route winds through the grass, passing California poppy and sidalcea, and then meets a spur road, left at mile 0.8, that climbs through the upper prairie. Gould Road branches right and immediately crosses a spring-fed bog. The remnants of a small orchard struggle for survival downslope to the right.

firecracker flower
(Dichelostemma
[or Brodiaea] ida-maia)

These gaudy, red and yellow, cigar-shaped flowers indeed look as if they'll explode come July. Clusters of them dangle alluringly from long stalks, waggling in the wind above open, grassy areas. A story has it that when a stagecoach driver located the flower for a plant collector, the beneficent botanist returned the favor by naming the find after the driver's niece, Ida May. The plant's underground stem, called a corm, can be eaten when roasted; the seeds are also edible. [blooms May-July]

The road passes through a small, wooded stream canyon and emerges onto the site of the Hazelton-Bull Creek Ranch. Several fruit trees and a mass of rock rose mark the location of the ranch yard, while beyond them is the tiny, ramshackle Upper Gould Barn. A Monterey pine, planted by Don Gould over 40 years ago, now rises tall from the hillside below the barn.

Leaving the ranch site, the road runs through more prairie and then crosses another shaded creek; wood rose, California hazel, California laurel, scrub oak, gooseberry, snowbrush, and yerba buena are found near the streamside. The route briefly turns to mud as seep-spring monkey flowers line the accompanying ditch. In the middle of more meadowland, mile 1.2, the route meets South Prairie Road.

RIDING HERD ON THE BULL CREEK RANCH

When Don Gould returned from the Navy at the end of World War II, his parents had a little welcoming present waiting for him: almost 3,000 acres of land in upper Bull Creek. Much of the property had once been the old Hazelton Ranch, and the younger Gould would now have a chance to run the spread.

Gould quickly made improvements, putting in roads and building two barns and a ranch house. He called the place the "Bull Creek Ranch," and although it never held more than a hundred head of cattle, the location did serve as a dude-style getaway for Gould's friends from Eureka. Judges, sheriffs, and other luminaries of the city would come south to sample ranch life, often relaxing at the hunting camp that Gould had built below Grasshopper Peak. Don's father and uncle came too, and the three men would saddle up horses with names like Brownie and Big Red and then gallop off across the prairie as if they were some latter-day riders of the purple sage.

Much of the ranch was forested, and the Goulds vigorously cut both timber and tanbark on the steep hillslopes. The tanbark was first hauled out by mules and later by truck; it sold for $5.00 a cord. All too soon, it seemed, the ranch itself was sold—the Park acquired it in the 1960s as part of the program to protect upper Bull Creek from further logging.

Little now remains of the main ranch except a small, dilapidated barn, which stands bravely beside an ominously eroding section of hillside. Inside, the empty stalls seem almost expectant in the enduring stillness, as if awaiting the whinny that will never come again.

Ready to ride at the Bull Creek Ranch—left to right:
Don Gould on "Brownie," Chauncey Gould on "Big Red," Dallas Gould on "Friday"

KEMP ROAD

Summary: This rugged road winds its way up the west side of the Bull Creek watershed; a long prairie near its start offers a view east towards the site of the old Hazelton-Bull Creek Ranch.

Distance: 3.7 miles, one way

Elevation Change: 1,800-foot gain, east to west

Location: The lower end of Kemp Road starts at mile 3.8 of Bull Creek Road; the upper end meets Mattole Road at Panther Gap, 14.4 miles southwest of the 101 Freeway.

Description: The route immediately descends to a rock-filled ford across Bull Creek and then rises to reach a flat west of the crossing. A side road exits left at 0.1 mile; this is an earlier version of Kemp Road which follows Panther Creek southwest before switchbacking north to rejoin the new route.

Leaving the flat, Kemp Road ascends sharply through madrone, tanoak, and snowbrush, reaching a second junction with the older road, left at mile 0.5. The course continues its climb, levelling somewhat at a large, unnamed prairie, 0.7 mile; in summer, the pale grass is speckled with the bright flecks of many winecup clarkias.

winecup clarkia
(Clarkia purpurea)

Like remnants of some picnic on the grass, the winecup Clarkia is found scattered across sunny prairies, its pinkish flowers so stained with purplish spots that it in fact resembles an undrained cup. Over the summer, the "cups" turn into capsules, with each leathery container eventually releasing its cache of small brown seeds. This charming flower is one of a large genus named for explorer William Clark of the Lewis and Clark Expedition. [blooms May-July]

Across the canyon to the east are the steep, cut-over hillslopes of what was formerly the Hazelton-Bull Creek Ranch; grassy openings brighten the surrounding second growth. Kemp Road continues rising through the prairie until it re-enters woodland at mile 1.2. The route now climbs, drops, and twists through small tanoaks and madrones until it reaches, mile 2.2, the first of several grassy openings. The road soon passes a pile of pale gray timbers, left at mile 2.5; opposite the debris is a large patch of vanilla leaf that brightens the shaded roadside. Douglas fir predominates along the ensuing uphill stretch, which is punctuated by a view down towards Bull Creek at mile 3.4. Kemp Road then rises along shady switchbacks to reach its terminus at a junction with Perimeter Road and Mattole Road, mile 3.7, just beyond a locked metal gate.

PERIMETER ROAD

Summary: This ridgetop ramble skirts the southwestern rim of the Bull Creek watershed; a lovely prairie and views of the King Range add interest.

Distance: 6.8 miles, one way

Elevation Change: 520-foot gain and 960-foot loss, west to east

Location: The route's western end is at a junction with Mattole Road and Kemp Road, 14.4 miles southwest of the 101 Freeway; its eastern end is at the top of Bull Creek Road.

Warnings: *1) The western part of the road passes through stretches of private property; "No Trespassing" signs are posted and the land-owners have been known to deny access—check with Park officials for current information. Perimeter Road's eastern end, including the section that connects Bull Creek Road with Tanbark Road, is entirely within the Park. 2) Motor vehicles, including logging trucks, travel the road.*

Description: The road runs south from its start at Panther Gap as creambush and Indian pink decorate the top of a low bank, right. The route soon moves into mixed forest.

California Indian pink
(Silene californica)

This bright scarlet flower is called a "pink" not for its color but for the shape of its petals, which are notched as if cut by pinking shears. Hispanic colonists avoided this confusion by naming the pretty plant *yerba del Indio;* they brewed it into a tonic tea that was also used to heal ulcers. [blooms May-August]

After moving along a pleasantly level course on the Bull Creek side of the ridge, the road reaches a saddle, mile 1.0, and crosses into the Mattole River drainage; the King Range looms in the distance to the southwest. On the roadbank, left at mile 1.4, the pink petals of farewell-to-spring shimmer throughout most of the summer.

A pair of wrecked cars at 1.8 miles bracket the junction with a ranch road, right, that leads out onto a spur ridge. On the main route, a "Keep Out - No Trespassing - Deedholders Only" sign discourages passage at mile 2.0; just ahead, an aging house and two other structures decay by the roadside. Property owners have been known to prohibit travel along this stretch of the road. The route then runs across a lengthy series of gentle dips and rises, punctuated at mile 2.5 by a concentration of canyon live oak and at mile 2.8 by a grassy opening. At mile 3.6 the road arrives at a junction beside a large, ridgetop prairie. To the right, the

**farewell-to-spring,
herald-of-summer**
(Clarkia amoena)
[blooms June-August]

more heavily used route begins a descent to the Mattole River, passing several private residences. Perimeter Road branches left along the ridgetop, moving across the upper side of the meadow. Canyon live oaks line the edge of the opening, and western blue flax, lupine, and brodiaea mingle with the grasses.

A short climb at 4.3 miles leads into a grove of Douglas fir and canyon live oak; the route returns to the prairie and reaches another junction, mile 4.5. The way right drops down the hillside through a continuation of the grassland, while Perimeter Road climbs the ridgeline to the left. The road enters more meadow at mile 4.7, rising steeply until mile 5.1. It soon descends to a sunny saddle, mile 5.3, where Tanbark Road exits to the left.

Perimeter Road continues east from the junction, rising out of the saddle and then bending right, mile 5.8, to enter the Salmon Creek drainage. On an exposed bank, right at mile 5.9, is a plethora of plants: true baby stars, snowbrush, creambush, wild strawberry, goldenback fern, bracken fern, poison oak, vetch, and clover. Opposite the botanically brimming bank are pair of Oregon white oaks. In the middle of the road, struggling for survival, is a blue witch.

Presently the route divides, its two branches rejoining 50 yards down the hillside at an intersection. A private road, right, drops to a locked gate while Perimeter Road runs left along the hillslope, passing gooseberry, yerba buena, western blue flax, true baby stars, firecracker flower, snowbrush, and California hazel. The route drops downhill, mile 6.1, as Indian pinks brighten the way.

blue witch
(Solanum umbelliferum)

A member of the nightshade family, this plant has a lavender-hued, pinwheel-shaped flower with a bright yellow center. While its name suggests an inhabitant of dark and dismal places, the blue witch actually prefers sunny, rocky slopes, often enjoying the company of neighboring oaks. Like other nightshades, it is high in solanine, a poison which can cause several problems, including death. [blooms April-July]

At mile 6.5 the road rises out of another saddle and soon comes to a vista of the Salmon Creek watershed, right. Canyon live oak, California laurel, and California black oak enhance the forest mix as the road again drops to a saddle. Perimeter Road ends at a junction with Bull Creek Road, left, mile 6.8. A route to the right descends from the ridgetop and leaves the Park.

SOUTH PRAIRIE ROAD

Summary: This challenging course climbs and winds through mixed woodlands and tumbling prairies before it reaches the Bull Creek-Canoe Creek divide.

Distance: 2.0 miles, one way

Elevation Change: 1,110-foot gain, east to west

Location: The western end of the road departs from mile 4.7 of the Bull Creek Road; the eastern end meets Grieg Road.

Warning: *Unless recently rejuvenated, the extremely steep lower section of this route is in very poor condition; it could be dangerous for downhill cyclists.*

Description: The unmarked route exits from the east side of Bull Creek Road opposite a metal Park road sign; it starts as a faint track that moves up the hillside through straw-mulched grass. The road is badly eroded and heavily overgrown; it rises relentlessly northeastward through mixed forest and a scattering of snowbrush.

Several California black oaks provide shade at 0.4 mile; the route continues climbing at an alpine angle until mile 0.7, when it reaches the bottom of a large, tumbling prairie. Gould Road exits, left, next to an old and often overflowing bathtub-size watering trough. A stream descends the hillside above the trough, its course marked by cascading clumps of California rose.

California rose
(Rosa californica)
[blooms May-August]

Giant chain fern adds to the creekbed foliage while California poppy, western verbena, and bindweed abound in the surrounding grasslands.

South Prairie Road now turns right and heads east on a more gentle grade along the hillside.

The incline again diminishes at 0.9 mile; California black oaks occupy the slope to the left. The route then drops slightly, passing, on the right, an older version of the route. The road levels and crosses an unnamed creek, mile 1.2, amid snowbrush, giant horsetail, bracken fern, and giant chain fern; at mile 1.3 tarweeds rise from the shaded roadbank.

Soon South Prairie Road emerges from the trees to pass over another branch of the stream. A bizarre forest duo dances at the right of the roadside, 1.6 miles, where a large madrone has joined its limbs to encircle a small Douglas fir. Another meadow then opens before the roadway; in the distance to the right are the headwaters of Bull Creek. Canyon live oak and California poppy pop up midway through the prairie, as the route continues climbing. At mile 2.0 South Prairie Road reaches the tree-crowned ridgetop and connects with Grieg Road.

tarweed
(Hemizonia corymbosa)
[blooms May-September]

Oregon grape
(Berberis nervosa)
[blooms March-June]

TANBARK ROAD

Summary: This twisting traverse of the upper Bull Creek watershed arrives at a ridgetop rendezvous with Perimeter Road.

Distance: 3.0 miles, one way

Elevation Change: 1,290-foot gain, north to south

Location: The northern end is at Bull Creek Road, 5.0 miles south of Mattole Road; the southern end is at Perimeter Road.

Description: Tanbark Road exits south from Bull Creek Road, dropping in a hundred feet to a bridge crossing of Bull Creek. The road soon passes an old slash pile and then runs southwest above a small stream, right. At 0.2 mile the route makes the first of three hairpin turns; it rises into mixed forest, encountering, at mile 0.6, right, a good-size grouping of Oregon grape.

Presently the road crosses a small stream, and after another creek crossing at 0.9 mile, the route begins climbing more steeply, levelling out a bit at mile 1.2. Tanbark Road makes a sharp turn at mile 1.5 and another at 1.8 miles as it rises to reach the end of a ridge. From here the course runs south up the rising ridgetop, occasionally dropping into a saddle and usually accompanied by mixed forest.

A steep climb commences at mile 2.5; the road turns left and crosses through a dark thicket of Douglas fir, mile 2.7. Redwood inside-out flower lines the roadway at 2.9 miles, followed by a beautiful bankside clump of crimson columbine. Fifty yards ahead, Tanbark Road ends at a junction with Perimeter Road, mile 3.0.

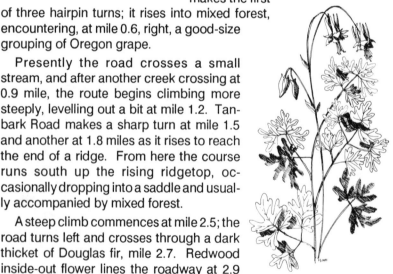

crimson columbine
(Aquilegia formosa var. truncata)
[blooms April-July]

SOURCES OF INFORMATION

Many sources were consulted in preparing the book; among the most valuable were the following:

General Information:

The *Eel River Current*, an annual publication of regional state park interpretive associations, appropriately provided "current" information about the Park. The *Living Museum*, the journal of the Humboldt Redwoods Interpretive Association, had useful articles in several issues.

Natural History:

Alt, David D., and Donald W. Hyndman. *Roadside Geology of Northern California*. Missoula: Mountian Press Publishing Company, 1975.

Balls, Edward K. *Early Uses of California Plants*. Berkeley: University of California Press, 1962.

Benyus, Janine M. *The Field Guide to Wildlife Habitats of the Western United States*. New York: Fireside, 1989.

Brockman, C. Frank. *Trees of North America*. New York: Golden Press, 1968.

Burt, William H., and Richard P. Grossenheider. *Mammals*, 3d ed. Boston: Houghton Mifflin, 1976.

California. University of California, Berkeley. School of Forestry. *A Symposium on Management for Park Preservation: A Case Study at Bull Creek*. Berkeley, CA, 1966.

Elias, Thomas S. *Field Guide to North American Trees*, rev. ed. Danbury, CT: Grolier Book Clubs, Inc., 1989.

Grillos, Steve J. *Ferns and Fern Allies of California*. Berkeley and Los Angeles: University of California Press, 1966.

Hewes, Jeremy Joan. *Redwoods*. London: Bison Books Ltd., 1981.

Johnson, Hugh. *Hugh Johnson's Encyclopedia of Trees*. New York: Gallery Books, 1984.

Lyons, Kathleen, and Mary Beth Cooney-Lazaneo. *Plants of the Coast Redwood Region*. Boulder Creek, CA: Looking Press, 1988.

Keator, Glenn. *Pacific Coast Berry Finder*. Berkeley: Nature Study Guild, 1978.

_____, and Ruth M. Heady. *Pacific Coast Fern Finder*. Berkeley: Nature Study Guild, 1981.

Mathews, Daniel. *Cascade-Olympic Natural History*. n.p.: Raven Editions, 1988.

Murphey, Edith Van Allen. *Indian Uses of Native Plants*. Ukiah, CA: Mendocino County Historical Society, 1959.

Niehaus, Theodore F., and Charles L. Ripper. *A Field Guide to Pacific States Wildflowers*. Boston: Houghton Mifflin Company, 1976.

Parsons, Mary Elizabeth. *The Wild Flowers of California*. San Francisco: California School Book Depository, 1925.

Peattie, Donald Culross. *A Natural History of Western Trees*. Boston: Houghton Mifflin Company, 1953.

Petrides, George A., and Olivia Petrides. *Western Trees*. Boston: Houghton Mifflin Company, 1992.

Peterson, Roger Tory. *Western Birds*, 3rd. ed. Boston: Houghton Mifflin Company, 1990.

Rickett, Harold William. *Wild Flowers of the United States*, vol. 5, New York: McGraw-Hill Book Company, n.d.

Russo, Ron, and Pam Ohlhausen. *Mammal Finder*. Berkeley: Nature Study Guild, 1987.

Scott, Shirley L., ed. *Field Guide to the Birds of North America*. Washington, DC: National Geographic Society, 1983.

Spellenberg, Richard. *The Audubon Society Field Guide to North American Wildflowers: Western Region*. New York: Alfred A. Knopf, 1979.

Watts, Phoebe. *Redwood Region Flower Finder*. Berkeley: Nature Study Guild, 1979.

Watts, Tom. *Pacific Coast Tree Finder*. Berkeley: Nature Study Guild, 1973.

Whitney, Stephen. *Western Forests*. New York: Alfred A. Knopf, Inc., 1985.

Whittlesey, Rhoda. *Familiar Friends: Northwest Plants*. Portland, Oregon: Rose Press, 1985.

Human History:

Baumhoff, Martin A. "California Athabascan Groups." *Anthropological Records* 16:5. Berkeley and Los Angeles: University of California Press, 1958.

Grant, Madison. "Saving the Redwoods." *Zoological Society Bulletin* 22, no. 5: 90-118.

Heald, Weldon F. "Who Saved the Redwoods?" *Natural History* Jan. 1953.

Nomland, Gladys Ayer. "Sinkyone Notes." In *American Archaeology and Ethnology*, edited by A. L. Kroeber, R. H. Lowie, and R. L. Olson, vol. 36. Berkeley: University of California Press, 1940. Reprint. New York: Kraus Reprint Corporation, 1965.

Pritchard, Susan. "Life Along the South Fork: A History of Humboldt Redwoods State Park." Photocopy. [available at the Park Visitor Center]

In addition, the *Humboldt Historian*, published by the Humboldt County Historical Society, contained many helpful articles, including ones authored by Addie Chadbourne, Harold Fisher, Jane Logan, Ellen Murray, and Margaret Pritchard. The clippings files located in the Humboldt County Collection at Humboldt State University in Arcata, California was another invaluable source, as was the indexed version of the *Susie Baker Fountain Papers* found in the Humboldt Room, main branch of the Humboldt County Library, Eureka, California. Also highly informative were the *Annual Reports* and the *Bulletin* of the Save-the-Redwoods League. Information on the Lolangkok Sinkyone Indians was found at the Indian Action Council Library in Eureka.

Many individuals generously provided primary historical information for the authors; they are:

Darrell Beasley, Bill Beat, Roberta Curless Beat, Verda Chadbourne Bishop, Joann Smith Brekke, the late Dave Chadbourne, Richard Childs, Robert Childs, Velma Childs, Max Crismon, Harold Fisher, Jane Bryant Fisher, the late Don Gould, Linda Moore Hillbrun, Dorothy Rose Baxter Johnson, Al Lewis, Ed Lewis, Mel Martin, Lloyce Moore, Marie Moore, Carol "Mori" Morrison, Alice Mortenson, Geraldine Stockel Myers, Henry Perrott, John Perrott, June Ruggles, Angus Russell, Blanche Lewis Tompkins, Clara Luke Trapier, James Trapier, Lucille Vinyard, Hershell D. Wheeler, and Irving Wrigley.

Roads and Trails:

Public roads were driven by car, with mileages computed by car odometer and roadway milepost markers. Park roads and trails were either hiked by foot, with mileages computed by pedometer, or cycled by mountain bike, with mileages computed by cyclometer. Elevation changes were determined by referring to USGS topographic maps and to the Humboldt Redwoods State Park map.

Index to Plants

All plants indexed below are illustrated; those with an asterisk (*) are also profiled in a short commentary.

* * * * *

left to right: Larry Eifert, Gisela Rohde, Jerry Rohde

In 1972, Jerry and Gisela Rohde met in the San Bernardino Mountains of Southern California; they have been enjoying the outdoors together ever since. The Rohdes relocated to Humboldt County in 1979 and began exploring the North Coast's forests, mountains, and shorelines. A few years later they happened upon Humboldt Redwoods State Park, which soon became a favorite hiking spot and later the setting for their first book. Gisela, who took to the trails of her native Germany at age two, now works at Humboldt State University's library. She is an avid gardener, jogger, and cyclist. Jerry currently writes full-time; he was previously the coordinator for a network of environmental organizations. His weekly column, "Tales and Trails of the Redwoods," appears in southern Humboldt's Redwood Record. The Rohdes live in the woods near Clam Beach with their cat, Shinto.

Disciplined by his family in both art and nature, Larry Eifert has spent the past twenty years painting and learning about coastal redwooods. His intent is not to simply portray these great forests, but to know them as family. Commissioned by a number of America's greatest national parks, including Yosemite and Redwood, Larry has painted projects that serve both as art and interpretation of nature. The Eifert Gallery in Ferndale is very close to Humboldt Redwoods State Park and Larry continues to cultivate an affection for this unique place. The book's cover painting is part of an ancient forest display in the Park's Visitor Center, one of many exhibits he has helped establish there. Larry also writes and edits the journal for the Humboldt Redwoods Interpretive Association, uncovering the wonders of this world-class park.

In creating this book, Jerry, Gisela, and Larry have developed a remarkable partnership that will obviously lead to other projects.